Learning and Development

Learning and Development

Making Connections to Enhance Teaching

Sharon L. Silverman

Martha E. Casazza

Jossey-Bass Publishers • San Francisco

Excerpts from P. R. Pintrich & D. H. Schunk's *Motivation in Education* are reprinted by permission. Copyright © 1996 Prentice Hall.

Excerpt from "Rethinking Nigrescence" included in *Shades of Black: Diversity in African-American Identity* by William E. Cross, Jr. is reprinted by permission of Temple University Press. Copyright © 1991 by Temple University. All rights reserved.

Jossey-Bass books and products are available through most bookstores. To contact Jossey-Bass directly, call (888) 378-2537, fax to (800) 605-2665, or visit our website at www.josseybass.com.

Substantial discounts on bulk quantities of Jossey-Bass books are available to corporations, professional associations, and other organizations. For details and discount information, contact the special sales department at Jossey-Bass.

 Manufactured in the United States of America on Lyons Falls Turin Book. This paper is acid-free and 100 percent totally chlorine-free.

Library of Congress Cataloging-in-Publication Data

Silverman, Sharon L., date.
  Learning and development: making connections to enhance teaching / Sharon L. Silverman, Martha E. Casazza.
    p. cm.
  Includes bibliographical references and index.
  ISBN 0-7879-4463-7 (hc)
  1. Developmental studies programs. 2. College teaching. 3. Adult learning. I. Casazza, Martha E., date. II. Title.
LB2331.2 .S55 1999
378.1'2—dc21   99-6611

FIRST EDITION
HB Printing   10 9 8 7 6 5 4 3 2 1

The Jossey-Bass
Higher and Adult Education Series

Contents

Preface

This book is based on the idea that learning is best experienced in settings that acknowledge the uniqueness of individuals and that using a variety of different instructional approaches enhances learning. Teachers are expected to have competence in their subject matter, and often it is assumed that this is sufficient; however, competent teachers must go beyond content knowledge and explore the full range of human understanding in teaching and learning.

We believe that no one viewpoint or explanation of behavior can fully account for learning. An integrated approach is richer and more useful than one that stands alone. When different perspectives are combined to provide an explanation, we are better able to reconcile inconsistencies in observations, address problems in instruction, and work through puzzling situations. For example, to understand why some students learn easily in a particular setting and others struggle, many factors must be considered. One viewpoint is usually not enough to explain a complex situation, whereas a combination of views often yields explanations that address a variety of possible circumstances.

Our view of learning includes many educational environments—traditional college and university settings, community-based organizations, continuing and adult education programs—any setting in which individuals pursue education past secondary school. In all of these environments, the focal point is on learning inside and outside the classroom and on how these experiences affect the other. We focus on many contexts—formal and informal, academic and nonacademic, present and past—and emphasize the belief that learning in one setting often affects the learning that occurs in another. We use the terms *students* and *learners* to describe those seeking learning and employ the terms *teachers, educators, instructors,* and *facilitators* synonymously.

Our primary purpose is to present and integrate information from theory and research concerning learning and development and to apply this information to practical situations that teachers face every day. We include information from the fields of psychology, college student development, adult learning, and higher education research. We present theory and research in six areas: (1) self and identity, (2) motivation, (3) interaction with the environment, (4) ways of knowing, (5) learning styles and preferences, and (6) self-regulation and goal setting. Each of these areas is large enough to be the topic of one or more volumes, but our goal is to take the critical ideas of each topic and present them within a framework for application to teaching practice.

The framework we use is the TRPP model (theory, research, principles, and practice). Throughout, we use the six case studies presented in Chapter One to connect the findings of theory and research to practice. We show how the TRPP model can be used to strengthen the foundation of teaching and provide guidance for promoting successful student learning.

This is not a book about techniques. Too often techniques are embraced as quick fixes to problematic concerns. We do not presume to know how to handle all frustrating or challenging situations. There are as many ways to approach teaching and learning as there are teachers and students. In his recent book, *The Courage to Teach,* Parker Palmer (1998) stresses the importance of teacher identity and integrity in the formation of uniquely creative teaching practice. Effective teachers are fully aware of their own strengths and weaknesses, have a firmly grounded value system, and are ethical and honest. Successful teachers are on a journey of discovery; they are uncovering new truths about themselves and the students they encounter. Teachers who risk the journey and are open to its discoveries are likely to be more satisfied and to advance student learning, but the journey can be lonely and sometimes frightening. What if the journey reveals that established ways of teaching are no longer as effective as newer methods? What approach is needed for a new group of students who seem quite different from those in the past? Who can help when new approaches are tried but there is uncertainty about the results?

When faced with these questions, it is helpful to be able to make connections to others and to what is known about learning and development. Our goal is to provide information and a process to help make these connections and to examine practice in order to enhance student learning.

Focus and Audience

Our focus is learning in postsecondary education in the broadest sense, including all places where such learning occurs—in colleges and universities, in proprietary schools, in the workplace, and in informal places where no predetermined structure is required. Throughout, we interchange the terms *educators, teachers,* and *instructors* to mean anyone who is involved with student learning. This book is intended for those who interact with students in the classroom, and the content is designed to benefit their daily teaching practices. For example, research on motivation emphasizes the importance of mastery goals over performance goals to increase engagement in learning. Mastery goals emphasize learning for its own sake, as opposed to performance goals, which center on student comparisons. In addition, consistent feedback regarding goal attainment and opportunity for individual choice and control over learning activities is known to increase motivation. Knowing these research findings and applying them to practice is more likely to promote student learning.

Other audiences for this book include educational administrators, student affairs professionals, and policymakers who interact with students and are responsible for developing programs to strengthen their learning and development. These persons may not always face students in the classroom, but they influence the nature and structure of educational experiences. For instance, orientation programs are developed to help students move into new educational environments. When the content and format of these programs are based on what is known about student development, program goals are more apt to be achieved. Research in higher education has shown that social integration and sense of community are linked to persistence in college. Residence hall directors can use this information to form positive environments for students while contributing to student retention. Directors of programs for returning adults need to know the importance of providing environments that allow for autonomy and self-direction. When this knowledge is applied to program development for adults, successful outcomes are more likely. These are just some examples of how theory and research are important to nonteaching staff in postsecondary education and how the contents of this volume may be useful.

Organization of the Book

We have organized the contents into three parts. In Part One, we begin by addressing the foundation of learning and development. Chapter One introduces demographic and descriptive information about students and personalizes some of these data with the presentation of six student stories; the students are from different backgrounds and educational situations. We use these case studies throughout the book as the focus of discussion about how theory and research are applied to student learning and development. Chapter Two includes an overview of theories covering three of the six areas related to student learning: self and identity, motivation, and interaction with the environment. In Chapter Three we discuss the other three basic topics: ways of knowing, learning styles and preferences, and self-regulation and goal setting. Chapter Four then presents the TRPP model (theory, research, principles, and practice), which provides a framework for applying theory and research to practice.

In Part Two, we focus on specific research findings in the six topic areas. Findings of recent research as well as those of classic studies are included. In each of the six chapters, we recap briefly the theories from Part One, selected research findings, and an application to practice using the TRPP model, along with the case studies from Chapter One. Last, we provide reflection questions for further application to the reader's unique situation.

Part Three has two main goals: (1) to guide readers to critically reflect on the material presented throughout the book and (2) to help readers begin a process of change. In Chapter Eleven, we present a five-step procedure, ReCreate, for organizing new information and include a set of six surveys, each focusing on one of the topic areas from Part Two. The surveys are for use in collaboration with peers to better assess teaching effectiveness and promote and strengthen student learning. Chapter Twelve is designed to stimulate thought about the expanded role of the educator as researcher, innovator, and change agent and to encourage the development of these three components of an educator's role. It provides questions for the future, and we discuss ways to answer those questions.

Concluding Thoughts

We are grateful for the many researchers who have contributed so extensively to the literature in student learning and development. They have shown that success and failure in learning do not occur by chance. It is not simply lucky when labors succeed and ill-fated when they do not. Success is the result of understanding how learners conceive of themselves and persist toward their goals.

Finally, there are no universal prescriptions for success. Basic principles provide guidance, but each teaching and learning situation is unique and is the personal creation of those experiencing it. This is an invitation to experience the journey of teaching and learning and to delight in its wonders and challenges. The journey is never-ending and worthwhile as long as students want to learn, and we join them actively in the pursuit.

In Appreciation

We want to thank many individuals who in different ways contributed to this work. First, we are indebted to all of the students we have taught and who have shown us that helping them learn is extremely rewarding and meaningful. We have learned so much from them and continue to marvel at their curiosity and productivity while sometimes facing significant barriers and challenges. In addition, our professional colleagues have been enormously supportive and encouraging. While observing them, we have been inspired to emulate their successes and advance our own practice. The collegiality experienced in interaction with peers in our own offices and in other postsecondary institutions and organizations has stimulated and motivated us to write this book. We especially thank Juele Blankenberg for her tireless reading of our early sections and her thoughtful feedback. To Erin Neumeir, who thought she would never leave the library where for hours she copied microfiche documents, requested books, and searched the ERIC database, we offer our sincere appreciation. Other students whose dedication seemed endless include Kathryn O'Connell, Joanna Krzywdzinska, and Dagmara Wisniewska. Without Lillian Hardison, the manuscript would never have been input and formatted in such a timely fashion. At the end, and across the oceans, it was Karen Kruse, Rose Novil, and Linda Sweeney who did the detective work that helped us complete some elusive citations. We thank administrators at our own institutions, Loyola University Chicago and National-Louis University, who support our daily work and encourage us to think beyond the present and plan for the success of students we have yet to meet. In addition, we acknowledge our colleagues in South Africa who provided the opportunity for us to use material from this volume in faculty and staff development. We also fondly remember the vervet monkeys who visited us there while we were making final manuscript revisions. They certainly helped us keep our sense of humor. With support from the Fulbright Commission, University of Port Elizabeth, and others in South Africa, we were reinforced that student learning and development have global commonalities. Applying theory and research to practice is important worldwide.

Finally, we are grateful for the love and support of our families. Martha especially thanks Larry, who regularly provided encouragement as he patiently waited to regain his space at the desk. We both thank our children Joshua, Daniel, Christopher, and Justin, who have been our best teachers, showing us always that what matters most are the connections made and maintained with those you love.

August, 1999
Chicago, Illinois

SHARON L. SILVERMAN
MARTHA E. CASAZZA

The Authors

Sharon L. Silverman is formerly director of the Learning Assistance Center at Loyola University Chicago. She has taught in the School of Education at Loyola and in the developmental studies graduate program at National-Louis University. Silverman received her doctoral degree (Ed.D.) from Loyola University Chicago in educational psychology and a master's degree in learning disabilities from De-Paul University. Silverman regularly presents workshops on teaching and learning in higher education and is currently a Fulbright Senior Scholar at the University of Port Elizabeth in South Africa.

Martha E. Casazza developed and now directs the developmental studies graduate program in the adult education department at National-Louis University (NLU), Chicago. She received her doctoral degree (Ed.D.) from Loyola University Chicago in the area of curriculum and instruction. Her master's degree is in reading. Casazza regularly consults in the areas of reading strategies, teaching and learning, and program evaluation. She speaks and writes frequently on the value of integrating theory and research with practice. She is one of the founders and is currently the coeditor of *The Learning Assistance Review* and serves on the editorial board of the *Journal of Developmental Education*. She has been active in establishing standards as well as a process for program certification for the field of developmental education through her committee involvement with the National Association for Developmental Education (NADE). She currently serves as the president of NADE and was recently named a Fulbright Senior Scholar to teach and conduct research in South Africa.

Understanding Learning and Development

In Part One, we begin the discussion with ways to enhance learning and development for all students. We present the view that theory and research have much to offer in guiding choices for meeting educational challenges. This discussion is needed because much has changed in recent years, and expertise from many different disciplines is required to address these changes. Students today are not like those in the past. Individual differences are more pronounced than ever before, and these differences must be considered in all learning situations. Teachers, administrators, staff developers, and student affairs professionals are facing many demands, including the need to retain students to degree or certificate completion, to be accountable for achievement of learning objectives, and to prepare competent employees for the workplace. We confront these challenges here in Part One.

The primary purpose of this section of the book is to set the stage for using theory to enhance student learning and development. We begin with demographic information about today's students and then provide six case studies illustrating these data; we continue with a discussion of theory as it helps explain the dynamics of learning. The discussion of theory is divided into two chapters: personal development and cognitive development. We emphasize, however, that personal and cognitive development occur together and should not be viewed separately. Finally, we present the TRPP model, which includes the components of theory, research, principles, and practice, and demonstrate how the model works using the case studies. Later, in Part Two, research takes center stage and is connected to theory in a dynamic process using the TRPP model.

Demographic information centers on students in the United States, and the student stories reflect those in U.S. culture. We recognize that many learning and development concerns are universal and hope the reader will find the stories applicable to students in a more global environment. For example, students of color in the United States are considered minority students, but in other nations they are the majority. Regardless of the population proportion, histories of disadvantage or lack of opportunity have very similar learning outcomes.

Chapter One

Today's Learners

Everyone seems to bemoan the fact that students just aren't what they used to be—that they are not as prepared or as motivated as they were in the "good old days" of teaching. Perhaps the reader has had similar thoughts. Even though the changes may be difficult to articulate, they are real. Today's students represent a wide range of learners who bring with them unique experiences and expectations.

In a classic text, *Beyond the Open Door,* K. Patricia Cross (1971) introduced the "new" students of the 1970s. These were students who were often the first generation in their families to pursue education after high school. They were also students who scored in the bottom third on traditional tests of academic ability but who saw education as "the way to a better job and a better life than that of their parents" (p. 18). In the 1990s, teachers have come to expect these "new" students; in fact, this picture has become rather a common one.

How is today's picture different? Who are the new students of the 1990s, and what will students be like in the decades to come? A brief summary of the demographics related to education in the United States will provide a more focused lens through which to view today's learners. By reviewing the completion rates at different levels of schooling in addition to the changing population groups who are accessing postsecondary institutions, teachers in all settings will be better prepared to understand the needs of their students

The numbers show that high school enrollment increased 13 percent from 1984 to 1994. Although the number of white youths has declined in this population, the participation of blacks and

Hispanics has been growing. From 1972 to 1992 the percentage of black high school seniors increased 6 percent, and for Hispanics the growth was 15 percent. Along with this increased enrollment have come higher completion rates. There has been a 12 percent increase for black students from 1975 to 1995. For Hispanics, the rates are more varied, but in 1995 the completion rate was 58.6 percent—an increase of 4 percent from 1990 (Hussar and Gerald, 1996, p. 9).

Not only are more students graduating from high school, but increasingly they are planning to pursue higher education. The proportion of high school students, including all racial and ethnic groups, expecting to graduate from college has risen 20 percent since 1972. The percentage of graduates going directly to college following high school was 62 percent in 1994, compared with 47 percent in 1973. This rate varies, however, among ethnic groups from 62 percent for whites to 50 percent for blacks and Hispanics. College enrollment for students of color increased almost 68 percent from 1984 to 1995. From 1990 to 1995, Hispanics had the largest gain among the four major ethnic minority groups, with an increase of 39.6 percent. The number of Asian Americans in higher education more than doubled from 1984 to 1995 (Carter and Wilson, 1996–97, p. 2).

The numbers also indicate that high school students are taking more rigorous coursework than in the past. The "New Basics" curriculum has placed an emphasis on academic course taking; the requirements are four years of English, three years of science, and social sciences and math. In 1982 only 14 percent of those in high school took such a stringent curriculum; in 1996, 61 percent enrolled in college preparatory courses (Fiore, 1998). According to a 1996 government report, "From a course-taking perspective at least, it appears that all racial and ethnic groups are better prepared for college today than they were in the early 1980s" (Carter and Wilson, 1996–97, p. 6).

The same report states that the reading skills of seventeen-year-olds have improved since the mid-1970s, with greater increases being seen in the test scores of black and Hispanic students than in those of white students. In addition, the math proficiency levels of seventeen-year-old blacks and Hispanic students have risen to narrow the gap that formerly existed with white students. At the same time, the mean SAT scores have increased significantly for black students and decreased slightly for white students.

College completion rates in 1993 increased for all ethnic and racial groups, especially females, compared with those in 1981. The percentage of change was 131.5 percent for Hispanics, 35.5 percent for blacks, and 27.7 percent for whites; women earned the majority of degrees at both the bachelor's and master's levels. These numbers reflect growing diversity; however, there is still a significant disparity among completion rates for minority groups. For students whose goal in 1989–90 was to obtain a bachelor's degree, by the spring of 1994, 61 percent had obtained it or were persisting in their efforts to do so. Of these persisters, 69 percent were Asian/Pacific Islanders, 65 percent were white, 52 percent were black, and 34 percent were Hispanics (U.S. Department of Education, 1995, p. 16).

Although the traditional time for completing a bachelor's degree has been four years, this is changing significantly. Only 36 percent of students complete their degree in four years or less; 26 percent take more than six years. This too can be analyzed by ethnic group: about 36 percent of whites and Asian/Pacific Islanders take four years or less, whereas about 24 percent of blacks and Hispanics complete a degree in this time (U.S. Department of Education, 1995, p. 22).

Also contributing to the new enrollment figures in higher education are the increasing numbers of immigrants entering the United States whose first language is not English. In 1994, 8.7 percent of the U.S. population was foreign-born; this figure has doubled since 1970. Seventy-six percent of the immigrant population is considered LEP (limited English proficient)—a growth of 43 percent in the last decade (Chisman, Wrigley, and Ewes, 1993, p. 1). In 1990 immigrant children were enrolled in high school at the rate of 93 percent, and they were more likely than their native peers "to make choices consistent with eventually pursuing a college education" (Vernez and Abrahamse, p. xiii). As they graduate from high school, they are more likely to attend college and to stay continuously through four years than are their native counterparts (1996, p. xiv). The "in-school" rates of eighteen-to twenty-one-year-old immigrants increased from 55 percent in 1980 to 65 percent in 1990 (p. 38). ESL (English as a second language) programs at the postsecondary level have grown commensurately, with 40 percent of all community colleges offering them in 1991, compared with only 26 percent in 1975 (Gray, Rolph, and Melamid, 1996, p. 74).

Students with disabilities are continuing their education further than they did in the past. Starting in 1991–92, their graduation rates from high school increased, with the largest number of the "exiting" population being those with learning disabilities. In 1978 freshmen who reported having a disability made up 2.6 percent of first-year college students; in 1994, this had jumped to 9.2 percent. One-third of these students were learning-disabled, and by 1994 learning-disabled students made up 3 percent of all college freshmen. This population is more likely to be male, older, and from lower-income backgrounds than the general college population.

Another part of the new diversity is age-related. From 1980 to 1990, college enrollment figures show an increase of 34 percent for those twenty-five and older. By 1993 those forty years and older represented 11 percent of the postsecondary population—an increase of 235 percent from 1970 (The Institute for Higher Education Policy, 1996, p. 14). Seventy-nine percent of this population is enrolled part-time, and over half attends two-year schools. A typical profile of this population is female, married, white, and working at least thirty hours a week. Only 39 percent of older students complete their studies in four years; less than half talks to faculty outside of class; and 93 percent never use student assistance services (p. 17). These students seem to be crunching their education into an already crowded schedule and have little time to participate in activities designed to facilitate success.

It is clear from these statistics that the overall participation in postsecondary education has ballooned way beyond the 1947 prediction made by the President's Advisory Commission on Higher Education; it estimated that 49 percent of the population could profit from at least two years of post–high school education and that 32 percent had the capacity for four years. Not only have the numbers increased dramatically, but the learners are coming from increasingly diverse populations that include more varied ethnic and cultural backgrounds, immigrants, students with disabilities, and those over twenty-five years old. The kinds of faces and styles of learning are multiplying, and the time spent working toward a degree has lengthened. Students today, more frequently than before, include part-timers with high expectations for themselves who are committed to continuing their education but are often unable to make it the primary focus of their lives.

These "new" learners of the 1990s are somewhat different from those of the 1970s, but like those of the 1970s, they continue to stretch teachers' abilities and expectations. How do teachers ensure that a learner whose first language is one other than English understands the handouts and participates in class discussions? How do teachers facilitate collaborative learning and active participation with those whose cultural expectation is that teachers are authority figures with all the answers? What do teachers do to integrate part-timers who arrive at the last minute and leave as next week's assignment is being given out? And how about learners who may be underprepared either in academic skills or in the culture of the postsecondary environment—or both?

How far has our educational system really come from Cross's concern in the 1970s that our "college programs are not prepared to handle the learning needs of these New Students to higher education" (1971, p. 6).

Putting a Face on the Numbers

In order to look for answers to these and other questions and to make the numbers come alive, we now introduce six students who characterize many of the learners enrolled in postsecondary systems today. We describe their general circumstances, goals, backgrounds, and current educational status. Each embodies many features of the students with whom teachers work daily. As readers review these brief histories, they will probably find that the stories sound familiar.

These students serve as case studies throughout the book. As the integration of theory, research, and principles is discussed across the various components of teaching, we will refer to these students to clarify the connections. Readers are encouraged to reflect on their own students in a similar way to ensure a relevance and clarity that comes with such a concrete application. These case studies do not specify racial and ethnic backgrounds, with the exception of Jadwiga; we've done this on purpose in order to facilitate the broadest connections for the reader.

Jadwiga

Jadwiga is a former ESL student who has recently completed her English language coursework. She had been living in the United States for a year when she first enrolled at Urban Commuter University (UCU) three years ago. Before that, she had immigrated from Poland with her family to join extended family members who lived in a large metropolitan area of the Midwest. Jadwiga spoke little English, and her parents spoke none at all. Because they lived in a Polish American community and it was easy enough to find jobs for which English was not required, learning English was not a priority.

After a year, Jadwiga began to feel the restrictions associated with her job in the neighborhood and the missed opportunities due to her lack of English. She discovered through friends that UCU had a good ESL program, but she was a little afraid. Her family did not see the need for her to leave the community; after all, she had a good job and was in a secure environment. After much encouragement from her friends, however, she went to UCU and was assessed by the ESL faculty. They placed Jadwiga into level one of the five-level English language program, and she diligently worked her way through all five levels.

It took her almost two years to complete the coursework by attending classes in the evenings. She worked full-time during the day and joined her growing group of young classmates in the evenings. She looked forward to meeting them for dinner to practice her English before going to class. Jadwiga was finding less time for her family, and when she was home she spent most of her time studying. As much as she wanted to help, she became increasingly resentful of the additional family responsibilities she had to assume due to her increasing proficiency in English. She also wanted to speak English while at home, and she offered to help her parents learn. She found, however, that speaking Polish provided a comfort zone and a tie to their heritage that her family did not want to give up.

Shortly before completing the fifth level of English study, Jadwiga moved into an apartment downtown with some of her friends. She found a new job near school where she had to speak English, and she chose a program of study at UCU that would lead to a career in medical technology. Although she was excited and extremely proud of her accomplishments, her family did not want to talk about it and spoke very little when she came home to visit.

Mike

Mike is struggling to run his own auto repair business. He went to work full-time at his uncle's auto body shop after his graduation from high school. High school had seemed pretty easy to Mike; after all, he had been advised in his freshman year to focus on vocational-technical courses. He had grown up spending a great deal of time in his uncle's shop; he felt very comfortable in the shop atmosphere of these classes and often felt that he knew more than the teachers. Mike and his friends, in fact, developed a reputation for being confrontational and difficult, both in the classroom and outside. Their attitude was that they were already doing "real" work in their part-time jobs as mechanics, and there was nothing relevant going on at school. Mike rarely did homework and often skipped class or was asked to leave when he became too disruptive. Teacher expectations were low. In spite of this, he passed all his classes and graduated in four years.

This experience in school left Mike with the feeling that formal education was for others; he would rather learn on the job where the work was exciting and fulfilling. He worked long hours for his uncle, and because of his dedication and growing expertise the customers often asked for him specifically. At the end of two years he was working on the side for so many customers that his work week had stretched to an average of sixty-five hours. He began paying his friends to help him out with the extra work and eventually rented space in an empty garage down the street from his uncle's where he worked evenings.

After feeling pressure from his friends to cut down on his hours, Mike decided to leave his uncle's shop and direct his efforts solely at developing his own business. He figured that he already had plenty of customers and good, dependable help from his friends. What he didn't have, and didn't know he needed, was formal training in the various components of running a small business. He knew his trade, but he needed a framework for budgeting, marketing, accounting, and training. The first year was tough because he had to depend on others for this expertise. Many of his friends left because he wasn't able to pay them on a regular basis, and Mike became frustrated when he couldn't adequately communicate with his business staff.

Mike asked his uncle for advice and, after listening to him, decided to go back to school in the evenings and take a few classes. He registered in the continuing education program at his high school for an accounting class, where he immediately began to experience the old feelings from his high school days when the assignments seemed irrelevant and he felt inadequate. He struggled with the math examples from the text and wondered what they had to do with his goal of running a business.

Sabina

Sabina is frustrated by her experiences in a graduate-level class taught through distance learning. She graduated from college with a major in English literature and went to work for a small company that specialized in corporate training. Her job was to write up the proposals that were sent out to potential clients; she primarily worked alone and at her own pace. She was quite successful, and her interest in writing continued to grow. After ten years, however, Sabina grew tired of this position and also felt that she needed to spend more time at home raising her two children.

She decided that returning to graduate school might be the answer; it might provide her with the opportunity to refocus her career and at the same time allow her to meet the increasing demands of her family. She found a program that seemed to be a good fit; it had a writing specialization and offered the option of an interactive video delivery system. That meant Sabina would not have to spend time driving thirty miles to class; rather, she could simply go to the interactive video classroom at the local community college and be connected to her classmates and teacher through a video camera. All instruction originated from the primary site, and most of the students attended there; in fact, Sabina was the only student who was not present in the community college classroom.

Even though Sabina had no prior experience with technology, and the monitors and cameras scared her a little, she welcomed the opportunity to be a part of this new distance learning process. She quickly learned how to work the controls and participate in discussions. She had always been resourceful and independent, so she was accustomed to figuring things out on her own. Soon, however, she began to notice the informal conversations going on among her classmates before the teacher arrived. And even though she was always included in group projects and activities, she felt a little like an outsider as she watched the others handling and distributing the materials for a presentation that she had helped to create.

One evening, the teacher invited a guest speaker to class who had never experienced an interactive delivery system. Sabina was present via camera, but the speaker kept forgetting about her and rarely looked in her direction as she spoke to the group. Sabina was able to ask questions at the end, but it was still unsettling to feel so removed. It was then that she decided to make the trip and attend the next class session thirty miles away at the primary site. She had never met her teacher or classmates face-to-face, and she felt she needed that connection.

Linda

Linda is an eighteen-year-old, first-year student living in the residence hall at Urban Residential University (URU). Her goal has always been to become a physician like both of her parents, and she chose URU because of its fine reputation in pre-med education. Her course enrollment for the first term includes biology, chemistry, psychology, English, and calculus.

When Linda was in junior high school, she was diagnosed with a learning disability in reading and worked with a learning disability specialist for three years. Her reading improved, and she received no help for her learning disability after her sophomore year in high school. She always excelled in mathematics, enjoyed science, and especially wanted to be a physician so she could help others.

Linda had never lived away from home before attending URU and was somewhat homesick from the beginning. She called her parents almost every day and often went home for the weekend because her parents lived only an hour away. Her involvement in campus activities was minimal; she found that she needed to study a great deal and felt more comfortable at home on the weekends.

Academically, the coursework was more challenging than Linda expected. Her grades in high school were mostly A's and B's, but at URU she received mostly C's and was in danger of failing her chemistry class. The large lecture classes were markedly different from her small classes in high school, and she felt intimidated by her professors, most of whom didn't know her by name. The reading assignments in all of her classes were extensive, and Linda fell significantly behind. She attended all of her classes regularly and hoped that the information from her lecture notes would make up for the reading that she had not completed.

Linda kept her academic performance concerns a well-guarded secret. When her parents asked, she always said that everything was fine. She didn't seek assistance from others and always studied alone. Because of her increasing concern about grades, she retreated from her fellow classmates. Anxiety about test performance was building as the term moved along toward final exams, and this fear made it difficult for Linda to concentrate. Her study time steadily decreased because of these difficulties. She knew that her goal of going to medical school required very good grades, and she was becoming increasingly concerned about what would happen if she performed poorly. She was especially worried about what she would tell her parents and was having difficulty sleeping and eating because of this anxiety.

Charles

Charles is a twenty-five-year-old student who is taking classes at the technical institute in order to learn computer technology skills that will help advance him on the job. He was working as a data entry clerk, but a higher-level position in data analysis opened up and he wanted to apply for the position. His company supported continuing education and paid the tuition for Charles to learn new skills.

Charles attended classes three nights a week for a total of six hours of class time weekly. This meant that for three nights he went to class directly after work and didn't get home until after his two-year-old daughter had gone to sleep. Because he had to leave very early for work, he didn't see his daughter in the morning which greatly reduced the amount of time he had to spend with her.

Class time was only one factor. Charles found that the coursework required many hours of outside reading and study which he usually completed on the weekend. His wife would have liked to go on family outings during the weekend, but Charles needed to study; there was tension between Charles and his wife because of his time away from her and their daughter.

To compound Charles's problems, there was difficulty at work. Other employees in his department complained that Charles was not alert at his computer and was making numerous entry errors. His boss spoke with him about this, and he was feeling pressure to improve his work performance.

In evening class, Charles found the work interesting and challenging. But after a long day at work, he found it difficult to concentrate and sometimes wished he could be at home with his wife and daughter. The mathematical background required for the data analysis work was significant, and Charles discovered that he needed to review more and more in order to be able to complete the class assignments. He noticed that other students seemed to grasp concepts much more quickly, and he was beginning to feel discouraged. The teacher was usually in a hurry to leave class at the end, so there was no available time to seek extra help.

Because his company was paying the course tuition, Charles had to demonstrate success in the course. If he failed to finish it satisfactorily, he would have to pay the tuition himself. This additional financial concern added to the worry and pressure to achieve.

Teresita

Teresita is in college to complete a bachelor's degree in early childhood education after successfully completing an associate's degree in the same field five years earlier at a neighboring community college. Her husband is not supportive of her educational pursuits and tries to discourage her. Nevertheless, Teresita is determined; she has agreed to maintain all of her household responsibilities as well as her part-time child care job while going to school.

Her enthusiasm was high as she began her coursework. She loved learning and was an excellent student. But she began to feel the stress of trying to meet all her responsibilities at home, work, and school. Her grades began to slide and she didn't know how to turn things around.

At home, her husband was telling her that she was wrong to try to return to school and that was why she wasn't doing well. According to him, she should just stick with her part-time job and be home with the children and everything would be fine.

In a private meeting with the director of the early childhood education program, Teresita cried, saying that she thought she would have to give up her dream of earning this degree. She didn't know how she could catch up with the course assignments and was worried about keeping peace at home.

How Can Theory Help?

If readers will "take these students along" as they proceed, the theoretical constructs described in Chapters Two and Three will seem more relevant and directly connected to teaching. By continuously asking questions raised by the various theories and then critically reflecting on how they could directly enhance the learning and development of these students, the reader will begin to experience the value of integrating theory with practice.

Some of these questions can be directly related to the individual students we described. For instance, in Chapter Two Sternberg's concept of the triarchic mind or Tennant's adult learning theory will raise questions related to Mike's failure with formal schooling and success in the workplace. More important, these theories will lead to reflections on how Mike's needs could be better met if formal educational practice were reexamined and made more relevant.

When the constructivist theories and their relationship to collaborative learning are described, think about Sabina and how this applies to her distance learning situation. Ask how collaboration and connection with students who may not be physically present in the classroom might be facilitated. Reflect on both the positive and negative outcomes of drawing Linda into an interpersonal relationship with either a small group or an individual tutor. Ask if she might need an external mediator, as Vygotsky suggests in his zone of proximal development.

When metacognition is discussed, think about how Charles needs to develop the strategic component of self-regulation in order to manage his stress and organize his time. Ask how Brookfield's concept of cultural suicide may affect each of these students as they lose their traditional family support. Using McClusky's theory of margin, look for the elements of load versus power that each of these students carries.

Another set of questions and reflections could be related more generally to the variables we have embedded in our student descriptions. One of the most farreaching variables that generates many unanswered questions is that of instructional delivery method. Great differences in student backgrounds, for example, will continue to have an impact on teaching practice and on questions related to the learning environment this creates; the interaction of individual learning styles, the effect on interpersonal relationships, and the effect on active, collaborative learning must be addressed.

An increasing number of postsecondary learners will have English as their second language and bring cultural expectations for teaching and individual development that may not easily fit into traditional learning settings. How can teachers integrate a range of cultural imperatives with theoretical perspectives on active learning, constructivism, and different ways of knowing? Can there be a comfort zone that acknowledges and respects a wide range of needs and expectations while challenging learners to expand their

meaning systems? How is the balance between support and challenge created? Do teachers' assumptions about learning and the
environment match those of the students?

Conclusion

These and many more questions will be raised throughout this volume in order to guide a reflection on teaching practice and the
construction of a theoretical framework to facilitate student learning and development.

Chapter Two

Theories of Personal Development and Learning

Our goal in this chapter is to begin laying the groundwork for an integrated approach that will advance learning and development; here we present three of the six theories that underlie the topics in this volume; we discuss the other three in Chapter Three. The six topics that form the basis of research related to learning and development are

1. Self and identity
2. Motivation
3. Interaction with the environment
4. Ways of knowing
5. Learning styles and preferences
6. Self-regulation and goal setting

These are not the only topics related to learning and development, but they are primary considerations that help to improve practice. In this chapter, we present an overview of the theories relevant to the first three of the six topic areas; the last three appear in the next chapter.

Even though we discuss theory separately, it is not to be viewed in isolation. We begin with theory in order to provide a basis for understanding and discussion. In our discussion we use the case studies from Chapter One to illustrate how theory helps explain specific learning situations. In Part Two we review the relevant research and link it with the theories presented here.

Self and Identity

When facing any group of learners, it is important to acknowledge their varying backgrounds and previous learning experiences. As teachers, it is not enough to be ready with course content, syllabi, exams, and grading procedures. What is offered to students is only part of the equation. What students bring to the learning experience is equally critical. Too often the delivery of instruction is primary; little attention is given to the reciprocal nature of learning and to examining teaching as it is likely to be received by students.

Individuals bring many different qualities to the learning environment, and the more teachers understand diverse backgrounds, experiences, and needs, the more likely they are to teach effectively. As illustrated in the case studies in Chapter One, many factors influence what students bring with them. Social, emotional, intellectual, and cultural influences all contribute to diversity in the classroom.

Jadwiga is representative of an increasing number of students new to the United States who must overcome the challenges of learning a new language. As they become more proficient in English and pursue advanced education, these students continue to need help with both written and oral communication skills. In addition, they often experience tensions associated with moving away from their traditional cultures. New information presented to students who are not from the predominant culture is likely to be received in different ways.

Another way to understand the effects of culture and identity on learning is to examine the characteristics of cultural groups. Asians, for example, value collective benefit over individual gain. They are more socially and psychologically dependent on each other, reflecting a view of self that is less individualistic than that traditionally found in Western cultures (Pai and Adler, 1997). Educationally, it has been shown that Asian students may profit from their emphasis on interdependence. Treisman (1986) found that Asian students surpass black students in academic performance because the Asian students work together to help each other and learn cooperatively, whereas the black students are more isolated.

Chickering's Theory of Identity Development

Chickering (1969) originally focused on the importance of the development of autonomy and independence; however, in recognition of cultural differences, he revised his notion of development to include the idea of moving through autonomy toward interdependence, acknowledging that total autonomy and independence is not the desired goal (Chickering and Reisser, 1993). Chickering's theory includes seven vectors that describe psychosocial development during college; each is briefly described here.

1. Developing competence is concerned with three areas: intellectual, physical and manual, and interpersonal. Intellectual competence is the acquisition of knowledge and skills related to specific content material. Physical and manual competence involves participation in recreational and athletic activities. Interpersonal competence is acquired through interaction with others and the development of communication and leadership skills.

2. Managing emotions involves the ability to recognize and accept feelings and to appropriately express and control them.

3. Moving through autonomy toward interdependence is the ability to separate from parents and family while still remaining linked to them and the development of confidence without the need for consistent reassurance and support.

4. Developing mature interpersonal relationships includes the development of recognition, tolerance, and appreciation for differences. In addition, there is growth in healthy and intimate relationships with friends and partners.

5. Establishing identity is built on the previous vectors and includes acceptance and comfort with oneself. Identity is established in the areas of gender and sexual orientation, cultural heritage, and a sense of one's role in life. Of particular importance is the development of positive belief in oneself.

6. Developing purpose is concerned with the future directions. It involves the ability to make decisions even when facing opposition and deciding to propose a course of action consistent with one's personal motivations.

7. Developing integrity involves the development of a value system that considers the needs of others as well as one's own interests.

Chickering offers the following suggestions for promoting development in these factors. There should be opportunity for student and faculty interaction, clearly defined goals reflective of the institution's values, a curriculum that reflects diverse perspectives, instruction that includes opportunities for active learning and respect for individual differences, and collaborative programming between academic and student affairs.

Concepts of self and identity are closely tied to a person's heritage and upbringing and are important components of what the learner brings to any experience. As course requirements and learning assignments are developed, it is important to consider how students from varying backgrounds are likely to respond. For example, learners who value cooperation and interdependence are likely to respond positively to group projects, whereas those who favor individual competition will not. Ideally, all learners should have opportunities that are comfortable for them while being gently challenged to experience activities outside their comfort zone. Effective teaching takes into account what the learner brings; the teacher seeks to build on that while promoting exploration into new, less familiar territory.

Marcia's Theory of Identity Formation

Marcia's theory of identity formation defines four stages of self-views: (1) foreclosure, (2) moratorium, (3) identity diffusion, and (4) identity achievement (Marcia, 1966, 1980). Each stage occurs as a result of the presence or absence of a crisis and a commitment. For example, in the stage of foreclosure an individual makes a premature commitment to a goal or vision based on parental wishes. In this stage, the person may forestall the search for a true identity of self only to find later that problems arise. In the moratorium stage, one delays commitment to a goal while exploring different alternatives. Sometimes this becomes problematic when the individual continually explores avoiding commitment altogether. The stage of identity diffusion is characterized by feelings of apathy. No direction is taken, and the individual remains stuck, evading the issues of true identity formation. Finally, the stage of identity achievement is reached; the person clearly has a sense of direction and purpose after having considered different alternatives. Although these commitments have strength, they are not unchangeable and they allow for modification over time.

The individual's understanding of self is a key part of what is brought to the learning environment. Mike, for example, views himself as a practical learner and one for whom formal education is not particularly well suited. His past experiences in high school vocational classes reinforced his notion of self as someone who learns best when content is immediately applicable to relevant, practical situations. Faced with learning that emphasizes concepts and theories, he has difficulty seeing their relevance.

In Marcia's terms, Mike's identity stage is one of moratorium; in his new academic venture there is a period of unresolved crisis, and attempts are being made to reach a resolution. Should he persist in the formal learning setting and struggle with concepts and theories even though he doubts their relevance, or move away from that setting and give up the idea of running his own business?

Linda is also experiencing identity issues. Her issues, however, are what Marcia would term *foreclosure* because she has made a commitment (to become a physician) based on her parents' wishes. A crisis is beginning to develop as she experiences academic frustration that causes her to doubt her ability to succeed. When someone is experiencing frustration or unresolved conflicts, the teacher's responses are critical and can help determine learning outcomes. Overall, identity development is a powerful influence on learning.

Mezirow's Theory of Transformation

Learners in every situation bring with them certain schemata or meaning systems composed of sets of beliefs or assumptions based on their experiences (Mezirow, 1981). These schemata form filters through which new information is received and interpreted.

For example, Mike's schemata include beliefs about the relevance of concepts and theories to practical situations. His assumption that information is valuable only if it can be easily applied to real-life situations is problematic in his current learning situation. Mezirow would say that Mike needs to engage in a process of critical reflection in order to transform his assumptions. In this way, he would find ways to make connections between what he is learning now and how it may be useful to him. The teacher could meet with Mike individually and help him imagine succeeding with his own auto repair business and applying some of the course content to this venture.

Motivation

Cultural and social expectations and self-perceptions are only some of the critical factors in learning and development. Motivation also plays a significant role and affects performance. For example, some people ascribe their learning outcomes to external factors ("The teacher was unfair," "I was not lucky that day," or "There was not enough time"). Others focus on internal factors ("I did not study enough," "I need more background for this course," or "I was careless when reading the test questions").

Rotter's Theory: Locus of Control

This phenomenon of attributing learning outcomes to either internal or external factors is referred to as *locus of control*—the place where the student puts responsibility for performance results (Rotter, 1966). According to Rotter, how one perceives learning outcomes and attributes responsibility for them influences self-concept and motivation to succeed.

Linda attributes her academic struggles to required reading that is too long and difficult, believing that if only the reading were more manageable she would be successful. Instead of focusing internally on her own need to improve her reading proficiency, Linda avoids reading and feels increasingly powerless. If she were more centered on her own need for developing reading skills and less focused on external factors such as assignment difficulty, Linda would be more likely to seek help and improve her academic performance. Her beliefs about causality are keeping her from making satisfactory progress.

Weiner's Attribution Theory

Attribution theory (Weiner, 1984, 1990) states that the explanations one gives for successes and failures actually influence subsequent performance. For example, individuals prone to failure tend to cite inadequate ability as causes for failure and luck or mood as causes for success. Therefore, any future successes are seen as outside their personal control and dependent on chance. Conversely, students oriented toward success connect ability and diligence to success and lack of effort to failure. Successful experiences reinforce self-esteem and self-control, and failure leads to a need to try harder next time. What is known from attribution theory is that how a person explains success or failure is more important than how often he or she has succeeded or failed (Covington, 1993). A person's own emotions and the emotional reactions of others contribute to the development of our self-perceptions.

The power of self-belief is very strong. For example, even if individuals succeed, it may not be reinforcing or encouraging for future tasks if they believe that success is due to circumstances outside their control. Why try again in the future if the result is due to chance? Linda, for example, has newly formed perceptions about her ability to succeed now that she is in college. She has lost faith in her academic ability, and even though she did well on her most recent chemistry exam, she attributes this to luck in that most of the test material was from the lecture notes. Because she lacks confidence in her ability and credits her last exam result to luck, she is not putting forth effort to complete the course readings and increase her study time. Her anxiety around performance is increasing and is immobilizing her.

When faced with a learner's poor performance, teachers may believe that the learner is not motivated, lacks drive, or just does not care. However, explanations for poor academic performance are not often readily apparent and frequently involve the interaction of many complex factors. Sometimes what appears to be lack of effort is really fear of failure.

Weiner and Covington: Self-Worth Theory

Self-worth theory (Weiner, 1984, 1990), closely connected to attribution theory, is another framework through which to view motivation and behavior. With this perspective, self-acceptance becomes equal to succeeding academically in a competitive environment. According to self-worth theory, we are not just dealing with lack of motivation. "Poor performance is as much the result of being over motivated, but for the wrong reasons, as it is of not being motivated at all. The real threat to learning occurs whenever the individual's sense of worth becomes tied to the ability to achieve competitively . . . once failure threatens a self-image of competency, with its legacy of shame and anger, students will likely withdraw from learning" (Covington, 1993, p. 75).

Bandura's Self-Efficacy Theory

Related to, yet different from, attributions about performance is the concept of self-efficacy or one's belief about the ability to be successful in a given situation (Bandura, 1977). When barriers begin to impede progress, self-efficacy beliefs help determine how much effort will be expended in learning. In the academic arena, an individual might have low self-efficacy beliefs in particular subject areas and high self-efficacy beliefs in others.

What influences an individual's self-efficacy beliefs? According to Bandura (1986) there are four sources of efficacy beliefs: (1) mastery experiences, (2) vicarious experiences, (3) social persuasion, and (4) physiological and emotional states. Mastery experiences are those that reinforce beliefs of competence. Successes tend to raise a person's level of self-judgment, whereas failures tend to lower it. Individuals with a strong series of successful experiences are usually able to tolerate an occasional failure with little or no overall effect on their positive self-efficacy beliefs. Easy successes, however, do not facilitate positive self-efficacy beliefs and should not be encouraged as a way to change self-judgments.

Vicarious experiences influence self-efficacy beliefs by offering individuals the opportunity to observe others similar to themselves performing well. It has been noted that observing others as they model successful behavior can help raise a person's own self-appraisal if there is some recognition of similarity between them.

The third type of influence—social persuasion—is somewhat helpful in countering a person's self-doubt, but it is not effective alone. Social persuasion involves pressure to meet expectations of others to perform or belong. For example, participation in a group learning activity can be facilitated by others in the group seeking a common goal. In order to produce a change, social persuasion must be accompanied by other influences.

Reducing stress and negative emotions can also help combat negative self-efficacy beliefs. It is known that anxiety, frustration, and depression are all influenced by one's beliefs of competence. When learners are in supportive psychological environments, they tend to have higher self-efficacy beliefs that enable them to better handle difficult situations when they arise (Multon, Brown, and Lent, 1991).

The effects of high and low self-efficacy beliefs are significant. High self-efficacy beliefs result in enhanced effort during difficult tasks, reduced stress in taxing situations, and the choice of goals that are challenging and that sustain interest and involvement. Low self-efficacy beliefs result in reduced effort, tendencies to give up when faced with difficult tasks, increased attention to personal deficiencies, the development of avoidance behavior, increased anxiety and stress, and the likelihood of lowered aspirations (Bandura, 1986).

Some of the case studies nicely illustrate how the perspective of self-efficacy beliefs helps promote understanding of their learning situations. For example, previous successes and failures help determine an individual's self-efficacy beliefs. When faced with repeated failures, learners may take beliefs of incompetence and integrate them with their concept of self, thus making it difficult to separate self from belief (Nisbett and Ross, 1980). Mike's situation represents this phenomenon. He has come to believe that he is not academically adept and will only be successful in practical situations. This belief is central to his idea of self so, when faced with traditional academic activities, he sees them as too challenging and he retreats.

Linda had a series of unsuccessful learning experiences and is developing negative self-efficacy beliefs about her ability to perform well in college overall and in chemistry specifically. Because she has kept her failure a secret, she is not able to receive support from others and finds herself in an environment filled with anxiety, frustration, and doubt. Because she has not revealed her failure, encouragement from others is not forthcoming, and she is also not observing those with whom she identifies achieving well. None of the four influences on developing positive self-efficacy beliefs are operating for Linda. In addition, her anxiety is causing problems with eating and sleeping, and this further contributes to her learning problems.

Maslow's Needs Satisfaction Theory

Another perspective through which to view motivation is that of needs satisfaction. Maslow (1970) presents a needs hierarchy that shows how individuals are motivated to have their needs met in a hierarchical fashion, from most basic needs (safety, food, shelter) to higher-level needs (love, esteem, belonging). Maslow's hierarchy focuses on the importance of recognizing that when lower-level needs are not satisfactorily met, performance on tasks dependent on higher-level need achievement is compromised. For example, in Charles's situation, his basic need for sleep and time with his family are being compromised by the time he is spending in school at night and the time he spends studying. Because he is not spending the necessary time with his daughter and wife, he is experiencing tension and frustration at home that is making it difficult for him to concentrate on his studies. On the surface, it might appear that Charles's poor academic performance is due to lack of motivation or laziness when, actually, he is unable to concentrate because his more basic needs for sleep and feelings of love and belonging with his family are not being fully met.

Teresita's situation can also be understood through Maslow's hierarchy. Even though she had great enthusiasm at the beginning of her learning experience, the strain of duties at home and the need to work have overtaken her higher-level need to achieve academically. Until she is able to resolve these more basic concerns, it is likely that her academic success will continue to be thwarted.

Teachers are not always aware of the many personal factors contributing to lack of success. Often, close involvement with students and knowledge of the circumstances leads to better understanding. When confronting a student's poor performance or apparent lack of motivation, it is helpful to remember that there are many possible explanations for the behavior.

Interaction with the Environment

In addition to past experiences, cultural and social expectations, beliefs, and motivation, the specific learning environment and the individual's response to it has a powerful effect on learning. It has long been acknowledged that there is a strong connection between environment and behavior. Over sixty years ago, Lewin (1936) put forth the idea that behavior is a result of person-environment interactions. Some learners thrive in small, intimate settings but are not successful in less personal situations with large numbers of students. Lewin's idea of the importance of person-environment interaction is embraced by many who believe that the right match between an individual and a particular environment will produce optimal opportunity for learning. It is also known that a reciprocal effect exists between students and environments, each affecting the other (Kaiser, 1971). For example, physical environments with open spaces designed for interaction promote student engagement. When students congregate and interact with each other, the result contributes to a more open and inviting atmosphere, fostering the exchange of ideas and influencing the learning environment. How campuses, classrooms, and learning settings are constructed influences both the learners and the overall educational atmosphere.

For instance, the developmental instruction model (Knefelkamp, 1984) shows that an open environment for discussion is important to helping students explore identity issues. This model includes four variables related to challenge and support: structure, diversity, experiential learning, and personalism. *Structure* is the framework and direction given to students; *diversity* is the degree to which alternatives to learning are presented and promoted; *experiential learning* is the degree to which students have direct involvement in activities; and *personalism* is the notion that a positive environment provides for safety while encouraging risk taking.

In Linda's case, her residence hall lacks educational programming to promote growth and independence. Instead, students are basically left alone to find their own way. Linda has withdrawn and is not developing relationships of support. She is floundering in an environment that offers little opportunity for growth and development. In addition, her classes are mostly large lectures. She knows few of her fellow students and has not connected with any of her teachers. According to Moos (1986), whose work was focused on residence hall life, the learning climate is greatly affected by the relationship dimension or the degree to which persons help each other feel free to express themselves. In Linda's situation, this relationship dimension is greatly lacking and contributes to her lack of success.

Educators must recognize situations in which relationships are needed to build success; they should seek ways to provide opportunities for these relationships to develop. If a learner is feeling isolated from her peers and unknown by her teachers, she may need help in developing connections to promote learning success. Taking a personal interest in students and discovering those who can benefit from interaction with others is part of the responsibility of effective teaching.

McClusky's Theory of Margin

Another concept of environmental influence on learning is that of power versus load. McClusky (1970) puts forth the idea that there must be a balance between load and power in the learning environment, and he calls this a theory of margin. *Load* is all that dissipates an individual or creates stress, and *power* is all that contributes to strength in dealing with the load. When there is a lack of balance and load outweighs power, learning often suffers.

Charles is the twenty-five-year-old student taking computer classes while working full-time. McClusky's theory of margin, as applied to Charles, suggests that the balance between power and load is more heavily weighted toward load. The pressures of family, work, and finances bear hard on him and make it very difficult for him to concentrate on his studies. McClusky might suggest that Charles reevaluate his situation and reduce some of the load in order to increase his learning success.

What role can the teacher play when a student is overcome with load to the degree that learning suffers? First of all, just recognizing and acknowledging the situation can be helpful. Meeting with the student to discuss reasons for poor performance and asking questions that may reveal learning constraints can be a good first step. When the environment allows for personal interaction and the development of relationships, it is possible to know more about individual learners and identify ways to help them. In a meeting with Charles, the teacher might agree to adjust some of the assignment due dates and offer suggestions for how to make the best use of the available time. If it does become necessary for Charles to withdraw from the class, the teacher can serve as a support and encourage him to try again later.

Moos's Theory of Social Climate

The social climate of learning environments is significant as it pertains to individual learner comfort. As noted earlier, Moos (1986, 1979) constructed a model of social climate. This model includes the degree to which persons help each other express themselves, the opportunities for personal growth and development, the way the learning organization is managed and controlled, and how clearly the goals of the institution are communicated. This idea of social climate is particularly pertinent to the success of individual learners. For example, classrooms that emphasize social engagement through collaborative learning projects tend to encourage free and open expression and minimize individual competition in favor of group interaction.

Which learners in Chapter One would be most comfortable in such a setting? Linda, who is experiencing academic difficulty and frustration and is retreating socially, might initially find this learning environment uncomfortable and threatening. However, in a situation requiring group interaction and mutually supportive learning, she could begin to gain confidence, develop social skills, and, in a noncompetitive environment, be able to learn with less anxiety. But if her feelings of failure have become so overwhelming that they inhibit her ability to interact at all, she may be unable to profit from such a situation.

Fit or match between an individual learner and a specific learning environment is a complex phenomenon. We know that learners possess different learning styles (Myers and Briggs, 1985; Canfield, 1988; Witkin, 1976) and that one's learning preference influences level of comfort in educational settings. These ideas of individual learning styles and different ways of knowing are explored more fully later in this chapter. For now we examine just how important it is that learners feel comfortable while learning and whether or not it is necessary that their learning environments match their learning styles or preferences.

One illustration is Sabina, who is studying in a distance learning environment. Sabina chose the opportunity to participate in distance learning because she was unable to travel to the classroom site. Her learning style is such that she prefers active group interaction and opportunity for free and open expression. Having become familiar with interactive video technology, she hoped that she could be an active participant even though she was located miles away from the classroom. As it turned out, Sabina became increasingly frustrated with the distance learning environment; she felt ignored by one of the guest speakers and left out when her fellow classmates were able to handle and distribute materials not immediately available to her. In this case, the distance learning environment contrasted sharply with Sabina's learning preference for inclusion and active participation.

Even though it is recognized that learners are most comfortable in environments that closely match their learning styles, it is not always feasible or even desirable to attempt to achieve perfect learner and environment fit. Brookfield (1995) points out that the real world does not always allow for fit between individual preference and reality. By accommodating learner preferences in the environment, educators are not fully preparing students to meet real situations outside the classroom where they will be required to adapt to uncomfortable situations. Instead, Brookfield recommends that students be helped to become adaptable. They need to become aware of those situations that provide comfort and those that produce tension and learn coping strategies for times when environment and individual preference are in conflict. Going to great lengths to assess individual learning styles and match teachers and students who share similar preferences is neither practical nor pedagogically desirable. Instead, both teachers and students benefit from becoming more aware of individual differences, accommodating to different styles, and making environmental adjustments when feasible. Given this understanding, how could Sabina's situation be improved?

Recognizing Sabina's frustration and feelings of separateness when her classmates are actively engaged with concrete materials, the teacher might be more attentive to planning each class session in advance and sending materials to Sabina at the distance learning site. Instructors who have taught in distance learning environments agree that the teaching is more demanding and that advanced planning and distribution of materials is a particular challenge. Here the burden of overcoming barriers in the learning environment falls heavily on the instructor.

Purposeful interaction with the environment is essential to effective learning and development. The more actively the learner participates, the more effective the result. The challenge is to help learners move from passive behaviors, including quiet listening and silent reading, to more active engagement such as questioning, summarizing information, organizing material into manageable chunks, and critically reflecting. This is further discussed in Chapter Three when self-awareness and self-regulation are emphasized, but it is important to think of active learning in connection to forces in the environment that either encourage or hamper it.

Conclusion

We have explored the theoretical foundations of self and identity, motivation, and interaction with the environment. Now, in Chapter Three, we continue with the theories underlying ways of knowing, learning styles and preferences, and self-regulation and goal setting.

Theories Related to Cognitive Development and Learning

In this chapter we explore the last three of our six major topics: ways of knowing, learning styles and preferences and self-regulation and goal setting. We begin by looking at various ways of knowing, including components of intelligence, how learners understand knowledge and, based on that, how they engage in the process of learning.

Ways of Knowing

Chances are that when teachers prepare a class or lead a workshop, they design instructional materials that fit their own learning styles and ways of knowing. They may carefully reflect on what has been most effective in their personal learning experiences and, feeling comfortable with it, adapt it to the subject at hand. For instance, if they have always found visual reinforcement helpful, they probably enter the classroom armed with a folder of carefully constructed overhead transparencies. If they go beyond this, the preparation may include what was heard at the latest professional conference where research was presented confirming that the lecture was dead and collaborative learning was the way to go. With this information, they systematically design small-group activities and let the students work on their own. Alternatively, maybe colleagues have suggested that one particular method works best for a particular discipline. In a workshop on time management or a chemistry lab, for example, there may be a tried and true set of materials developed around a formula that presumably "works for everyone," along with a syllabus that everyone is expected to use.

What is missing from these assumptions is a theoretical framework that informs about the learners' different understandings of what knowledge is and also how they approach the task of learning. Once teachers have a better idea of the variables affecting the many ways of knowing, they can construct a more effective range of instructional approaches that will meet the needs of the increasing variety of learners pursuing their education.

Relevancy and Experience

Mike seems to be most successful when he is involved in an environment that is relevant to his interests. Brown, Collins, and Duguid (1989) suggest that learning is highly effective when the learner is engaged in realistic, messy problems rather than those that are more linear and predictable, as is the case so often in formal educational settings.

From their work with "Just Plain Folks," Brown and others conclude that cognitive apprenticeships where the learner is engaged in authentic activities in a relevant context helps to foster learning. For Mike this suggests that he would learn best through an internship or independent study situation with a plan of study that includes at least several hours a week at a work site under the guidance of an expert in the field. If this is not possible, perhaps a simulated work environment would be effective. In this way, teams of students are created in the classroom, they are asked to design a business plan, and then are expected to find solutions to realistic problems associated with their "own" businesses.

If Mike were engaged in such a learning environment, his practical intelligence would be highlighted and perhaps serve as positive reinforcement that would further motivate him. In other words, even though he may not do well in the analytic tasks required of him in school, he excels in an environment where practical performance is valued.

Tennant and Pogson's notion of tacit knowledge (1995) supports this idea. He contends that adults develop expertise in domains indirectly through experience. Often they are unable to articulate their knowledge base; rather, they depend on an implicit memory that does not diminish with age. He refers to the importance of procedural (how to do something) rather than declarative (body of information) knowledge.

Components of Intelligence

Howard Gardner's (1983) ideas also contribute to an understanding of Mike. His theory of multiple intelligences describes an intelligence as a set of tacit knowledge related to performance in a particular domain. Gardner outlines seven intelligences: linguistic, logical-mathematical, spatial, musical, bodily kinesthetic, interpersonal, and intrapersonal. Mike is most likely strong in several of them, including bodily-kinesthetic (physical involvement in an activity) and interpersonal abilities.

This new way of looking at intelligence leads to Sternberg's (1988) triarchic theory. He contends that intelligence consists of three components: analytical, synthetic, and contextual intelligence. The analytical piece is best reflected in traditional approaches to learning in formal settings. There the learner frequently processes information by analyzing how to solve a given problem and then monitoring and evaluating the effectiveness of the solution. Following this, the solution is implemented, and, subsequently, knowledge is acquired by sorting out the most relevant information for storage and connecting it to prior knowledge. The process here follows a linear format and is characterized by an internal, mental methodology.

Sabina has always been successful in this area, as measured by her standardized test scores and consistently high grades. For Mike, however, this area causes the most trouble. He is not particularly interested in learning through an internal, mental analysis of information that is presented to him. This would account for his low grades and for low performance on standardized tests. Mike's performance in the second area—synthetic intelligence—is probably higher. Here is where many traditionally high achievers in school experience difficulty; they cannot go beyond what is given them in order to create solutions to novel situations. The internal world of mental processing often collides here with the external world of messy, complicated situations in which neatly learned solutions don't work. Mike's ability to deal effectively with the daily problems of his business indicate his strength, not only in this second component but in the third piece of Sternberg's theory—the contextual.

The contextual piece is where one is able to adapt successfully to the everyday world and to go beyond adapting to actually selecting and shaping the environment. Here again, traditionally successful students may run into trouble.

For instance in the case of Linda, she has been a high achiever throughout her high school years by studying hard and performing well on tests that have been based for the most part on information that was given in class or that came straight out of a textbook. Now in college, she is expected to go beyond the text and synthesize by connecting ideas from various sources. This was not an expectation in her high school studies, and she has not been taught how to learn this way. She also does not know how to adapt to this new environment; she was taught that the more time she spent alone memorizing information, the better she would do. No one told her that seeking academic assistance or working collaboratively were acceptable ways to adapt to and to shape the learning environment to her advantage.

Emotions can also contribute to a person's cognitive processing. Mayer and Salovey (1997) describe this concept as emotional intelligence and define it as a developmental process. It starts with learners perceiving and accurately expressing the needs related to their emotional state and then moves to a level at which they consciously regulate emotions and reflect on them regularly.

In the case of Sabina, she seems to be able to understand and to express her needs related to distance learning. She understands that her feelings of isolation and lack of involvement stem from her physical separation from the larger group of learners. She does not attach these feelings to resentment of the instructor or to any inability to understand the content.

It is likely that Sabina has moved through level two of Mayer and Salovey's emotional intelligence development, as she has allowed an analysis of her feelings to help her direct attention to the significant variables in the situation; she is evidently a learner who enjoys collaborative processing, and she realizes that she must change things in order for that to be satisfied. If she were at the highest level of emotional development, Sabina would be able to consciously detach herself from the negative feelings she attaches to this method of instruction through a process of reflection and concentrate on the positive, utilitarian aspects of it that led her to enroll in the first place.

Likewise, if Charles had been able to access his emotions ahead of time to help him anticipate how going back to school would really feel, perhaps he would have been more prepared and better able to deal with the impact it has had on his life. It may have caused him to focus on different aspects of his situation, which could have led him to make another decision.

Meaning Systems

These components of intelligence all affect how an individual understands. Mezirow introduced the concept of "meaning systems" that act as filters through which learners take in information and try to make sense of it. Individuals construct these systems, based on their own experiences, to develop sets of beliefs, theories, and assumptions. These in turn become the filter through which incoming information is processed. If the beliefs are distorted and organized without careful thought—or critical reflection, as Mezirow describes it—new experiences will be processed in the same way. Cross and Steadman (1996) also talk about the organization of information and refer to it as schemata. Without schemata, learners must rely on memorization for learning. They provide a good image for this by their description, "Our existing knowledge base is the Velcro of the mind to which new information sticks. However, in the same way that lint can keep Velcro from sticking, misconceptions in a schema can interfere with connecting new information to existing knowledge" (p. 41).

Collaboration and Constructivism

The work of Vygotsky (1965) helps our understanding of the significant role played not only by the overall environment but by the facilitators in that environment. He describes an individual's zone of proximal development as being the area between latent ability and realized potential. He theorizes that guided instruction leading one across that zone is a necessary ingredient for learning and that intelligence is most related to performance following this mediation. Vygotsky's framework outlining the effectiveness of an external mediator who gradually releases the responsibility of learning to the learner relates to the concepts of collaboration and constructivism.

Although there is no one constructivist approach to learning, most emphasize social interaction and adaptability. To view learning through this lens, it is necessary to rethink the traditional idea of what knowledge is. In the traditional view knowledge is considered foundational; most often the expert, or instructor, uses Freire's "banking concept" by making "deposits" of information into a willing, passive recipient—the learner. This exemplifies Linda's understanding of the educational system; she waits for the instructor to simply fill her with information. The constructivist viewpoint, however, suggests that knowledge is nonfoundational and is "a socially constructed sociolinguistic entity and that learning is inherently an interdependent, sociolinguistic process" (Bruffee, 1993, p. 3). Bruffee discusses this approach as it relates to collaborative learning. He makes the assumption that learning occurs as people talk and work toward a consensus about the knowledge they need for the task at hand. He suggests that when heterogeneous groups of learners work together, the zone of proximal development expands due to the varied experiences of all members in the group and consequently increases the potential learning power of the individual.

If Linda's instructors set up the expectation that study groups were a positive element of learning and actually began the process with in-class, small-group activities, perhaps she would develop relationships that would keep her on campus more often and help her find the support she needs. She would also begin to understand "knowing" in a different way; she would see herself as an active participant in constructing her knowledge base.

Field Dependence-Independence

Related to Bruffee's emphasis on individuals learning from each other is the work of Stephen Brookfield (1986), who has described adult learners using Witkin's (1949, 1950) concepts of field dependence and field independence. In the field of adult learning, there is often the assumption that self-directed learning is a sign of maturity and that being characterized as a field-independent learner is more likely to lead to success. Field-independent learners are considered to be more analytical, inner-directed, and individualistic and to have a stronger sense of self-identity, whereas field-dependent

learners are extrinsically oriented, that is, in need of external reinforcement and more structure from a mediator (Brookfield, 1986).
Brookfield's work has shown that successful self-directed learners
exhibit characteristics of field dependency rather than independency. "Their learning activities are explicitly placed within a social context, and they cite people as the most important learning
resource. Peers and fellow learners provide information, serve as
skill models, and act as reinforcers of learning and as counselors
in times of crisis" (p. 44).

Sabina's plight is that she is expected to be self-directed while
sitting at the far end of a camera, but she does not feel the connectedness she needs from her peers. She needs their reinforcement and more direct opportunities to collaborate in order to
effectively process information. The distance acts as a barrier to her
learning. Likewise, Linda finds herself in large lecture classes with
no direct offer of learning assistance and assumes that she should
be mature enough to direct her own learning. By continuously
going home to escape her misery, she allows herself no opportunity
to become part of a social setting where she might be more influenced by peer modeling and receive the advice and reinforcement
that could facilitate her success.

View of Knowledge

Constructivism has much to do with how the learner understands
what knowledge is. A good example of this comes from reading
comprehension theory. Schraw and Bruning (1996) discuss readers' implicit models of reading and explain how the different perspectives regarding knowledge that a person brings to the task of
reading determine how the reader attempts to understand. The
transmission model has the reader acting passively with the purpose of simply extracting information from the text.

This sounds like the perspective Linda brings to her studying,
probably as a consequence of the positive reinforcement she received in high school for memorizing facts and then restating them
on tests. She most likely also relied on the translation model in
which meaning is completely within the text—the task being to de-
code the message without connecting it to previous knowledge or
experience. If Linda's instructors did not encourage her to inter-

pret the information, she did not consider it her right to evaluate it critically or to raise questions about the material as it related to her own experiences. Her understanding of knowledge is that someone else has it, and she needs to collect it.

Another model of reading comprehension that connects directly to a constructivist point of view is the transactional model. This perspective assumes that comprehension results when a reader actively engages in the process of building meaning by setting goals and purposes and relating new information to prior knowledge. Schraw and Bruning (1996) contend that most readers are not conscious of the perspective they bring to the reading task and that this often leads to their comprehension being author- or text-centered. This implies that instructors need to provide some direct instruction on how to read a text before making assignments. They could direct students to set a purpose for reading by outlining critical questions beforehand and directly articulating expectations for connecting new material to prior knowledge.

For Teresita, this would be particularly motivating because she recently completed coursework in early childhood education and has her own small children at home. It would be a simple and most likely affirming process for her to see her knowledge base being valued and serving as a foundation for new ideas.

Cognitive Development Continuum

Some of these ways of knowing and various understandings of what knowledge is can be related to the developmental stages through which a learner moves. This notion began with the work of William Perry (1970) when he established the now classic stages of cognitive development. According to his research, learners progressed through four major categories of knowing: (1) absolutist or dualist (viewing the world in terms of right or wrong, with experts holding the "right" answers); (2) multiplicity or problematic (uncertainty creeps in); (3) relativism (knowledge becomes contextual and learners make their own judgments); and (4) commitment, in relativism, which leads to a personalized set of values and identity.

Mike probably functions at a dualistic level when he is in a formal learning situation; he seems intimidated by his instructors in part because he sees them as authorities who hold the answers. He becomes frustrated when he cannot seem to find "their" answers, and that is when he returns to the "real" world. In the context of his world of mechanics, his level of knowing may be at the level of relativism, as he makes judgments regarding work to be done based on varying sets of conditions. He has sufficient experience and knowledge to know that repairs frequently are personal judgments and not set in stone. Perry's levels are most useful if they are applied, not developmentally but within a context, as a way of understanding different thinking patterns.

Whereas Perry's work was primarily conducted with males, Belenky and others (1986) extend the notion of various ways of knowing to females. Even though they do not suggest that these ways are developmental, they have been widely interpreted as such. The positions include (1) silence (a person feels voiceless), (2) received knowing (knowledge comes from an external source), (3) subjective knowing (knowing is intuitive rather than based on evidence), (4) procedural knowledge (procedures for processing information are developed), and (5) constructed knowledge (knowledge is contextual and the knower is part of the context).

More recently, Baxter Magolda (1992) has looked at college students' ways of knowing and reasoning. She discovered patterns of thinking that are related to but not dictated by gender. She argues that gender is primarily a social construct and that differences between the sexes result from interactions within particular contexts that vary by gender. She identifies four stages that evolve from simple to more complex. Within the stages, she describes patterns of gender differences. The stages—absolute, transitional, independent, and contextual—are similar to those of Perry and Belenky, but the patterns within them make them significantly different.

According to Baxter Magdola, at the *absolute level* the learner sees knowledge as being held by an external authority. Females at this level tend to function as receivers, taking notes and studying to do well; whereas males function in a mastering pattern, exhibiting more verbal interaction with the instructor. At the *transitional level* females tend to exhibit an interpersonal pattern by relying on the opinions of others through dialogue and the collection of others' ideas to help construct their own knowledge; males more often engage in an impersonal pattern, with the opinions of others used as material for debate or challenge. At the *independent level* of knowing females are often engaged in an interindividual pattern, whereas males tend to use a pattern of independent processing. Within the interindividual pattern, learners have their own interpretations but value an exchange of ideas; the individual pattern focuses more on the learners' own independent thinking. The *contextual level* is generally characterized by thinking in which a person can make informed judgments and evaluate distinctions among perspectives. According to Baxter Magolda, it rarely appears during the undergraduate years, so she does not suggest any patterns within this level.

We have discussed some of the psychological, emotional, and developmental bases for the way a person approaches a learning task. Closely related to these ways of knowing are individual styles and preferences that affect behavior in a variety of situations. They are less related to age, maturation, and context than the various ways of knowing and, consequently, are perhaps more deeply embedded and more difficult to modify. These learning styles are the focus of the next section.

Learning Styles and Preferences

We discuss the significance of learning styles and preferences within a framework composed of four components: cultural, physiological, personality-based, and instructional preference. These factors are not discrete; they overlap and influence each other regularly, and they are not hierarchical.

It may be helpful to look at the factors through a model in which culture provides a generalized context for the physiological and personality-based traits to become operationalized through instructional preferences. The cultural component can be likened to a battery that energizes the other parts. Also like a battery, it may weaken over time and gradually have less impact. The parts do not in any case operate separately, and although some generalizations can be made based on the administration of assessment measures, for each person the synthesis of all factors is truly unique.

Cultural Factors

Students bring with them a wide range of variables related to their diverse backgrounds, many of which can significantly affect their approach to learning. Stephen Brookfield (1990) suggests that students may be committing "cultural suicide" (p. 153) when the values of the learning community conflict with those of the external community of peers and family. The student may resist the demands of the institution if she is afraid of losing the traditional support system that she has relied on for years. Two of the students we described in Chapter One, Jadwiga and Teresita, dealt with this in very different ways.

Jadwiga, when faced with dwindling support at home, constructed a new network of support. She turned to friends who were experiencing similar attitudes from their families, and together they gave each other support. Teresita, however, has not been able to substitute another support system for the one she is rapidly losing. Her difficulty may be due to having more responsibilities at home with her young family than Jadwiga and consequently not having the time or freedom to find a new network.

Different systems of communication seem to be at the heart of many of the cultural and ethnic differences that affect the learning environment. Bruffee (1993) discusses the impact of ethnicity and culture on collaborative learning. Although he argues that diverse groups "invigorate the conversation," he also talks about how difficult it is for students who come from a background where decision making is top down, with participation and consensus building forbidden (p. 33). It may also be difficult for students who come from cultures in which silence is valued. Goldberger (1996) describes the Native American system of communication in which talk can be considered a waste of time and individuals see the "advantages of silent and respectful listening rather than confrontation" (p. 343). She goes on to say that particularly in cultures that "stress interdependence and social connections rather than independence and autonomy, the rules of speech tend to be more tightly regulated by relationships and statuses, for example, one keeps one's place in the social hierarchy and does not speak out of turn" (p. 344).

Pai and Adler (1997) also look at the effects of culture on communication style. They too note that it frequently depends on the nature of social relationships. They characterize these relationships as either hierarchical—the communication is one way and flows from top to bottom—or egalitarian—there are fewer formal codes. The latter is true in the United States. Because U.S. schools most often reflect the egalitarian structure, students are expected to express themselves directly, make eye contact, and engage in serial exchanges in which taking turns prevails. This may be in conflict with values that students have been taught in their native communities. For instance, according to Pai and Adler, the Asian American family is structured around a hierarchical system in which roles are established according to age, sex, and status. Direct expression of ideas is discouraged. In the African American family, nonverbal exchanges are highly significant, and eye contact is less frequent when individuals speak to each other. The Hispanic American community is often more concerned with interpersonal relationships than with impersonal facts alone and may express their ideas along with personal feelings.

Pai and Adler also discuss language in terms of its styles. They outline five styles that serve various functions and are valued differently: (1) formal (lecture); or (2) frozen (print) styles of communication, which are often found in schools; (3) intimate (private jargon); (4) casual (insider talk), and (5) consultative (specific information). Learners who come from backgrounds in which interaction is valued will have difficulty when there is an emphasis on formal and frozen communication.

Teachers can deliberately plan to integrate various styles of communication into their classrooms; perhaps even more important, they can openly discuss the different styles with students. For instance, with a lecture the session can begin with an explanation of how this format represents a formal style of communication but that it will be followed by a more consultative one. At the same time, students can be guided to engage in a silent, casual conversation during the lecture by writing questions and making personal notations as they listen. This information will help to set the more formal expectations in the classroom while sending the message that various styles of communication are valued.

Wlodowski and Ginsberg (1995) have developed a framework for what they call culturally responsive teaching that attempts to model "how to create compelling learning experiences through which learners are able to maintain their integrity as they attain relevant educational success" (p. 27). They argue that motivation and learning are inseparable and that the following conditions must intersect to enhance learning for a diverse set of learners: establishing inclusion where everyone feels respected, developing positive attitudes by giving learners a choice and ensuring relevancy, enhancing meaning so that the values of the learners are included in the process, and engendering competence that communicates to learners how they can be effective in learning something of personal value (pp. 27–28).

Physiological and Personality-Based Styles

One way to look at the physiological component of learning preferences is through the theory based on left-brain–right-brain research. This theory was first suggested in the nineteenth century when it was found that damage to one hemisphere of the brain selectively affects brain functions. When the left side of the brain suffers an injury, there is often language loss; when the right side is damaged, visual-spatial recognition is affected. Since the time of that discovery, research has been conducted under the premise that the left hemisphere functions more like a computer, with analytical, linear thought processes, and that the right side is more like a kaleidoscope that uses a creative, synthetic approach to thinking (Kitchens, Barber, and Barber, 1991).

Formal schooling frequently places a greater value on left-brain thinking, and individuals whose thinking is more influenced by the right hemisphere may "have developed an attitude of learned helplessness which becomes self-fulfilling and thus a formidable barrier to their learning" (1991, p. 3). Kitchens, a mathematics instructor, contends that it does not matter whether or not each hemisphere actually determines how one thinks but what is important is that individuals approach problem solving from different perspectives. She recommends that teaching include "lateralization," that is, using strategies that encompass both types of thinking, and that students be made aware that the differences reflect styles rather than abilities.

Looking back at Mike, it seems that he is more influenced by the right hemisphere; his ability to synthesize and create solutions to problems in the auto body shop outweighs his ability to process information that is handed to him in a more linear style. Linda, however, has always succeeded when achievement was based on analyzing information presented in a straightforward, linear manner.

It is when she is required to go beyond the facts that she runs into trouble. She is most likely functioning with a left-brain preference.

Personality-based styles, often referred to as cognitive personality styles, "tend to be central to the development of preferences or organizational patterns for learning. They not only influence characteristics at other levels, they are also more stable than other characteristics" (Bonham and Boylan, 1993, p. 2). Before looking at models that fit this definition, a few words of caution are in order. Personality-based styles are not ways of learning; rather, they influence a person's approach to learning. Measures designed to assess learning styles should not be used to create labels for individuals but to show patterns of preferences located on a continuum.

Several models can facilitate thinking about personality-based styles. One of the most extensively studied is that of Witkin (1976), who developed the bipolar concept of field-dependent and field-independent learners. Recall that we used Witkin's work also to understand ways of knowing. Learners who are more sensitive to their surroundings, including people, and who tend to need their surroundings for processing information are field dependent. Those who tend to work more autonomously with less regard for external factors are considered to be field independent. Again, a word of caution: individuals fall along a continuum and not at one end or the other of this construct.

Looking back at the case studies, we see that Teresita tends to fall at the field-dependent end of the continuum. She has difficulty as she tries to focus and concentrate when studying alone. When she attended community college (before starting her family), she was always part of a study group that also became her primary social network. She no longer has time for this, and the lack of it contributes to the stress she feels in school and, generally, in life. Sabina is also more field dependent and struggles with her distant learning situation. She would prefer to have more interaction with her peers and is quite sensitive to the fact that she attends class by sitting alone in an empty interactive video room miles away from everyone. She originally thought she could handle this because at work she functioned pretty much on her own. Why can't she do it now? Part of the reason could be that when she worked, she was able to leave at the end of the day and participate in her social activities. The need for external dependence was satisfied by this portion of the day. Now, with her small children, she is no longer able to nourish that need, and she spends much of her time during the day without peers.

Another model for examining personality-based styles is that measured by the Myers-Briggs Type Indicator (MBTI) (Myers and Briggs, 1985). This instrument is based on variations in the way people prefer to take in information, make decisions, and in general perceive the world. It consists of four dichotomous scales:

1. Extraversion (E)—energies are directed toward the external world—versus introversion (I)—interests lie in ideas and concepts.
2. Sensing (S)—experiences are processed through the senses—versus intuition (N)—attention is directed more to inferences and possibilities.
3. Thinking (T)—judgments are made through logic—versus feeling (F)—personal values play a more significant role.
4. Judging (J)—a need exists for planning and controlling—versus perception (P)—being flexible and more spontaneous and open to events.

Being careful not to pigeonhole, take a look at Jadwiga's personality style, based on the MBTI, to see if it helps to explain some of her actions. She recently completed the inventory, and the results indicate an ENFJ profile. From what is known, she does tend toward extraversion (E). When she went to school to learn English, much of her success was due to her interest in making new friends and constructing a new world for herself. She was very much energized by the external world that she discovered beyond her Polish community. When she decided to leave home, her reasoning was based more on intuition (N) than her senses because she couldn't be sure what the future would bring. A reliance on her senses may have kept her at home, as that would have been the safest thing to do. Her behavior also relates to her values (F) and how important it was to her to become independent and take the chance of going out on her own. Making her decision based on pure logic may have kept her at home. On the judging versus perception scale, Jadwiga comes out slightly higher on the judging (J) dimension. She needs to take control of things, her life in particular, and she does plan and make decisions for which she follows through. A part of her, however, does enjoy spontaneity, especially if it fits into her overall plan. As is the case with all learners, she cannot be neatly pegged into one profile.

Instructional Preferences

Instructional preferences are the external, observable components of a learner's style. They result from the complex interaction between a person's physiological and personality-based styles that exist within a cultural context. Unlike the other styles discussed, instructional preferences are less deeply embedded and consequently more likely to change over time and in different circumstances.

A comprehensive model for looking at instructional preferences has been provided by Canfield (1988). He developed an instrument—the Canfield Learning Style Inventory—that has four scales. The first is for learning conditions and includes affiliation (need for personal relationships), structure (need for detail and organization), achievement (desire to set goals and be independent), and eminence (orientation toward authority and competition). The second scale looks at learner preference for content: numerics, qualitative, inanimate, and people. The third scale focuses on the learner's preferred mode; this scale includes listening, reading, iconic, and direct experience. Last is the expectation the learner has for a particular grade.

By applying these scales to Charles, it is clear how these preferences may change, depending on the learner's circumstances. When Charles was younger and in undergraduate school, he was fairly competitive. He had to be, as he was competing with his peers in a very tough job market—computer programming. He considered himself independent and always set goals for himself. He needed very little structure in his classes because he enjoyed going beyond the assignments and discovering new ideas on his own. He expected high grades and usually received them.

Charles's context for learning has changed this time around. He is in school because his employer strongly suggested he do it if he wants to move ahead. His employer will reimburse his tuition only if he maintains a C average, and that has become his goal; he does not have enough study time to achieve a higher grade. Although he used to enjoy reading beyond the expected assignment, now he prefers listening to the instructor, taking notes, and hoping that will be good enough to get him through. His circumstances have changed and so have his instructional preferences.

It is evident that everyone does not approach learning and understand knowledge from the same perspective. It would facilitate the learning process, however, if individuals were more aware of how they learned. Once individuals become aware of their processing strategies and levels of cognitive development, they can begin to see where the gaps are between instructor expectations and their own. They can then take action that will help them adapt to the environment.

Self-Regulation and Goal Setting

People may not be aware of the different ways they process information. Because information is being processed all the time, it's easy to assume that the behavior is automatic and that everyone else behaves (processes) the same way. It's not until something is particularly difficult or out of the ordinary that people begin to question why they aren't "getting it." Then they may start to critically reflect on the individual nature of their own strategies and styles, as they relate to learning.

For example, when finishing a chapter in a book, a reader might realize that she remembers nothing from the chapter. What is the first thing to do in that situation? Most likely, she will apply certain reading strategies when she reviews the text. She may become aware of subtitles, boldfaced or underlined phrases, italics, introductory paragraphs, and summary sections; she may try to connect the content to her prior knowledge. Perhaps she will reflect on the purpose for reading the material in the first place.

If people engage in these activities, they are demonstrating metacognitive knowledge—an understanding of how to evaluate and regulate learning. Garner (1987) describes three highly interactive components of this concept: knowing about oneself, knowing about the task, and using one's own repertoire of learning strategies. In the example given earlier, the reader examined her own knowledge base and tried to make a connection. She reflected on her purpose for reading and on the task and then reviewed strategies that had worked in the past when comprehension was difficult, such as carefully reading introductory and summary sections.

It is evident that a person's ability to monitor his or her own learning is not a unitary phenomenon; it has several components, including evaluation of the learning process and subsequent regulation of it. In order to effectively engage in the evaluation component, learners must have a set of standards or goals against which to measure their progress. To be most effective, these standards should be flexible and adapted for specific purposes. Following the evaluation, learners need to have a repertoire of "fix-up" strategies available to make any necessary changes. This whole process assumes that learners see themselves at the center of the learning process and in control of the outcomes; it cannot be dictated by an external agent such as an instructor or even a peer. Sabina is a good example of a learner who assumes such control. Once she evaluated what was missing in her learning experience, she regulated it by rethinking her goal of attending class close to home and made the necessary modification. Linda, however, has so far been unable to focus her anxieties and evaluate her situation. She feels totally out of control and responds by fleeing to the safety of her family.

Metacognition—the self-awareness of cognitive processing strategies and the ability to control them—plays a significant role in most theories of learning. It's the executive control function in information processing models whereby the learner regularly makes decisions regarding the organization of incoming information. It has also been referred to as comprehension monitoring in cognitive reading theories and has been labeled as a management strategy by Weinstein within her eight categories of learning.

Weinstein and Mayer (1986) maintain that for comprehension monitoring to be effective, learners must establish learning goals, assess whether or not they are being met, and then modify their approach to learning if necessary. In Weinstein's model of strategic learning (1997), she emphasizes the importance of understanding the interaction between the learners' cognitive strategies and the specifics of the learning situation. In other words, even though learners should have an overall process for evaluating their performance that can be applied across all learning activities, they need to be flexible and modify it based on their goals in a particular area and the demands of the task itself.

Linda, for instance, has set a long-term goal of becoming a physician, but she has done very little to adapt or connect this goal to her current learning situation. She still relies on study strategies that were successful in high school even though they no longer work. She is not evaluating her new environment; rather, she is letting her anxiety about failing consume her and lead her to believe that she is probably not capable of succeeding in it.

Pintrich (1995) expands this concept of self-awareness, labels it self-regulated learning, and states that it is "the active, goal-directed, self control of behavior, motivation and cognition for academic tasks by an individual student" (p. 5). This definition suggests a direct link to the learner's behavior and motivation in addition to a working knowledge of cognitive learning strategies. Pintrich explains that to regulate behavior, learners must have active control over the resources available to them. For instance, they must know how to manage their own schedules and study environments and also how to access appropriate support systems. If Linda were regulating her behavior, she would explore the opportunities for learning assistance available to her, and she would also look into alternate scheduling possibilities. Possibly, she could enroll in non-lecture-style courses or at least find those that offer tutorials or some type of supplemental instruction.

Pintrich (1995) suggests that learners must be able to control and productively use their anxieties to regulate their motivation and affect toward learning; they should make changes to their belief systems about their own abilities and be willing to adapt their goals. Here, Linda could analyze her anxiety and try to pinpoint its cause. To do this, she may need to find a support network composed of peers. She may also want to seek out professional counselors in the counseling center where support groups may be formally organized. Once she is able to evaluate what causes her anxiety in particular learning situations, she can begin to develop strategies to control and regulate it. As she begins to take charge, she will gradually become more confident about her ability to succeed. She may also need to analyze her long-term goal of becoming a doctor, break it down into smaller parts, and find a way to connect it more directly to her current coursework. If she can do this, she may become less anxious and more excited about her work.

When learners apply such self-regulatory processes, they become tools for self-improvement as they encourage the learner to "direct attention, to set and adjust their goals and to guide their course of learning more effectively" (Zimmerman and Paulsen, 1995, p. 175). Some of the ways learning can be enhanced within this framework include distinguishing between effective and ineffective performance and then linking it back to identify the behavior that may have caused it, identifying inadequate learning strategies, managing study time more efficiently, and fostering reflective thinking. We contend that an added benefit is often increased self-efficacy, as the learner may discover she is making unexpected progress toward her goals. When this occurs, self-monitoring strategies are likely to be employed more frequently; likewise, when learners find a lack of progress, it can affect their self-efficacy in a negative way and self-monitoring activities may cease. With Linda, if she begins to network with other first-year students, she might be surprised to find that her progress is normal. In fact, if she speaks with her instructor, she might be pleased to hear that even though her grade may not be what she was hoping for yet, he has seen some good thinking in her work and that with a little assistance in writing, she will do quite well.

Zimmerman and Paulsen (1995) outline four phases for facilitating a process of self-regulated learning. First, learners must establish a baseline of expectations for themselves in a given learning situation from which they can set goals. For instance, Linda could begin to monitor herself and record how long it takes to complete certain types of assignments and which types are most difficult for her. Second, she could be shown how to structure her monitoring activities with a protocol such as a self-questioning strategy that provides immediate feedback on her learning. She could regularly ask herself to articulate the main theme of a class lecture or to summarize a chapter in the text. Next, she would need to become more independent and prepare protocols that are more individualized for her needs. Finally, she may arrive at a level of self-regulated monitoring, be able to generalize the process, and transfer it to her other courses.

A basic assumption reflected in all self-regulating activities is that the learner has established a set of goals. Without goals, there are no standards against which to evaluate one's performance. Two types of learning goals that are frequently described include mastery and performance. Hagen and Weinstein (1995) describe mastery goals as having a primary focus related to learning the material at hand; performance goals focus on the outcome, with learning serving only as a means to an end. When the learner is engaged in trying to attain mastery goals, she is more apt to seek out challenges and put forth effort. These goals are also more often associated with a regular process of self-monitoring. With performance goals, however, learners more often give up when they experience difficulty and do not tend to look for alternative strategies. These learners also do not frequently apply the cognitive strategies of planning and monitoring their learning activities.

Cross and Steadman (1996) label goals as either learning-oriented (mastery) or grade-oriented (performance). They contend that students with learning-oriented goals tend to be more relaxed and less anxious, more collaborative, and better able to use effective study methods than those who are motivated simply by grades. Grade-oriented learners who are driven by performance goals frequently conclude that failure is due to their inadequacies, and this belief may cause them to exhibit patterns of helplessness in future learning situations. This tendency may explain their lack of persistence when difficulties arise. These students would rather avoid failure than admit feelings of low self-worth. If they are not aware of their ability to control learning through the application of different strategies, they attribute their lack of achievement to an overall lack of ability and adjust their goals accordingly.

Although Teresita has established a long-term goal of working in the field of early childhood, she also loves learning for its own sake and has set mastery goals for each of her classes. She enjoys the process of discovering the theory behind working with preschoolers, and the final grade is less important to her than understanding the material. Earlier, when she was attending community college, performance goals were much more significant to her, as she needed to attain a certain grade point average in order to transfer to her current four-year institution. Charles, however, has returned to school as a condition for promotion at work. He cannot really afford it, financially or personally, and his company will not reimburse tuition if he receives less than a C average. His goals are completely performance-oriented; he is ready to give up because he cannot achieve this, and he is unwilling to invest the time to evaluate his situation.

To maintain a risk-free environment, grade-oriented students may either construct goals that are so low that they are assured of meeting them or are so high that failing is almost expected (Atkinson and Feather, 1966). For instance, a student with little background or achievement in science has little to lose when setting a goal of becoming a doctor. The goal is most likely so far out of reach that no one could reasonably expect him to reach it, and consequently it involves little risk. If this same student constructed a more realistic goal of becoming a paramedic—a goal he could reasonably be expected to meet—there is more risk involved and, therefore, a greater threat of failure.

Performance that is related to goals construction is similar to performance based on feelings of self-efficacy or on a belief in one's ability to accomplish a task. Hagen and Weinstein (1995) discuss how students with low-efficacy beliefs tend to be less persistent than those with high-efficacy beliefs. When these beliefs are associated with particular types of goals, learner behaviors are quite different. For example, when students who have low-efficacy, performance-type goals, their behavior becomes one of helplessness when difficulties arise; students with similar beliefs about their abilities but who construct mastery goals often persist until they have achieved success.

A look at the behaviors of Charles and Teresita demonstrates this. Charles has serious doubts about his ability to succeed in school at this time in his life. His goals are driven by a need to please his supervisor in order to receive a promotion at work. The content of the coursework has little direct relevance to the skills required on the job, and his supervisor only cares about Charles's final grades. Charles is feeling total helplessness and lack of control; consequently, he will most likely drop out in the near future.

Teresita is also doubtful about her ability to succeed at a four-year institution, but in contrast to Charles, she is driven by mastery, or learning-oriented goals. She is so eager to learn everything she can about the practice of early childhood education that she is working hard to overcome her feelings of doubt and to find better strategies for learning.

To successfully engage in a process of self-regulated learning, students must believe that they are active partners in the learning process. They must see themselves as being in control of their learning and have access to a repertoire of strategies that can be used when modifications are needed. To be successful monitors of their own learning, they also need to construct goals that provide an appropriate set of standards against which to evaluate their progress. These behaviors are essential to effective learning, and they must be taught and integrated into all learning environments.

Conclusion

In Chapters Two and Three we have examined a variety of theoretical perspectives in order to better understand the learners of today (see Table 1). We have looked at theory through an interdisciplinary lens that has allowed us to cross traditional boundaries and perhaps bring ideas together in novel ways. For example, we have not limited ourselves to cognitive psychology or reading theory. We have combined them with nontraditional ideas about intelligence and attitude and motivation. We have included the effect of culture and personality-based factors when thinking about how a person learns best. We have also looked at gender patterns and the effect of environment among many other factors.

In order to make the theory come alive, we have applied it to the case studies described in Chapter One and have invited readers to make connections to their own students as well. Now we move into additional connections—those related to research, principles, and practice. Through a model for effective practice (TRPP), we demonstrate in Chapter Four how the theoretical framework that we have constructed with the six topics in these two chapters can be strengthened by research and used to develop principles for a more effective practice.

Table 1. Summary of Components
of Theoretical Foundation.

Theoretician	Application to Practice
Self and Identity	
Treisman	Cultural interdependence
Chickering	Autonomy-interdependence
Marcia	Identity development stages
Mezirow	Meaning systems and critical reflection
Motivation	
Rotter	Locus of control
Weiner, Covington	Attribution
Weiner	Self-worth
Bandura	Self-efficacy
Nisbett, Ross	Self-concept
Maslow	Hierarchy of needs
Interaction with Environment	
Lewin	Behavior-person-environment
Kaiser	Student-environment reciprocity
Moos	Model of social climate
McClusky	Theory of margin
Canfield, Witkin	Learning styles
Brookfield	Environmental coping strategies
Ways of Knowing	
Brown, Collins & Duguid	Cognitive apprenticeship
Tennant & Pogson	Tacit knowledge
Gardner	Multiple intelligences
Mayer & Salovey	Emotional intelligence
Sternberg	Triarchic theory of intelligence
Vygotsky	Zone of proximal development
Bruffee	Constructivism
Brookfield, Witkin	Field dependence-independence
Schraw & Bruning	Models of reading
Mezirow, Cross & Steadman	Schemata
Perry, Belenky, & others	
Baxter Magolda	Cognitive development

Table 1. Summary of Components of Theoretical Foundation, Cont'd.

Theoretician	Application to Practice
Learning Styles and Preferences	
Brookfield	Cultural suicide
Bruffee	Collaborative learning
Goldberger, Pai & Adler	Communication and culture
Branch-Simpson, Fordham & Ogbu	Cultural identity
Wlodowski & Ginsberg	Culturally responsive teaching
Kitchens	Left-brain–Right-brain research
Witkin	Field dependence-independence
Canfield	Learning style inventory
Myers-Briggs	Personality-based indicator
Self-Regulation and Goal Setting	
Garner	Metacognition
Weinstein & Mayer	Comprehension monitoring
Pintrich, Zimmerman, Paulsen	Self-regulated learning
Hagen & Weinstein, Cross & Steadman, Atkinson & Feather	Goal orientation

Chapter Four

A Framework for Effective Practice

Understanding theory and recognizing the many possible factors that help explain individual differences in learning are only part of the story. Translating understanding into meaningful and effective action is the challenge. It is not always apparent how instruction can best be designed to meet the varying needs and concerns of students. Instructors often use trial and error in hopes of finding an approach best suited to most learners. At other times, educators choose methods that they find most appealing and expect the students to adapt. Sometimes this is successful, sometimes not.

Effective instruction and successful learning are not achieved by chance. We offer a framework called TRPP (theory, research, principles, and practice) as a guide for designing teaching and learning situations in order to maximize student potential (Casazza and Silverman, 1996) (see Figure 1). The TRPP model promotes (1) connecting information about the learning process, (2) integrating knowledge about learning from many sources, (3) reflecting critically about theory and research, and (4) constructing a framework for practice. When using the TRPP model, educators develop their own unique approaches built on a foundation of what is known about the learning process.

TRPP is useful as a dynamic framework. It requires awareness of new research and new ways of viewing theories about learning, as well as the examination of long-standing practices that may need to be revisited. To remain vibrant and enthusiastic, educators must be engaged in a continuous quest for refining and improving the teaching and learning process. This does not mean that old ways

Figure 1. The TRPP Model.

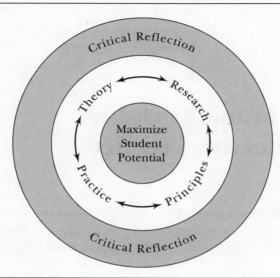

of teaching need to be discarded, but it does mean that they should be reviewed and evaluated in terms of what is currently known about the learning process and the specific settings in which learning occurs. Professional educators make decisions about instruction based on theory and principles of practice supported by research. The TRPP model offers an effective way to engage in this decision-making process.

Teachers are usually knowledgeable about the content they teach; however, they are not always aware of different instructional methods and forms of pedagogy. The natural inclination is to teach the way one was taught. The TRPP model is designed to promote awareness of learning theory and research for use in practice. For those with background and expertise in this area, the model should be a motivating force in the continued investigation and integration of theory and research into teaching practice.

The four components of TRPP—theory, research, principles, and practice—interact to help explain why certain practices are preferred and why one approach may be more effective than another. One purpose of the TRPP model is to provide a way of integrating different theoretical perspectives in order to better understand what educators do, why they do it, and how it ultimately leads to learning outcomes. An underlying assumption of the model is that no one theory adequately explains all behaviors in every situation. An eclectic approach that includes facets of different theories is most useful in developing instructional strategies for increasingly diverse groups of students.

The four components in the TRPP model function together within a framework of critical reflection. Beginning with any of the components, it is possible to move through the model to develop an approach connected to theory and research. For example, a teacher may begin with a situation requiring a new method for practice, look up research to support the method, connect the research to theories of learning and development, and finally construct a principle based on this information to guide the new method. The following example demonstrates this process.

Situation: A teacher of an introductory course in natural science is frustrated. Students seem to be learning material in a rote manner and do not see the relevance of the course to their own lives. There is a general sense that students are mechanically absorbing information but not processing it in a meaningful way. Although the lectures are well prepared and organized, they do not stimulate student interest and enthusiasm. Frustrated with this situation, the teacher consults others, who suggest that she needs to try a different approach in addition to her lectures. Some colleagues stress that it is important for students to connect the material to their own experiences. In addition, activities need to be developed so that students are not just swallowing facts and spitting them back. After discussions with her peers, this teacher explores what is known about different ways of teaching and learning and comes across the following research findings.

Research findings: When students are actively engaged in the learning process, they learn more than when they are passive recipients of instruction (Cross, 1987). Students report that they enjoy classes in which the instructor attempts to relate material beyond the classroom (Eison and Pollio, 1989). Finally, cooperative learning has been shown to effectively increase student achievement but only if group goals and individual accountability are incorporated into the methods (Slavin, 1989).

Theoretical foundations: The ideas of at least three different theorists are useful here. Lewin's theory (1936) is pertinent, as it puts forth the idea that behavior is a result of person-environment interaction. Structuring the learning environment to provide for connections to real-life experiences promotes person-environment interactions that produce meaningful behaviors. Moos's theory (1986) of the learning environment emphasizes the importance of the relationship dimension or the extent to which individuals help each other. Vygotsky (1965) promotes the idea of guided instruction such that responsibility for learning is gradually released to the learner. The notion of collaboration and constructivism inherent in Vygotsky's theory emphasizes the importance of social interaction in learning.

Principles: Given some of the research findings and theoretical foundations related to the idea for practice, the educator could then develop some principles for instruction. For example, Slavin's research finding that group goals must be combined with individual accountability in cooperative learning would direct the teacher to develop the principle of providing for both of these factors with an instructional plan. Vygotsky's theory would direct the teacher to incorporate the principle of slowly releasing responsibility to the student so that active, collaborative learning activities would be more closely directed at first. Gradually the teacher would move into the background.

Practice: Returning to the situation that prompted a need for change, what can the teacher do now? She might begin by sharing her frustration with the students and asking for their cooperation in shifting to a different class format. She could share that she discovered some new ideas for making the course material more interesting and relevant and would like their help in trying them. She might also begin by shortening her lecture presentations to no more than fifteen minutes and providing discussion questions prior to the lecture. Following the shortened lecture, students would form small discussion clusters to answer the questions. Each cluster would identify a spokesperson who, at a designated time, would report back to the larger class and answer one of the assigned questions. This would be a step toward releasing responsibility to the students and promoting active participation. More active engagement in learning should stimulate interest in the subject as well.

However, the issue of relevance to personal experience is still of concern. The teacher might consider constructing some natural science case studies based on real situations in the community. For example, a recent outbreak of Dutch elm disease in trees could be discussed as a threat to the quality of life for people living in the community. Another example might be aggression and territoriality among animals; connections could be made between this type of behavior in animals and humans. Case studies could be developed and distributed to students in small learning clusters for discussion and application to their own lives.

The example shows how each component of the TRPP model is combined with the others to provide guidance and support in instructional endeavors. The process of connecting these four components is driven by what we call critical reflection—a process of closely examining and analyzing something, searching for meaning, discovering inconsistencies, and questioning the basis for one particular approach. In the example, we examined the idea of introducing active, collaborative learning activities that are related to real-life experiences. Why would this approach be chosen? What is known about previous attempts in this endeavor? Using TRPP, these questions are posed and information is provided to support the idea. Last, critical reflections guide the process.

At the center of the TRPP model is the ultimate goal of maximizing student potential. The educator's purpose is to reach each learner and facilitate learning as much as possible. Given individual differences, including learning preferences, motivation, and competence levels, it becomes increasingly more important to engage in critical reflection in order to produce a successful learning experience for as many students as possible.

Applying TRPP to Case Studies

The example shows how a teacher used TRPP to plan instruction for an entire class. Now, how can TRPP can be used to address learning concerns with individual students? Remember Mike? He's the student who worked in his uncle's body shop but decided to return to school to learn accounting with the idea of moving into the business aspect of the body shop business. Unable to find relevance in the coursework, he struggles in the classroom. In the past, Mike's behavior in school was characterized by confrontational and disruptive behavior. He did not perceive himself to be a good student and sought recognition from nonacademic activities. He never conceived of himself as a real student; instead, he found success in hands-on work fixing cars. Motivated now to open his own business, he has returned to formal learning, hoping to learn the basics in order to be successfully self-employed.

How can the TRPP model help in Mike's situation and lead to a more successful learning experience for him? Any one of the four components in the TRPP model can be used to begin, so this time theory starts the process.

Theory: One theory that can help explain Mike's situation is self-efficacy, or the belief a person has about his or her ability to be successful in a given situation (Bandura, 1977; Weiner, 1986). Self-efficacy as described in Chapter Two is not the same as self-concept. Self-efficacy beliefs are specific to certain situations and do not represent a global belief about overall worthiness. Mike has high self-efficacy beliefs in the auto shop but low self-efficacy beliefs in the formal classroom setting. As previously described, Mike completed a vocational and technical program in high school and believed that formal education was not for him. He did graduate from high school but always believed that he was best suited to practical, hands-on work. Now after returning to night school in a formal classroom environment, Mike's belief in his ability to succeed in this setting is very low. He is not succeeding and feels discouraged and overwhelmed.

Motivation, identity development, and environmental factors are also pertinent in Mike's case. Theories of motivation are useful in that they help explain Mike's frustration with his current situation. In addition, identity theories show that how Mike views himself and perceives his "possible self" is connected to learning behavior. Finally, environmental theories provide a framework for assessing the effects of the situation in which Mike finds himself.

Research findings: Research in the areas of self-efficacy, motivation, identity, and environmental interaction are also to be considered. Studies in self-efficacy show that the more success a person has in a task, the greater his or her belief in the ability to perform that task. Repeated failures reinforce beliefs of incompetence and often result in withdrawal from the activity. This does not mean that learners always need to be successful to maintain their competency beliefs. Research has shown that when there are many successful experiences, occasional failures can be well tolerated without affecting positive self-conceptions (Bandura, 1989). In Chapter Two, we showed that stress and negative emotions are correlated with negative self-efficacy beliefs. In Mike's case, he is highly stressed by pressure from his friends and from his own poor classroom performance. Mike is in a cycle of failure. He believes that he is not capable in the formal classroom setting; he is frustrated with his poor performance and stressed by pressures and demands. These beliefs contribute to more negative self-efficacy beliefs and lack of success.

Research in motivation has shown that mastery goals promote success in learning more than performance goals (Pintrich and Schunk (1996). Mastery goals center on achievement for its own sake, whereas performance goals are focused on comparisons with others. Mike is struggling with tests that put him in competition with others in the course. Instead, he would be better off identifying specific concepts and skills to learn which are pertinent to his own specific needs of running an auto repair business.

Identity research says that support from teachers and mentors facilitates identity achievement and self-confidence (Baxter Magolda, 1998). Mike feels isolated from others and has no one encouraging his academic endeavors. Furthermore, self-esteem is enhanced by environments that are accepting and caring and that provide consistent and positive feedback. He is not currently experiencing this kind of nurturing environment.

Last, teachers who use concrete examples and make practical applications are more apt to promote student success. Mike is struggling with abstract ideas and sees no relevance between those ideas and his goal of self-employment.

Principles: Several principles emerge from the research. In order for Mike to succeed in the classroom, he needs a series of success experiences to build his confidence in his ability to perform. Given his frustration and very low confidence in this class, his toleration for failure is very low. Therefore, all activities need to be presented so that he is successful almost 100 percent of the time.

Another principle related to motivation is that Mike needs to develop mastery goals so that he can reduce the frustration connected to competing with others in the class. He needs to see that he can succeed at something related to his own needs and applicable to his personal aspiration of self-employment rather than having his work compared to others.

Identity research stimulates the principle of providing a caring, supportive learning environment that encourages self-confidence and success. Finally, research in teaching behaviors has indicated that the use of concrete examples and connections to practical applications promotes learning (Mayer, 1987). In Mike's case this seems particularly important.

Practice: How realistic is it for the teacher to be successful with Mike in the classroom setting? In Mike's case, the solution may be beyond the teacher. Usually it is not possible to provide instruction so that all students succeed almost all of the time. Although this is an ideal, realities of individual preparation, course requirements, standards of achievement, and time-limited course schedules do not always allow for its accomplishment. In some instances, tutorial support outside the classroom setting can help individual students fill in learning gaps and be successful. In other situations, learning gaps may be so great or levels of self-confidence may be so low that classroom instruction would best be postponed until the student is more self-assured and has the prerequisite background learning.

Challenge is important in learning but too much challenge can be defeating and lead to withdrawal. Too little challenge can lead to boredom and disinterest (Sanford, 1967). In Mike's case, theory and research help us understand that he initially needs much encouragement, support, and success to boost his low self-efficacy beliefs. His current classroom experience is not providing this, and he feels defeated. In practice, it would be best to prevent any continued experiences of failure and encourage Mike to withdraw from the course and receive intensive individual tutoring before trying the class again. This must be approached sensitively so that he is not discouraged; he should see that his own achievement is being promoted within a wider time frame and should include individualized help. The next time Mike enrolls in the course, he will be better prepared for the content and more confident of his ability to master it. Individual tutoring should also be considered as a continuing intervention when he enrolls in the course again.

The TRPP model is also useful in Linda's situation and sheds some light on how to help her maximize her potential. Remember that Linda is an eighteen-year-old, first-year student living away from home for the first time. She has a long-term goal of becoming a physician. Both of her parents are doctors, so it is likely that her goal has been influenced by their professional status. Although Linda did well in high school, she is not succeeding in her first term at college. She feels alone and much too worried about her performance to seek assistance or confide in anyone, including her parents. Rather than try to find a new group of peers at school, Linda maintains her ties to home by calling every day and going home each weekend.

Applying the TRPP model to Linda's situation, we begin by looking at a possible principle related to self-monitoring.

Principle: One of the common threads running through Chapter Three is that at the center of effective learning is an active learner—one who is aware of her progress and able to take some initiative to make changes when necessary. A useful principle for Linda's situation would be that the learner needs to be aware of how she processes information and be in control of a repertoire of strategies to apply. Linda seems unaware that her method of studying does not fit her current learning tasks. She believes that if she simply spends more time repeating the same strategies, she will eventually succeed. She has not learned to analyze her own style and to fit it to particular content demands.

Theory: The relevant theory suggests that learners need to have an overall self- management system through which they evaluate and regulate their learning. To evaluate it, they must have standards to apply along the way to determine their progress. Rather than waiting for the instructor or the final grade to determine success or failure, students must be able to analyze their own performance. If they find that they are not progressing satisfactorily, they need to take the responsibility for regulation. This regulation includes being adaptable to the particular task that is required in a content area and applying appropriate strategies. To do this, students must carefully review the assignment, the expectation, and their own prior knowledge base. When these factors have all been analyzed together, the appropriate strategy can be used. This implies, of course, that the student has an array of strategies and is willing to be flexible, depending on the context.

Research: Research has shown that students who monitor their learning have a better chance for success and also that this increases the transfer of knowledge across areas (Weinstein and Mayer, 1986). Successful students are usually very aware of their own processing strategies and what they must do to adapt to varying demands. They also have a repertoire of study strategies to apply, depending on the situation. They are actively in control and have taken responsibility for their own learning.

Practice: What does this mean in terms of practice related to assisting Linda? First, it would be helpful if she completed a learning styles inventory to help her assess her instructional preferences. With a learning specialist, she could discover that some of her frustrations reflect her preferred learning style, not her ability. Linda and the specialist could then discuss how she may need to adapt to the demands of some of her courses and use styles that are not familiar.

She may also want to meet with an academic adviser who could help her schedule more appropriate sections of classes in which tutorials or supplemental instruction options are offered. In addition to providing academic assistance, this would help her to form a smaller network within the larger class. Then she could begin to establish peer relationships and also become exposed to more effective behaviors. The academic adviser could also assist Linda by looking at her goal of becoming a physician, discussing her prior achievements in science courses, and then working out a long-term plan that would allow her to progress in a manner best suited to her needs. For instance, after discussing her strengths and weaknesses, they could schedule Linda's next academic term to include a chemistry course that has a tutorial attached. Also helpful would be a study skills course, a history course (a strength of Linda's), and a fine arts elective. By developing such an overall plan, Linda may find that it will take her longer than four years to complete her undergraduate studies, but she will also feel more relaxed when she sees how her strengths and weaknesses are interwoven. She will be moving toward her long-term goal, but along the way she will learn to adapt to her environment by shaping her schedule to meet her unique needs.

Another valuable component for Linda would include being part of a pre-med support group. Such a group of peers, meeting regularly with an adviser, could discuss their progress as well as their common concerns. These discussions would promote a sharing of strategies and a standard against which to compare progress realistically.

See Table 2 for a summary of the case studies, the issues they contain, and the relevant research that is described.

Table 2. Connections to Case Studies.

Case Study	Primary Issues	Theory-Research
Jadwiga	Language-culture	Pai & Adler; Goldberger, Brookfield
	Learning style	Bruffee, Wlodowski & Ginsberg
	Support system	Kaiser, Lewin
	Self-identity	Marcia, Mezirow
	Autonomy	Chickering
Mike	Goal orientation	Atkinson & Feather, Cross & Steadman, Hagen & Weinstein
	Learning style	Brookfield, Canfield, Kitchens
	Self-identity	Chickering, Marcia, Mezirow
	Self-efficacy	Bandura, Weiner; Rotter
	Failure of formal system	Gardner, Sternberg, Tennant; Brown, Collins, & Duguid; Cross & Steadman, Mezirow
Sabina	Learning environment	Lewin, Kaiser, Moos
	Learning style	Witkin, Canfield, Bruffee
	Emotional intelligence	Mayer & Salovey
	Goal orientation	Cross & Steadman, Hagen & Weinstein
Teresita	Support system	Brookfield, Maslow, McCluskey
	Goal orientation	Cross & Steadman, Hagen & Weinstein
	Self-identity	Chickering, Marcia, Mezirow
	Self-efficacy	Bandura, Weiner
	Emotional intelligence	Mayer & Salovey

Table 2. Connections to Case Studies, Cont'd.

Case Study	Primary Issues	Theory-Research
Charles	Goal orientation	Cross & Steadman, Hagen & Weinstein
	Motivation	Rotter, Maslow, Nisbett, & Ross
	Time management	Canfield, Pintrich, Zimmerman & Paulsen
	Anxiety and stress	McClusky, Lewin; Mayer & Salovey
Linda	Lack of affiliation	Lewin, Kaiser, McClusky
	Goal orientation	Cross & Steadman, Hagen & Weinstein
	Learning disability	Pintrich, Zimmerman & Paulsen; Weinstein, Garner
	Learning style	Bruffee; Kitchens; Canfield; Witkin

Conclusion

In this chapter, we used the TRPP model to construct a framework
for effective practice by actively connecting theory, research, principles, and practice. Using applications to Mike and Linda, readers
can jump into the model at any point and start making connections
to improve teaching. With Mike, the connections began forming
with the theory of self-efficacy; with Linda, connection making
started with the principle that learners must be able to regulate and
monitor their own behaviors if effective learning is to occur.

The TRPP model is significant because it is dynamic and the
components continuously affect one another; no one component
can function effectively without the others. In order for TRPP to
work, it is important to regularly reflect on practice by asking questions. In addition, teachers must analyze successes and failures to
maximize potential for all students.

∽

In Part One, we presented a theoretical framework for the practice of student learning and development. Moving into Part Two, we investigate current research that both supports and strengthens the theory. We apply the research implications directly to practice and use them to develop a set of principles to guide work with students.

Applying Research to Teaching

In Part Two we move from the theoretical foundation for practice to the research base that connects it even more strongly to practice. As long as discoveries are being made about what others have found through their work with students, new ideas emerge for practice. Research also validates, and in some cases refines, the theoretical models traditionally used as frameworks.

In these six chapters, the same areas of student learning and development that we outlined in Chapters Two and Three are revisited: self and identity, motivation, interaction with the environment, ways of knowing, learning styles and preferences, and self-regulation and goal setting. The research we report is not all-inclusive; we have selected research that we think will be the most valuable to those working with students in a variety of learning environments beyond high school. Our primary focus is on the adult learner, but often the most relevant research has only been done with younger students. We have included that research when it has implications for the work done with older students.

The reader will find overlap throughout the chapters both in the concepts we discuss and in the principles that follow. For example, it is difficult to discuss motivation without referring to goals. At the same time, the research related to self-regulation is tied directly to the construction of goals. The fact that goals become significant in at least two areas of research underscores their importance to the whole teaching and learning process.

In order to make the research as practical as possible we continuously connect it to the case studies. The reader might want to review the short histories in Chapter One before reading this section; the histories help the research come alive. Following descriptive summaries of the relevant research, principles for practice that emerge from a synthesis of the reading are outlined. They provide a framework for the critical reflection on practice that we discuss further in Part Three. Even though we make connections continuously with the case studies, we urge readers to visualize their own students in the examples and reflect on how this research is relevant and how it can help improve practice.

| **Self and Identity**

Learners' views of themselves and the educational settings they experience are often closely connected to learning outcomes. We discussed several aspects of self and identity in Chapter Two, including Chickering and Reisser's (1993) vectors of development, Marcia's (1980) notion of identity formation, and Mezirow's (1991) theory of schemata that form filters for interpreting experiences.

The power of self-belief is evidenced in many ways. For example, if a student believes she is not capable of writing well and dislikes the process, her feelings of inadequacy and trepidation will make it difficult for her to successfully accomplish writing assignments in a composition class. However, if a student believes he is a good writer and finds writing enjoyable, the same composition class presents an entirely different, more positive situation. His self-perceptions allow him to eagerly approach writing tasks with confidence, whereas hers function as potential impediments to learning.

View of self is a complex phenomenon and includes concepts that are not easily defined: self-esteem, self-efficacy, and self-concept. View of self is conceived of differently by different researchers, and the concepts it contains are not always clearly distinguishable from each other. The purpose here is not to discuss the fine distinctions among these constructs or to engage in debates over definitions. Instead, we present some basic definitions for the purpose of our discussion and review research with the understanding that definitions may vary in different studies. Finally, we present and discuss research in identity formation, which is closely related to views of self.

Self-Esteem

In Chapter Two, self-esteem was defined as a person's overall assessment of personal adequacy or worth. Studies have revealed that there is a consistent increase in self-esteem during the college years. This change occurs in relatively equal intervals and is understood to be developmental rather than revolutionary (Pascarella and Terenzini, 1991). It is commonly believed that if only we could help improve a person's self-esteem, things would be much better.

Self-esteem research has produced some clear findings in several areas: parental factors, social factors, relationship between self-esteem and success, personality characteristics, and consequences of self-esteem. Highlights of Mruk's (1995) meta-analysis of research in these areas are summarized here.

Research shows that active parental involvement tends to produce higher self-esteem; parental indifference or absence results in lower self-esteem. This factor, however, is not sufficient to enhance or deter self-esteem development. The quality of parental involvement is also important. For example, quality involvement is characterized by a parent who willingly accepts a child's strengths and weaknesses. Self-esteem is enhanced when a parent sets clear expectations within limits, treats children in a democratic fashion with opportunities to discuss matters, and behaves consistently. Last, birth order is associated with self-esteem in that first-born children are slightly more likely to develop positive self-esteem.

Linda's lowered self-esteem in her first year at college can be understood, in part, by focusing on the quality of her parents' involvement in her learning. Although they were actively involved, Linda's parents focused extensively on her learning strengths while failing to accept her weaknesses due to a learning disability. They pushed Linda to excel academically and to take courses in preparation for medical school. When Linda began to struggle and failed to meet her parents' expectations, she became despondent and reclusive and developed overriding feelings of lowered self-esteem.

Social factors connected to self-esteem are those associated with values and gender, as well as with racial, ethnic, and economic conditions. Although values are understood to be culturally related, some common values across cultures are viewed in connection with self-esteem. Some of these values include honor, self-discipline, courage, and caring for others. Persons with high self-esteem expect to be able to attain what is valued in their culture; the opposite is true for those with low self-esteem.

It is generally believed that racial and economic factors such as deprivation and lack of opportunity contribute to lower self-esteem. Research findings, however, have not supported this. Instead, results confirm that as long as people meet the criteria for success within their own reference group, self-esteem is positively affected. This is also true for the effect of poverty on self-esteem. When individuals meet the expectations of the smaller community to which they belong, self-esteem continues to flourish.

Successful experiences also lead to enhanced self-esteem. It is the ability to meet challenges in life and not material results that are most related to high self-esteem. Being valued by others is seen as a very important factor for positive self-esteem. A sense of having power or influence over events helps a person deal with life's challenges and in turn leads to enhanced self-esteem. Finally, one of the most powerful influences on positive self-esteem is when someone reaches a goal of personal significance that has been problematic over time.

These three factors—being valued by others, having a sense of power over events, and accomplishing a personally significant goal—are primary for understanding the relationship between success and self-esteem. There is a good deal of variability among individuals in terms of how much success in a particular area is necessary for a positive effect on self-esteem. One person may need a few successes in one area for self-esteem enhancement, whereas another may need many more achievements in a variety of different areas.

Linda's case is a relevant example. Excessive failures have contributed to her lowered self-esteem. However, once she changes her major and begins to study subjects that are more closely matched with her academic strengths, improved performance and increased self-esteem are expected. Of course, this will only be long-lasting if the expectations and beliefs of her parents also change, as she puts such a high stake on their involvement.

In addition, several personality characteristics are positively linked to high self-esteem. These characteristics include (1) positive affect (the individual approaches life with a good outlook in a way that is easy and spontaneous), (2) effective functioning (life's tasks and challenges are dealt with productively), and (3) autonomy or independence, particularly the ability to maintain opinions in the face of opposition. People with high self-esteem are more open to positive evaluations of their behavior than to negative feedback, whereas persons of low self-esteem take in negative feedback and often diminish what is positive. People with low self- esteem are thought to have feelings of insecurity and unworthiness and in the research reports are often described as being anxious or depressed.

Some of these personality characteristics are evident in the case studies. Take Jadwiga's case. Even though her family opposes her new academic pursuit, she has high self-esteem that is connected to her independence and autonomy. Jadwiga evidenced this by moving away from her family in order to continue her studies. Another student with lower self-esteem and lacking Jadwiga's independence would be more likely to retreat.

Knowing that persons of low self-esteem tend to be more cautious, self-protecting, and less likely to take risks, we can better understand Mike. In his new academic environment he is struggling and considers dropping out. He never thought highly of himself academically, and the challenges he is now facing seem overwhelming. His self-esteem is not strong enough to carry him through the difficult parts and risk failure. Realizing Mike's past feelings of academic inadequacy and knowing that lower self-esteem is linked with tendencies not to take risks, it might be expected that Mike will discontinue his studies.

It is generally accepted that high self-esteem protects people from stressful situations and that competence leads to positive self-esteem, which in turn reduces stress. In contrast, there is also a strong, consistent relationship between low self-esteem and high anxiety. High anxiety and stress tend to impede learning; therefore, low self-esteem is of particular importance in educational settings.

Charles presents an example of how stress and anxiety are related to self-esteem and, in turn, affect learning. He is struggling to handle many difficult situations in his work, home, and school environments. He is having trouble meeting all the challenges in these situations, is doubting his ability to achieve, and is overwhelmed with stress and anxiety. Understanding the dynamics of the situation is helpful, but he needs strategies he can use to address the problems.

Research shows that self-esteem can change, especially during major life transitions (Pascarella and Terenzini, 1991). Some of the most powerful enhancement techniques for promoting self-esteem include being accepting and caring, providing consistent and positive feedback, and giving positive self-feedback. In the case of Charles, using these approaches is recommended. For example, meeting with him to talk about his many responsibilities would be a good beginning. With a caring and accepting attitude, the teacher could provide an opportunity for Charles to share the many frustrations and challenges he is facing. Positive feedback about what he actually is accomplishing would be helpful; Charles could begin to develop a realistic view of his situation so that it doesn't look entirely bleak. Finally, Charles can be shown how to assess himself and provide his own positive feedback for what he is achieving rather than overemphasize areas of difficulty. Although this approach will not solve all of Charles's problems, it is likely to reduce some of the stress and anxiety so he can begin to make some balanced decisions about what to do next.

Self-Efficacy

Although it is similar to self-esteem, *self-efficacy* is what promotes belief in the ability to perform a particular task. The application of self-efficacy theory (Bandura, 1977, 1986, 1989) to academic performance is a growing area of interest and research. Recent research shows that self-efficacy beliefs are positively related to academic performance and that they account for about 14 percent of performance variance across student types, student ages, experimental designs, and academic performance measures (Multon, Brown, and Lent, 1991). Although self-efficacy beliefs are closely proximate to ability levels, there is a motivational effect for success at activities that are within the expected performance range of the individual. Bandura (1986) suggests that self-efficacy beliefs that are unrealistically high are likely to have a detrimental effect on student performance. Likewise, significant underestimates of ability and unrealistically low self-efficacy beliefs also have an adverse result. This may come about as a consequence of the student failing to attempt activities such as enrolling in college or performing poorly on a task within the student's capability.

O'Brien, Brown, and Lent (1989) investigated students who had been identified as underprepared for college on the basis of college entrance exam scores. The purpose of the study was to uncover the levels of aptitude-efficacy congruence that are most facilitative of academic performance for this student population. Results of the study indicate that self-efficacy beliefs that most closely approximate ability do facilitate academic performance and that overestimating one's ability is detrimental.

Again, one of the case studies helps in understanding this phenomenon. Mike is experiencing frustration in his math class. His past educational experiences were weak, and he is struggling now with course content. Mike has developed low self-efficacy beliefs concerning his performance in math. He hesitates to try math problems that appear difficult. This combination of weak preparation and low self-efficacy has inhibited his success. He is feeling defeated and may not muster the courage to try again. When the power of belief is coupled with poor preparation, it is easier to understand Mike's needs and plan intervention to target both problems.

Self-Concept

Self-concept refers to a person's judgment of his or her competence or skills in comparison to those of others (Pascarella and Terenzini, 1991). The concept includes the notions of academic self-concept and social self-concept. Social self-concept generally increases during the college years, with signs of the increase present by the end of the sophomore year. Academic self-concept also generally grows during this time but is characterized by early declines during the first year of college, with gradual increases through the remaining years (Pascarella and Terenzini, 1991). It has also been found that self-concept tends to become more differentiated during the college years, such that students have varying judgments about their competence in different areas of study. Astin (1993) believes that this phenomenon reflects students' increased sense of reality, as they have more exposure to diverse areas of study and interaction with more students.

In the review of research on self-concept, a multidimensional model is used that includes both academic and nonacademic self-concept (Shavelson, Hubner, and Stanton, 1976). Bachman and O'Malley (1986) analyzed longitudinal data to examine the relationships among academic self-concept, educational attainment, and global self-esteem. They studied whether or not academic self-concept is a function of the general ability level of students in a particular school. Results of this investigation reveal that the average ability level of students in the school does not affect an individual's level of academic self-concept. In other words, school ability contexts have no lasting effect on individual self-concept or self-esteem; however, academic self-concept is a function of individual academic ability and performance.

Knowing that the general ability level of a school context has little impact on individual self-concept is particularly pertinent for discussions in higher education. From this study, it might be assumed that students in community colleges, proprietary schools, public universities, and prestigious private institutions would have a range of academic self-concepts unrelated to the general ability of students in the institutions attended. We would therefore focus on individual student ability and academic performance as influencing factors to increase our understanding of self-concept as it relates to learning and development.

In contrast, some studies have investigated ways in which institutional differences play a role for certain groups of students (Smart, 1985; Smith, 1990). In particular, research on the effect of institutional character on self-concept has focused on comparisons between historically black colleges and universities (HBCUs) and predominantly white institutions (PWIs). Historically black colleges and universities have been under scrutiny regarding their contributions in higher education. Specifically, these institutions are seen as particularly advantageous for black students because they provide environments that support personal development.

Berger and Milem (1998) conducted a study comparing the self-concept of black students in both HBCUs and PWIs and found that black students who attended HBCUs are more likely than their peers at PWIs to report increased levels of social self-concept four years after entering college. The researchers suggest that black students are more likely to have opportunities to become involved in activities that affect self-concept development than their counterparts in PWIs. Although these findings support institutional type as a contributing factor to self-concept development, it is important to remember that the opportunity for involvement in the institution promotes self-concept development, which confirms the importance of these factors in any educational environment. In particular, when students receive faculty support for their academic and intellectual pursuits, their self-concept is enhanced. In addition, the opportunity for involvement in academics and student government is important. For black students, this involvement opportunity is greater in HBCUs and leads to an improved self-concept.

Another view of self-concept includes the idea of a "possible self"—the conception of the self in a future state. This view is rooted in the idea of self-schemas in which "generalizations about the self are derived from past experience that help one integrate and explain one's own behavior" (Yardley and Honess, 1987, p. 158). Self-schemas define both a past and present self and a future possible self. The possible self puts the self into action and is the bridge between the present and the future. Yardley and Honess describe the possible self as a "blueprint for action" (p. 158).

Empirical studies of possible selves have produced several findings: (1) positive possible selves are related to feelings of personal control, whereas negative possible selves are related to feelings of lack of control over the environment; (2) persons who report that a great many people depend on them have fewer positive possible selves; and (3) imagining a positive future leads to better performance than imagining a negative one (Yardley and Honess, 1987).

Related to yet different from the possible self is a concept known as the imposter syndrome (Brookfield, 1995). According to Brookfield, some people believe they are not to be taken seriously because they really don't know what they are doing. These persons believe that they must be very careful not to reveal their own incapacities. They feel they have no safe place to reveal their doubts and are therefore unable to receive feedback or suggestions for change.

Once again, the case studies provide opportunities to explore the idea of an imposter syndrome and the view of possible selves as it relates to performance. Sabina decided to return to graduate school and envisioned her possible self as someone who could advance in her corporate training career. She had already experienced success in her chosen career but was seeking more; she hoped graduate school would provide the opportunity for advancement. Even though she had two children who depended on her, she did not see this as a barrier to success. In addition, she enrolled in a program that used distance learning—an instructional medium she had never experienced. Because she viewed herself as an independent learner and wasn't resistant to technology, she went ahead and pursued her goal. When the distance learning method provided unsatisfactory, Sabina remained focused and did not give up. One explanation for her ability to stay focused and persist is that she maintained a positive view of her possible self and imagined a positive future.

Mike, however, was less successful. His view of his possible self was not as positive as Sabina's. He felt he had less control over his environment, and when his academic performance faltered he didn't persevere. Linda also failed to rise above her academic difficulties. Instead of facing them head on, she retreated into secrecy and isolated herself from others. Instead of moving to gain control over her environment, she became increasingly removed from resources that might have helped her succeed. Both Mike and Linda lacked positive views of their possible selves that could have helped them overcome difficulties in their academic pursuits. In addition, we might view Linda as an example of the imposter syndrome; she failed to accept herself as capable in her environments and was trying desperately to keep her difficulties secret.

Identity

After high school and in early adulthood, identity formations become particularly complex. As social contacts and relations become more varied, established family values and beliefs may be questioned. For example, as a new resident in the United States, Jadwiga began to increase her social contact outside her traditional Polish family. She ultimately found it necessary to move away from her family to pursue her own goals. Choices become crucial and are related to life decisions such as whether or not to get married, have children, or live in an urban or rural setting. The world becomes increasingly more complicated, and developing identities are formed through the process of making difficult decisions about how one chooses to live one's life. Pascarella and Terenzini (1991) presumed an identity status change during the college years, and almost ten years earlier, Waterman (1982) had stressed that the greatest change in identity formation occurs in college.

Identify formation is particularly complex in early adulthood when social interactions become more diverse and important decisions are made concerning career and life choices. Earlier we indicated that the greatest change in identity occurs during the years after high school, especially during the college experience.

Chickering's work (1969) focuses on the important years during college and gives a valuable framework for understanding how identity is formed during this time. (We described Chickering's vectors of development in Chapter Two.) In 1993 his work was revised in response to criticisms that suggested his earlier work did not successfully account for the differing development of women and students of color (Chickering and Reisser, 1993). His model is useful for understanding how students develop and how this development interacts with learning. It is important to remember that women and students of color may have different sociocultural experiences and to examine studies of psychosocial development and identity formation in these student groups.

Josselson (1987) is best known for her work on the identity development of women. Her research is based on Marcia's (1966) theory, which we described in Chapter Two. Using Marcia's term, *foreclosure,* Josselson describes women in her study who graduate from college without an identity crisis but with a formed identity. She characterizes women with foreclosure identity as having a strong sense of family and being primarily occupied with the care of others. But women who break away from the psychological bonds of their childhood are those she terms *identity achievers.* These women break away from parental expectations and forge new directions but often feel guilty. Support from others, including teachers and mentors, helps to dissolve the guilt and lead to a firm sense of identity in a career chosen of one's own free will. Identity achievers develop a strong sense of self-confidence and tend to be continually developing and maturing.

In the middle ground are women in the states of "moratorium" and "diffusion." Those in moratorium recognize the options available to them but have yet to choose one. Some move ahead into identity achievement and break the psychological ties with their families. Others move into foreclosure. Women in the state of diffusion have neither an identity crisis nor a commitment to identity. They remain unfocused and often tend to exhibit the most negative behavior characteristics, including high anxiety and personality disorders.

Linda can be viewed as someone in the foreclosure stage. She has firmly accepted her parents' values and aspirations for her future and hasn't begun to question them. Until she begins a process of self-evaluation and is confident enough to challenge her parents, she is likely to remain frustrated and troubled academically. Fully realized identity formation will elude Linda until this happens.

Several racial and cultural identity models have been proposed by different researchers. Cross's (1971, 1991, 1995) research proposes a model of Nigrescence, which delineates a five-stage developmental process for black students:

1. Preencounter stage: the person views race as unimportant and holds a generally Eurocentric view, including an idealization of white culture accompanied by anti-black attitudes.
2. Encounter stage: the individual experiences negative situations with whites and positive encounters with blacks so that previously held assumptions are challenged.
3. Immersion-emersion stage (marked by a deep involvement with black culture): the person begins to idealize everything black and devalue what is not; the individual continually weighs strengths and weaknesses of the black culture so that the end of the stage is characterized by a more balanced view.
4. Internalization stage: the individual integrates a black identity into the personality; a sense of inner pride in being black is coupled with a more flexible understanding and acceptance of group differences.
5. Internalization-commitment stage: includes behavioral action; the individual actively promotes social and political problem solving

Helms (1990) proposes a white identity model in which she identifies two major phases: abandoning racism and defining a non-racist identity. Helms uses the term *status* rather than *stage* to describe the phenomenon of a dynamic interaction between thought and feeling not limited to one point in time. Moving through six different statuses, the white person moves from a point of initial contact with black people in which views are not fully formed to the final status when white identity is internalized and black people are not seen as threats. In this final status, there is no need to idealize or oppress others because of race.

A third model of identity development results from Phinney's research (1990), which suggests that it is important for self-concept that a person have a well-developed sense of ethnic identity. In the process of achieving an ethnic identity, the individual resolves conflicts related to stereotyping and prejudice by the majority culture and clashes between the value systems of the majority and minority culture. Failure to achieve a sense of ethnic identity results in either foreclosure or in the acceptance of parental values without questioning them.

Using Chickering's framework and other identity models, researchers have studied the psychosocial development and identity formation of different student populations. Only recently have studies with special populations begun to be more prevalent, and some of these research results are presented here to advance the understanding of learning and student development and to better explain the behaviors of some of the students in the case studies.

In their study of women's development, Kenny and Donaldson (1991) found that women students are significantly more attached than males to their parents. Must women break familial ties in order to achieve emotional independence and autonomy? If so, does this move toward autonomy occur in the same way developmentally for women and men? Two studies show that the timing of autonomy development is indeed different for women and occurs after the first year of college (Straub and Rodgers, 1986; Taub and McEwen, 1991).

In a recent study of autonomy and parental attachment, Taub (1997) sought to answer whether or not autonomy and parental attachment vary by class year. In addition, she studied whether or not parental attachment varies by race and ethnicity. Taub's study supports previous research (Greeley and Tinsley, 1988; Taub and McEwen, 1991), which shows seniors to be significantly more autonomous than students in earlier years. In addition, Taub (1997) and other researchers (Greeley and Tinsley, 1988; Jordan-Cox, 1987; Straub and Rodgers, 1986; Taub and McEwen, 1991) found that women achieve autonomy later in their college years than men. The fact that women gain autonomy later than men was explained by differing socialization and development, as women value connectedness more than men do (Gilligan, 1982). Because of valuing connectedness, the move to detach and become more independent seems to occur later in women.

Chickering outlined the development of emotional independence from parents as occurring prior to that of independence from others; later, he placed greater emphasis on interdependence. In particular, he found that women grapple with detaching from parents while maintaining a level of attachment or interdependence. Taub (1997) found that women in her study achieved independence from peers before detaching from parents. The overall interpretation of autonomy development in women is similar to that found in Chickering's (1993) more recent works. Taub (1997) found that for women the process of developing autonomy does not necessarily involve detachment from parents.

Jadwiga is an example of a woman seeking some detachment from her family while still desiring a level of connection. In the process of developing autonomy, she has taken the bold step of moving away to live with friends, but she still needs the link to her family and culture. In order for her to achieve this degree of interdependence, she must find a way to balance these two needs.

In this chapter we have looked at research. Now we make connections. Using the TRPP model, we link theory and research to principles and practice.

Using the TRPP Model

The research findings and the theoretical foundations have led us to construct the following principles.

Principles

1. In order to reduce anxiety in learning, it is important to address issues of self- esteem.
2. Self-esteem is enhanced by environments that provide consistent and positive feedback.
3. Student achievement is facilitated when self-efficacy beliefs are most closely connected with realistic self-assessments of ability.
4. Opportunities for involvement in activities promote positive self-concept development.
5. Helping students develop positive images for a possible self encourages control over learning and development.
6. Support from teachers and mentors promotes identity achievement, self-confidence, and maturity.
7. Effective learning situations take into account differing developmental patterns and factors in women and persons of diverse backgrounds.

Applying Principles to Case Studies

Principle 1: In order to reduce anxiety in learning, it is important to address issues of self-esteem.

Some anxiety is expected and facilitates learning. Most people are anxious when faced with testing situations. However, anxiety in learning is counterproductive when its intensity interferes with the ability to concentrate and focus on the task. Students with lower self-esteem often experience counterproductive levels of anxiety. Their negative self-statements such as "I'm never going to get this" or "This is too hard for me" become self-fulfilling prophecies. In some instances, even when the student is capable of performing, negative self-statements and low self-esteem function as major barriers to success.

Mike's academic self-esteem is low, and he is struggling academically. His anxiety in testing situations has become overwhelming, and he finds that he cannot answer even the most basic questions that he has studied and learned the answers to.

The first strategy for helping Mike is to talk with him directly about his anxieties. In this discussion, the teacher explores Mike's feelings of competence, helps him identify the information he has learned and mastered, and guides him to make realistic assessments of his strengths and weaknesses in relation to the material. To help reduce anxiety, Mike and the teacher work together to select topics about which he feels most confident and focus on those first. Exams are broken into segments that include topics for which Mike feels the most readiness; gradually, more challenging areas can be added. This may not be feasible in all learning situations, but the principle of building confidence and self-esteem in particular content areas before testing those areas is a good one for reducing anxiety and increasing successful performance.

Principle 2: Self-esteem is enhanced by environments that promote consistent and positive feedback.

This principle underscores the importance of frequent feedback to enhance the self-esteem of students who are performing well and to communicate ways in which weak performance can be improved. Furthermore, it is important to help students learn how to assess their own performance as learning continues. The ultimate goal is to promote student self-assessment so that it is consistent with the instructor's assessment and the criteria of the course. Students who know what is expected of them and have a realistic sense of their own progress are most likely to have positive learning experiences and positive self-esteem.

Teachers can best practice this principle by having a systematic approach to student assessment and feedback. Some examples include weekly quizzes, scheduled meetings with students at designated points throughout the term, opportunities for viewing model answers to questions, and assignments that require students to conduct self-evaluations in which they communicate their own strengths and weaknesses in the course. Just as the course content is outlined in a syllabus, multiple forms of evaluation and feedback need to be included as well.

In Linda's case, regularly required meetings with her instructor would mean she could not avoid the reality of her poor performance. Personal meetings would communicate care and concern for her achievement while pinpointing weaknesses to be addressed. In these meetings, the instructor could suggest tutoring to address deficits while encouraging Linda in areas of satisfactory achievement.

Principle 3: Student achievement is facilitated when self-efficacy beliefs are most closely connected with realistic assessments of ability.

Theory and research have shown that realistic self-beliefs are associated with academic achievement. Overestimating or underestimating one's own ability is less desirable than more accurately determining the likelihood of success. In order to produce realistic self-efficacy beliefs it is important that students have information about their strengths and weaknesses. This may be accomplished in several ways. Academic advisers can collect records of past performance and test results that help to provide a picture of a student's academic achievement. In addition, the use of student learning style inventories and different study strategies are helpful. Individualized academic advising sessions are one of the most powerful ways to promote self-assessment and foster realistic self-efficacy beliefs. In these sessions, the adviser and the student review all useful information and in consultation make a determination of where the peaks and valleys of achievement are likely to occur.

It is unreasonable to expect that students completely on their own will be able to make the necessary determinations regarding their abilities to accomplish different tasks. The role of the academic adviser is crucial in helping make decisions about learning.

Principle 4: Opportunities for involvement in activities promote positive self-concept development.

Active learning refers to the dynamic involvement of the learner, as opposed to more passive activities in which information is given and the student absorbs facts and reproduces them on exams. Active learning requires the learner to develop questions about the material, find alternate ways of explaining the information to others, process information with peers, and critically evaluate new knowledge. In an active learning environment, students are engaged in the learning process and take control over their own learning with the guidance of a teacher.

Theory and research have shown that students develop more positive beliefs about themselves when they regulate their own learning and feel in control. Teachers who provide opportunities for learning that require students to learn material in a variety of different contexts and explain it to others give learners the opportunity to exercise more personal control, which leads to enhanced self-concept and achievement.

Principle 5: Helping students develop positive images for a possible self encourages control over learning and development.

The importance of a possible self is connected to realistic self-assessments, self-efficacy beliefs, and feelings of personal control. Being able to imagine positive possibilities in the future helps increase focus and motivation in learning. In a cyclical way, personal control over learning increases the likelihood of developing a positive possible self, which in turn leads to the desire to have more personal control. Linda is an example of how the lack of a positive possible self is connected to difficulty with personal control over learning and poor academic performance. Linda's career goal to become a physician was modeled after that of her parents. However, she has no view of herself in the future as a physician. Her learning disability has made it difficult for her to achieve in the science courses, she has not sought help, and she is experiencing a significant lack of personal control over her learning. The cycle of failure and the absence of a positive view of the future is well established in Linda. One way to break the cycle would be to counsel Linda about her academic strengths and weaknesses and help her develop an alternative view of the future that includes another version of a positive self. Once she can focus on achievable goals and imagine a future matched to her abilities, Linda probably will gain more personal control over her learning and will experience success.

Principle 6: Support from teachers and mentors promotes identity achievement, self- confidence, and maturity.

As individuals break away from their parents and move toward achieving interdependence and autonomy, teachers increasingly become important figures. Students often view teachers as persons to emulate, and teachers' praise and encouragement help students formulate views of themselves and establish beliefs about competence.

Jadwiga, the young Polish student, moved away from her family into an apartment with her friends. She persisted in her ESL program and gained entrance into a medical technology program of study. Jadwiga's parents and family did not understand her need to move away and study in college, and there was mounting tension around this. Jadwiga desperately needs the support and understanding of her teachers to help her persist toward her goal. Supportive teachers and others in her educational environment are crucial to her success. As Jadwiga develops a future identity as a medical technician, she needs others to encourage her and help her believe in herself. Ideally, there would be an adviser in the program who would meet regularly with Jadwiga to discuss her progress and assess her performance. In addition, there might be a group of students slightly ahead of her in the program who could include Jadwiga in gatherings and help her to feel like part of the program. If there were a student organization in the program, this would be an excellent place for Jadwiga to interact and begin to develop an identity as a medical technician.

Principle 7: Effective learning situations take into account differing developmental patterns and factors in women and persons of diverse backgrounds.

Individual differences are increasingly important in learning. We know that students approach learning in unique ways and that all approaches are not equally effective with all students. Teachers who instruct with a variety of different approaches, including lecturing, group discussion, collaborative learning, and student presentations, are likely to reach more students than teachers who are firmly wedded to one approach.

Remember Sabina, the student in a distance learning classroom: although the distance learning setting was convenient, it was not meeting Sabina's learning needs. She wanted more personal interaction and was frustrated when unable to participate as fully as she wished. If she cannot attend class at the primary site, modifications should be made to allow her more opportunity for participation and interaction with her classmates. Perhaps a distance learning specialist could work with the teacher to show how the technology could be used more effectively.

Reflections

The following questions can provide a starting point for further reflection on practice.

How consistently and frequently is feedback provided to students?

What kinds of learning activities are provided that actively involve students?

How are students personally supported in their learning?

What aspects of instruction reflect understanding of differing student backgrounds?

Chapter Six

| **Motivation**

We introduced several theories of motivation in Chapter Two. Currently, the most prevalent view is the cognitive perspective, which emphasizes the importance of student beliefs and self-perceptions. No one theory represents the cognitive perspective on motivation, but all cognitive views seek to understand why a person is or is not motivated. Some of the theories considered in the study of motivation include attribution theory and goal theory (Weiner, 1990), social learning theory (Bandura, 1982; Rotter, 1966), the theory of self-efficacy beliefs (Bandura, 1982), self-worth theory (Covington, 1992), and sociocultural theory (Wertsch, 1991; Sivan, 1986). We described the tenets of these theories in Chapter Two and briefly restate them here along with relevant research. We view motivation research from three perspectives: (1) goals, (2) self-perceptions and beliefs, and (3) contextual or cultural factors.

Goals and Motivation

The cognitive view of motivation focuses on goals. Pintrich and Schunk (1996) define *motivation* as "the process whereby goal-directed activity is instigated and sustained" (p. 4). Motivation is a process and not a product. It is something that is inferred from behavior. In the study of motivation, goal theory differentiates *mastery goals* from *performance goals*. Mastery goals are oriented toward self-improvement without comparison to others. These goals emphasize the use of comprehension monitoring, which includes elaborating, as well as organizing strategies for relating new material to past experience. In contrast, performance goals involve comparison with others and competition. These goals often focus on memorization without emphasis on problem solving or critical thinking and are directed toward short-cuts and quick payoffs (Maehr and Anderman, 1993). Students may be primarily oriented toward mastery or performance goals, or they may have a multiple-goal orientation if they have various goals in different learning situations.

Research on goals and learning has produced consistent results showing that an orientation toward mastery goals leads to more engagement in the learning process and a higher incidence of metacognitive strategies (Maehr and Pintrich, 1995). Schunk (1991b) found that the effects of goals on behavior depend on three properties: specificity, proximity, and difficulty level. *Specificity* refers to the degree to which goals are exact in nature; specific goals outline in detail what needs to be accomplished. The following shows how a teacher's instruction can convey a specific goal: "You will write a five-page paper and have the body finished in two weeks, the conclusion completed in three weeks, and the introduction and final product done in four weeks." General goals are less precise and would go something like this: "You will have the paper completed by the end of the term." Specific goals are known to increase motivation more than general goals.

Proximity refers to the extent to which goals are attainable in the future. Proximal goals are attainable within a relatively short period of time and tend to be specific. They contrast with distal goals whose attainment is further away and more global. A proximal goal such as "By tomorrow, you will all know the answers to the questions at the end of the chapter" contrasts with a general goal such as "You will take your licensing exam next year." Proximal goals are more motivating than distal goals. One explanation for this is that with the pursuit of a proximal goal, the individual readily experiences progress toward completion and receives feedback about performance in a more consistent and timely fashion. Distal goals do not provide the opportunity for evaluating progress in the same way that proximal goals do.

Motivation and proximal goal setting are enhanced when standards of performance are provided by the teacher before beginning an activity, according to Harackiewicz, Sansone, and Manderlink's (1985) research. By receiving the standard first, learners are able to monitor their actions during the activity and make assessments of their own performance.

Mike's situation is a good example of how proximal goals in the accounting course might have improved his learning. He is having difficulty seeing the relevance of the course to the ultimate goal of owning his own business. If accounting tasks in the course were structured to include real-life examples related to operating an auto repair shop, it is more likely that Mike's motivation to learn would improve.

Goal difficulty level was also found to be related to motivation. If students believe a goal too difficult and outside their perceived levels of ability and knowledge, they extend less effort to attain it. On the contrary, the amount of effort expended on a difficult goal is increased when students perceive their ability and knowledge to be up to the task.

Linda is a case in point. She has come to believe that the reading material in her courses is beyond her ability to comprehend. She stopped trying to complete the reading and is relying solely on material presented in lecture.

Results of a recent study of college freshmen reveal several things about goals in relation to motivation (van Etten, Pressley, and Freebern, 1998). The most prominent student goal is to get good grades or avoid bad grades, and for many students, getting good grades is more important than learning. Students in this study believed that good grades are the result of memorizing rather than actual learning, and they said that if there were no grades they would do little studying. In addition, they believed that effort should be counted in grading. Students reported setting grade goals for themselves and said that previous success experiences subsequently caused them to set higher goals. Receiving consistent feedback in relation to goal attainment increased motivation, and students said they were more motivated when targeting a self-set standard of achievement than when trying to compete against others. Most students reported that worrying about grades tends to motivate studying but said that excessive worrying could lead to the avoidance of studying. Finally, students said that thinking about distal goals and not proximal goals is counterproductive to studying. This supports the idea that proximal goals are more likely to increase motivation.

Students in the study who had a goal were more likely to have positive self-efficacy beliefs. This, in turn, led to greater participation in activities connected to goal attainment such as attending class, using effective study strategies, expending effort, and persisting in the learning process. As the students made progress toward goal attainment and received feedback regarding this progress, their self-efficacy beliefs improved. This helped increase motivation and the use of study strategies (Elliot and Dweck, 1988; Schunk and Swartz (1993).

This cycle of goal identification leading to positive self-efficacy and resulting in increased motivation is evident in Sabina's case. She has well-formulated goals to move beyond her position in a small company and to refocus her career, so she is motivated to pursue further education through distance learning.

Finally, because mastery goals are known to be linked to increased motivation, researchers have suggested strategies for teachers to employ (Ames, 1990). The following principles illustrate ways motivation can be fostered in the classroom (Pintrich and Schunk, 1996, pp. 248–250).

1. Focus on meaningful aspects of learning activities.
2. Design tasks for novelty, variety, diversity, and interest.
3. Design tasks that are challenging but reasonable in terms of students' capabilities.
4. Provide opportunities for students to have some choice and control over the activities in the classroom.
5. Focus on individual improvement, learning, progress, and mastery.
6. Strive to make evaluation private, not public.
7. Recognize student effort.
8. Help students see mistakes as opportunities for learning.

All of the students in the case studies would benefit from the use of these principles in their educational settings. For example, when Teresita met with her instructor privately, it was a good opportunity to evaluate her situation and plan for better results. The only effective way to provide useful feedback for her was a private meeting. Public feedback would have only made her more discouraged and frustrated.

Sabina is frustrated with her distance learning course and misses the opportunity to interact more fully with other students. Additional choices for learning could be provided, such as the opportunity to choose alternate assignments involving direct student contact. For example, she might have the choice of conducting some live student interviews as part of a course writing assignment. In this way, her feelings of isolation and separation could be addressed.

Two researchers (Locke and Latham, 1990) reviewed studies of motivation in the workplace. The results of their meta-analysis are applicable to formal learning situations as well. They identified two aspects of goal-oriented behavior: goal choice and goal commitment. *Goal choice* is the goal identified and its level of difficulty. *Goal commitment* is the degree to which a person is enthusiastic about the goal and the amount of determination put forth to achieve it. Eccles (1983) found that a value given to a goal influences both goal choice and goal commitment. Mood can also be related to goal choice, with a positive mood leading to the choice of higher goals (Locke and Latham, 1990).

Jadwiga exemplifies the degree to which level of goal commitment can lead to behavioral change. In order to achieve her goal of English proficiency, Jadwiga moved away from her Polish-speaking family. Even though she experienced lack of family support by moving away, her commitment to the goal was strong enough to sustain the loss. In her case, strong motivation is clearly connected to degree of goal commitment.

In Locke and Latham's research, factors related to the environment also influence goal choice and commitment. When individuals have higher norms for performance, they tend to set higher personal goals for themselves. The researchers also found that peer group support or lack of support on a task affects individual commitment. For example, if a group resists an assigned task, individuals in the group are likely to be less committed to the task. However, if the group is enthusiastic and supports the task, individuals are more likely to be motivated and engaged in achieving it (Locke and Latham, 1990). One implication for classroom instruction is the idea that cooperative learning groups have the potential to influence a reluctant student to be more engaged in a learning activity.

Locke and Latham also cite role modeling as an influencing factor. When a person observes another individual setting a goal and going about achieving it, the observing person is more likely to set a similar goal and attempt to attain it.

Linda's lack of reading in her courses is a good example for the use of role modeling. If she were in a small group or paired with others who complete the reading, it is more likely that she would rely less on her lecture notes and do the assigned reading. Through observation, she would learn how to approach the reading assignments and be more confident in her own reading ability.

Locke and Latham also found that the structure of rewards is an influential environmental factor. When goals are highly difficult, extrinsic rewards are helpful; however, when goals are easy or moderate in difficulty, incentives have a positive effect. In addition, unlike other motivational researchers, Locke and Latham found that competition, while not having an influence on goal commitment, has a positive influence on the level of goals set.

Last, the role of authority and type of feedback are of interest. It is generally believed that self-set goals are more motivating than goals set by an authority figure such as a teacher. However, studies in organizations outside education have found that goals set by certain kinds of authority figures may facilitate an individual's goal commitment (Locke and Latham, 1990). An authority figure who is seen as trustworthy, knowledgeable, supportive, and likeable, and who provides a convincing rationale for the goal, positively affects a person's commitment to its achievement. The type of feedback concerning goals is influential as well. When feedback includes self-efficacy information and emphasizes self-improvement, challenge, and mastery, it seems to influence goal commitment (Locke and Latham, 1990).

Understanding personal and environmental influences on goal choice and goal commitment is helpful, but it is also necessary to know how goal levels and goal commitment affect performance. In their literature review, Locke and Latham found that the higher the difficulty level of the goal, the more likely it is that performance outcomes will be better. This finding is valid, however, only when the difficulty level of the goal remains within the ability level of the individual. In addition, goals that are difficult and specific lead to better performance, whereas goals that are difficult and global do not. For example, a global goal level might be described as "do your best," whereas a specific goal level would include detailed standards of achievement. Detailed standards of achievement probably result in higher performance levels because individuals have particular information on which to monitor their behavior.

Again, all of the students in the case studies would benefit from having detailed standards of achievement for monitoring their progress. Charles, for example, would profit from a listing of the basic mathematical competencies needed for each of the course assignments. Before beginning each assignment, he could review the necessary operations and be able to monitor his achievement in relation to the underlying skills needed.

How does being committed to a goal influence performance? The findings are not as clear in that respect. In general, Locke and Latham (1990) found that when goal difficulty and goal commitment are high, the resulting performance is better. In contrast, when goal difficulty is high and goal commitment is low, performance is low.

As we mentioned, Locke and Latham conducted their study in the workplace. Even though there seems to be application to school and learning environments, their conclusions regarding goal choice and goal commitment were reached from workplace studies emphasizing productivity outcomes; they are not completely analogous to cognitive outcomes such as learning. More research is needed regarding these influences in classroom settings.

Using the work of Locke and Latham (1990), Pintrich and Schunk (1996) suggest four principles for classroom instruction: (1) set clear and specific goals, (2) make goals challenging and difficult but not outside the range of students' capabilities, (3) set both proximal and distal goals for students, and (4) provide feedback that increases students' self-efficacy for obtaining the goal.

The third principle, which emphasizes the importance of both proximal and distal goals, is based on Locke and Latham's finding that the efficacy of proximal goals over distal goals was not firmly established in their research review. We know, however, that Bandura (1986) found proximal goals to be more facilitative of self-efficacy and performance.

Self-Perceptions, Beliefs, and Motivation

Self-perceptions are connected to behavior. The theories of self-worth (Covington, 1993), attribution (Weiner, 1990), and self-efficacy (Bandura, 1977) all deal with individual self-perceptions. Self-worth theory is focused on ability perceptions and how they affect behavior. Research results have revealed that college students' perceptions of their abilities are the most prominent part of their self-definitions (Covington, 1993).

In an effort to better understand the dynamics of self-worth theory, Covington studied undergraduates at Berkeley (Covington and Omelich, 1991) using Atkinson's model of need achievement (1964) and identified four types of students: (1) the failure-avoiding student, (2) the overstriver, (3) the failure-accepting student, and (4) the success-oriented student. We describe the results of the Berkeley study and the typologies drawn from it briefly.

The Failure-Avoiding Student

The Berkeley study confirms results of earlier research showing that students who avoid failure doubt their ability to succeed (Laux and Glanzmann, 1987; Salame, 1984; Schmalt, 1982); have a great deal of achievement anxiety (Hagtvet, 1984); and do not feel generally prepared (Covington and Omelich, 1988). Students in this group exhibit poor study skills, high anxiety, much self-doubt about their ability, and they spend much time studying. In the Berkeley study, failure-avoiders were excessively worried about being discovered as poor performers. This worry intensified as testing situations approached. In attempts to minimize their anxiety, the students tried to attribute any potential failure to external factors such as a poor teacher or attempted to minimize the importance of the test. In addition, physical manifestations of anxiety presented themselves in the form of illness or headaches, causing them to spend less time studying as the test approached. Even though failure-avoiding students spent as much time studying as success-oriented students, they performed poorly because of their less effective studying in an anxiety-induced state.

It is puzzling to learn that failure-avoiding students tend to continue putting themselves in situations predictive of failure. One study of community college students found that students continue to enroll in courses after a succession of failing grades (Reagan, 1992). The explanation given was that for these students the need to maintain their image and status as college students supersedes the concern for failure.

The Overstriving Student

Overstrivers are characterized by good study skills, high anxiety, and a great deal of time spent studying. According to Covington (1993), "in self-worth terms, overstrivers attempt to avoid failure by succeeding" (p. 65). The behavior of overstrivers is defeating because they have a perpetual fear of not being able to continue to succeed. Overstrivers seek perfection and are characterized by high anxiety and concern about maintaining high levels of performance. Although anxiety is present in the overstriver, it functions as a catalyst for studying, and overstrivers spend more time studying than any of the other types of students. Covington (1993) also reports that students who are anxiety-driven to study often fail to deeply process material and rely more on rote memorization. Information not learned through deep processing is more likely to be forgotten later (Covington, 1985).

The Failure-Accepting Student

In contrast to overstrivers, failure-accepters doubt their own abilities, exhibit poor study skills, spend little time studying, and have low anxiety about their performance. According to self-worth theory, these students have stopped trying to use ability as a means to maintain their self-worth. Students in this group show neither pride in success nor shame in failure. Instead, they may be resigned to a state of mediocrity or they may have decided not to participate in what they view as a fruitless endeavor. The Berkeley study results confirm the idea that failure-accepters reach a state of general resignation. Failure-accepters exhibit behaviors like those found in the literature on learned helplessness; students come to believe that no matter how much they try, they are doomed to failure. The failure outcome is generally believed to be due to incompetence so that no amount of effort can compensate (Coyne and Lazarus, 1980; Miller and Norman, 1979).

Success-Oriented Students

Success-oriented students are self-confident, have good study skills and low anxiety, and spend a modest amount of time studying. These students seem less affected by competition in learning and show more interest in learning for its own sake. Covington and Omelich (1991) found that intrinsically motivated students are not affected much by tangible rewards so that when these external rewards are not present they continue to learn at optimal levels. Success-oriented students already know that they are learning well and do not need grades or other rewards for reinforcement.

In summary, the Berkeley findings reveal three main things. First, the process of achievement is a complex phenomenon and is connected to a person's beliefs and emotions. Second, poor performance is due to an inability to retrieve information because of anxiety, inadequate studying, or a combination of both factors. Covington (1993) emphasizes that it is important to understand the underlying causes of poor performance when helping students overcome test anxiety. Depending on the cause, different types of intervention will be necessary. Third, the Berkeley study helps explain why some researchers have found that having good study skills is not necessarily connected to academic performance. Even though students in that study may have known the strategies for effective studying, they were not using them because exerting effort in the learning process threatened their self-worth beliefs.

In addition to self-perceptions, beliefs are powerful in many ways and they help explain motivation; self-efficacy beliefs are motivating because they provide a context for what to expect in a task. When faced with a learning task, students have beliefs about how difficult it is, how much effort is needed, how long it will take to complete, which strategies are needed, and whether or not the task stimulates anxiety. Students with high self-efficacy believe they have the knowledge or skill to perform well and tend to choose difficult tasks, persist longer, choose appropriate strategies, and experience little anxiety. Schunk (1991a) found that motivation to learn is enhanced when a low-achieving student observes another low-achieving student successfully perform a task, with the student explaining to the observer how the task is approached and what steps are involved in completing it. Furthermore, research has shown that observing peer models increases efficacy and performance better than observing a teacher or no model at all (Schunk and Hanson, 1985). This finding helps support the need for tutoring programs and services in which competent peers can be models and help those in need.

Beliefs about control also influence student behavior. Early social learning theory (Rotter, 1966) used the term *locus of control* (see

Chapter Two) in reference to whether a person believes the outcome of an activity or attainment of a goal is due to personal effort and competence (internal control) or to outside factors such as teacher opinion or course difficulty (external control). In a study of motivation in college freshmen (van Etten, Pressley, and Freebern, 1998), students reported that feeling in control and taking personal responsibility for their behavior is positively associated with greater motivation. Other research has shown that when students have an internal locus of control they manage their time better and expend more effort when faced with difficult or boring tasks (Schunk and Meece, 1992).

Charles is an example of someone who lacks internal control and whose motivation is declining. The pressures of external factors were the reasons given for his lack of time to do school work. He needs to become more aware of how to set priorities himself and make choices about what is important. In this way, he can transfer the power he perceives to be from outside factors to himself.

Attributions are the explanations given for why a particular experience results in success or failure. Covington (1993) discusses attributions when he describes success-oriented and failure-avoiding students. Success-oriented students believe in their own ability and accept that effort is related to success. Success-oriented students attribute their learning outcomes to ability and effort. Conversely, failure-avoiding students have different attributions. They attribute success to external factors such as luck or easy assignments and failure to lack of ability. Effort is not part of the attributional belief system of failure-avoiders.

One researcher (Ames, 1990) cautions that teacher comments regarding effort can influence behavior. For example, students may already believe they are exerting the most effort possible. When the teacher says that poor effort causes poor performance, students who believe they are putting forth great effort may think ability, not effort, is the reason for their difficulties. It is important for teachers to know what attributions students make for their successes and failures and to communicate a need for reasonable effort along with the use of appropriate learning strategies. Just encouraging more effort may cause students to stop trying if they already believe they are exerting the maximum.

Telling Linda, who is already failing, that she needs to try harder is unlikely to produce a positive result. Linda may resist trying because she believes more effort might also result in poor performance. This could seriously threaten her own self-worth beliefs that are already vulnerable.

Effects of Contextual and Cultural Factors on Motivation

Motivation research that is centered on goals and beliefs is based on the belief that factors connected to what motivates a person are located within the individual. Another view, however, sees motivation as connected to culture and context and not solely within the person. For example, Sivan (1986) states that "motivation is inseparable from the instructional process and the classroom environment. The culturally determined joint activity between student and social context results in an internal state of interest and cognitive and affective engagement, and motivated behaviors, both of which can be considered cultural norms" (p. 209).

The sociocultural perspective on motivation embraces the cognitive view of motivation as an individual psychological construct, but it also places emphasis on student interaction with specific learning environments. In the sociocultural framework, motivation cannot be understood without analysis of the activity in a particular setting. Social interaction is seen as the basis for learning and development and is the foundation for higher-order thinking processes. Knowledge of context and cultural background is critical to motivational research in this framework, and, unlike cognitive research, sociocultural studies primarily use qualitative and observational methods. The research cited here, even though often conducted in lower-level educational settings, has relevance to the students in higher education whom we described in the case study examples.

Researchers using the sociocultural framework have contributed much to the increased understanding of motivation in student learning. Sivan (1986), for example, discovered that teachers in Western society have views of motivation that are based on notions from their own culture. This research reveals that teachers from elementary school through high school have consistent views of what constitutes a "motivated student." Teachers were found to view the motivated student as one who has an interest and eagerness and is actively engaged in learning for its own sake, puts forth effort on tasks, gets good grades, and seeks to form and maintain social relationships. These teacher-constructed views are important in that they form the basis for how teachers make judgments and develop expectations. Teachers in higher education often have similar views.

The complex nature of academic motivation is evident in the sociocultural perspective, which recognizes that academic motivation is often domain-specific. A student may be highly motivated in history but unmotivated in mathematics. For this student, it is likely that a mastery goal will be developed in history and a performance goal pursued in mathematics (Dweck, 1986, 1989). Specifically, the sociocultural perspective emphasizes the importance of classroom factors and their effect on motivation. Some of these classroom factors include the structure of the learning task itself, the way students are grouped for learning, the procedures used for feedback and evaluation, where the responsibility for learning is centered (in the teacher or the learner), and the quality of teacher-student relationships.

A number of studies have contributed to an increased understanding of the influences of educational environments on learning and academic motivation. Marshall and Weinstein (1984) present a complex interactional model of classroom factors and discuss how it affects student self-evaluations, which in turn influence learning and motivation. Marshall and Weinstein reviewed literature on students at all grade levels, but their findings apply to students in postsecondary education as well. In particular, the findings on locus of responsibility for learning, feedback and evaluation procedures, and quality of teacher-student relationships are relevant to higher education.

Locus of Responsibility

Traditionally, the instructor holds the locus of responsibility for learning and evaluation in the classroom. This has been called the teacher-centered approach. Sharing responsibility for learning by giving choices to students in situations such as sequencing tasks, pacing task completion, deciding which groups to work with, creating new learning tasks, and establishing goals moves the responsibility toward the student and creates a student-centered approach. Furthermore, the student-centered approach includes shared responsibility for evaluating learning as well. These evaluations may be the opportunity for students to check their answers against a teacher-prepared answer sheet or to prepare a set of standards on which to evaluate an assignment. When students establish and use their own set of evaluation standards, teacher participation is still present but the occasion for more self-evaluation with varied criteria helps to lessen student vulnerability to external pressures.

In higher education, the idea of students setting their own evaluation standards may seem odd. Traditional ways define the teacher as expert and the student as novice. The teacher decides the standard for excellence. When the locus of responsibility is shared with students, the teacher functions as a guide helping students identify basic requirements for excellence so that they are personally meaningful.

Feedback and Evaluation Procedures

Normative standards of performance stress comparisons among students, whereas mastery standards are less comparative and focus on concepts learned. Still, with mastery standards, students can make comparisons and see that some students are further along the mastery continuum. Both normative and mastery standards are externally imposed, and when students make comparisons between themselves and others, some may come to believe that they are less able. When teachers publicly display grades, the message of differing abilities and expectations is highlighted. In contrast, less visible displays of performance may take place in private meetings with students; emphasis is more likely to be placed on mastery of material, along with an opportunity for correction and encouragement. In private settings, students may be helped to understand their performance in light of past experiences and in relation to their own goals. This also advances the opportunity for connections to be made between effort and performance.

What a teacher says to a student can have powerful positive or negative effects. For example, it would be expected that a positive statement about ability ("You're very intelligent and should be able to think of the answer") would be likely to encourage a student. For some, the result might not be encouraging at all. The student may wish to avoid demands to achieve, and the teacher's statement may not match the student's own ability beliefs. In another example, it might be expected that a teacher's negative statement about ability would result in a lack of encouragement. But some students may be motivated to prove the teacher wrong and be even more encouraged to perform. And some individuals are not affected at all by teacher statements. Students who are intrinsically motivated are neither encouraged nor discouraged by teacher comments.

Quality of Teacher-Student Relationships

Students are perceptive. They are aware that teachers tend to have more positive interactions with high-achieving students. However, when teachers accept individual differences and structure instruction to allow for these differences, teacher-student relationships are likely to be more positive all around. Accepting and valuing differences is an important goal for promoting student learning and motivation.

Marshall and Weinstein (1984) emphasize all of the influences just cited as important in interactions; no single factor accounts for varying performance and degrees of motivation. An important goal in learning is to have all students view their abilities positively and realistically. In order to achieve this, teachers must examine their underlying beliefs about ability and know which instructional strategies support a multidimensional view of learning ability.

According to Marshall and Weinstein (1984, p. 321):

> When teachers conceptualize ability as a repertoire of knowledge that can be developed rather than as a single entity, and when teachers convey this conceptualization and the value of individual differences to their students, social comparison may not have deleterious results. However, it should be noted that information from sources other than social comparison needs to be taken into consideration. These sources include criterion-referenced tests or mastery learning as well as comparison to an individual's prior work.

The sociocultural perspective, with its emphasis on culture and context, also helps in the understanding of motivational behaviors in specific populations. Motivation in African American students was the focus of a literature review by Graham (1994) and resulted in findings particular to this culture.

Graham makes the point that African Americans make up a larger percentage of economically disadvantaged students and experience achievement failure in greater proportion than other students. This fact cannot be overlooked when viewing motivation in the black student population. The study of motivation in African Americans must take into account thoughts, feelings, and actions in response to failure.

Much of the research on motivation and social class has been based on the assumption that poverty and disadvantage result in failure to develop an achievement motive, lead to students feeling a loss of personal control, and foster negative self-perceptions. African Americans are over-represented in the lower social classes and were selected as subjects for research investigating social class and motivation. The results of this research are, in fact, results connected to social class and not to race. Middle-class blacks were not selected for studies on motivation and race, and the research findings attributed to race are believed to be invalid.

Graham's (1994) study reviews three factors related to African Americans and motivation: personality traits, internal locus of control, and self-views about competence. The literature review shows that African American individuals do believe in personal control, have high expectancies, and possess positive self-regard.

Graham's study does not support the assumption that African Americans have low self-esteem. Instead, it emphasizes the importance of self-perceptions for all persons regardless of race. When studying specific racial groups, it is important to recognize the function of self-perceptions as they relate to learning and motivation, just as with any other group.

When viewing African American students and all other students, it is important to incorporate the three cognitive variables: causal attributions, perceptions of control, and expectancy for success. These variables are interrelated and should not be viewed in isolation. Furthermore, research with this population must focus on affective variables related to achievement such as emotions of pride and shame; it should also focus on the results of other feelings such as anger, pity, guilt, and gratitude. Some researchers have suggested that African American students may be affected by competition from their peers more than other racial groups; however, little empirical research supports this.

To better understand motivation as it exists in the African American student population, it is important to study the effect of parent, teacher, and peer influences on achievement. In early research on motivation, it was recognized that cultural differences in parental beliefs and behaviors are connected to how children develop achievement motivation (McClelland, 1961). In general, however, it has been difficult to confirm that specific child-rearing practices are predictive of particular motivational characteristics. Graham suggests that it is now important to renew interest in the phenomenon of parent socialization and achievement motivation in African Americans. Graham reports that, unlike parents of white students, the parents of African American students are more likely to believe that their children are doing well in school and will continue to do well, even though evidence exists to the contrary. These optimistic beliefs could result in parents making fewer demands on their children to study and spend time on school work.

Research with African Americans should help promote the understanding of human behavior in all persons. Graham emphasizes the importance of studying subgroups of any type and relating the findings to those of general psychology. The main point of Graham's review of research is that it is important to recognize differences among diverse populations and to see similarities in how various constructs explain behavior.

Another way to view cultural factors and motivation is to compare and contrast collectivist and individualist societies by looking at their organizational structures and values as they relate to achievement and motivation. Collectivist societies are those in which members choose in-group goals over personal goals. Behaviors are focused around norms received from the group and emphasize relationships. Individualist societies are those in which the emphasis is on the self as an autonomous entity. Members of individualist societies choose personal goals over group goals, and they function according to personal preferences and needs. Behavior in individualist societies focuses on analyses of advantages and disadvantages of relationships with others; when a relationship is no longer believed to be advantageous it is terminated. Collectivists maintain relationships even when they are no longer seen to be advantageous. Competition in collectivist societies is characterized by intergroup competition, whereas that of individualistic societies is characterized by individual competition. Collectivists are more concerned about good social relationships than are individualists (Alexander and Barrett, 1982). The United States is an example of an individualist society; China is an example of a collectivist society.

How does this notion of collectivist and individualist societies relate to motivation? Triandis (1995) stresses that there are differing situations in which individualists and collectivists perform best and are most motivated. Collectivists are most motivated by their own groups. When their group norms emphasize achievement, they generally perform well. But individualists are motivated by their own internal processes and are most motivated when expected outcomes meet their own personal needs. When assessing motivation in different student populations, it is important to understand the effect of the culture and context. Students socialized in collectivist and individualist societies are likely to respond differently to particular instructional settings. For example, group work is more likely to be motivating to students from collectivist societies wherein the goal is to cooperate and achieve a goal together. Students from individualist societies, however, did not respond readily to group assignments, especially if the focus did not stress individual achievement within the group. Conversely, learning situations that emphasize individual competition without the opportunity for student interaction are likely to be less motivating for students from collectivist backgrounds.

Several cross-cultural studies have shown that Western notions of motivation and achievement are not easily applicable to the achievement behavior of students with non-Western backgrounds (Gallimore, 1981; De Vos, 1973; Gallimore and Howard, 1968; Salili and Mak, 1988). Stevenson and Stigler (1992) conclude that there are two types of achievement motivation: affiliative and individualistic. These two types are determined by sociocultural context and values and are important to the understanding of how motivation occurs in learning.

Another study emphasizes the importance of family duty in achievement motivation (Salili, 1995). In this study, Chinese students in a collectivist society where achievement had important implications for the family or group were significantly more achievement-motivated than British students.

Effort and hard work also have different cultural conceptions. With Chinese persons, for example, effort has a different significance than for Westerners; they believe that almost anything can be achieved through hard work and value it for the purpose of building character and carrying out one's duty. Westerners, however, see effort as useful for promoting one's own interests; even though hard work is valued, being successful or winning is more important (Spence, 1985). Ability, however, is not emphasized in the Chinese culture. Instead, they tend to believe that ability is controllable and can be changed through effort. Because of this belief, failure is not greeted with apathy because it is believed that repeated efforts will ultimately result in success. Westerners, however, have a more fixed view of ability and do not believe it to be so controllable. When Westerners ascribe failure to lack of ability, it generally leads to loss of self-esteem and a sense of helplessness (Hau and Salili, 1990).

The cultural value of education is connected to historical tradition in the society as well as social structure. It includes the value placed on education, as well as beliefs about effort and hard work. Chen, Stevenson, Hayward, and Burgess (1995) found a contrast between Asian and American cultures in relation to the value of education. Overall, East Asian cultures show a strong commitment to education. Although the American culture values education, it is not seen as the only way to succeed. Other paths, such as acquiring material goods and money, are identified by Americans as success-oriented values.

Overall, the value of education was found to be a significant factor in explaining cultural differences in achievement; however, no clear finding explains how this value is specifically connected to behavior.

The belief in the power of effort as it relates to achievement is also related to culture. It is known from attribution studies that when a student attributes success or failure to effort or lack of it, there is a tendency to continue to work harder. In contrast, the student who attributes performance results to ability is less likely to persist in the face of failure (Weiner, 1972, 1986). Studies have shown that group differences surrounding the efficacy of effort do exist. Spence (1985) reports that the American work ethic seems to have waned somewhat and that students increasingly stress the importance of ability over effort. As stated earlier, the Chinese place a great deal of emphasis on effort and hard work and are motivated to persist because of this belief.

Social support structures are also connected to achievement and motivation. Several factors have been shown to describe this phenomenon. Although family support of education is thought to be connected to achievement and motivation, the direct effects of this are not clearly evident. Studies have shown that family background cannot fully account for achievement differences among groups of minority and majority students (Howard and Hammond, 1985; Stevenson, Chen, and Uttal, 1990). Because of the lack of definitive differences in the sociological approach to understanding achievement, focus has shifted to an emphasis on parenting to explain achievement variance. An example of this emphasis is contained in a study investigating authoritarian versus nonauthoritarian parenting (Dornbusch, Ritter, Liederman, Roberts, and Fraleigh, 1987; Steinberg, Mounts, Lamborn, and Dornbusch, 1991). Students raised by authoritarian parents were found to perform better academically than students with nonauthoritarian parents; however, style of parenting is not sufficient to explain variations in academic achievement among different cultural groups. For example, Asian American students are generally successful academic achievers, yet they are least likely to come from authoritarian homes (Dornbusch and others, 1987; Steinberg and others, 1991).

Inconsistent results concerning the role of family and achievement motivation may be due to the fact that social support is provided in places other than the home environment. Peers and others in the community influence students' achievement motivation. For example, studies have shown that African American students may be seen by their peers as "acting white" if they perform well academically (Ogbu, 1990). This is particularly troubling because influence by peers may be even more influential than positive support from parents for academic achievement (Brown, Steinberg, Mounts, and Phillips, 1990; Steinberg and Brown, 1989).

Overall, Chen and others (1995) conclude that a great many variables interact to predict achievement in different cultures. A motivational explanation that may be valid in one culture is not necessarily useful in another. However, this does not negate the usefulness of motivational explanations. Rather, we need to understand the complexity of varying situations and be alert to inappropriate applications from one culture to another.

The literature on culture and context as it pertains to achievement and motivation is extensive. It is not possible in this chapter to present all representative samples. We have, however, touched on several aspects: classroom factors and motivation, motivation in

African American students, motivation in collectivist and individualistic societies, cultural beliefs about learning, and social support for academic achievement.

In this chapter, we have looked at research. Now we make connections. Using the TRPP model, we link theory and research to principles and practice.

Using the TRPP Model

The research findings and theoretical foundations have led us to construct the following principles.

Principles

1. Orientation toward mastery goals increases engagement in learning.
2. Consistent feedback regarding goal attainment increases motivation.
3. Individual choice and control over learning activities increases motivation.
4. Achievement motivation is affected when self-worth beliefs are threatened.
5. Observing peer models promotes self-efficacy and achievement motivation.

Applying Principles to Case Studies

Principle 1: Orientation toward mastery goals increases engagement in learning.

Linda is struggling and discouraged as she finds that she is performing less well than others in her courses. She is retreating from social interactions and losing motivation to persist. Overall, she lacks control over her learning and sees no way out. Guiding Linda to construct some mastery goals for her courses and become less focused on comparing her performance to others could help her regain motivation and persistence. For each of her courses, Linda could list the material she must master and make a plan for addressing it.

Developing a time line with tasks to be completed would help her stay centered on the goals. In class, it would be helpful if the grades of other students were not displayed for comparison. Instead, Linda and the other students should focus on mastering content and developing specific competencies.

Using mastery goals in the classroom is challenging because courses are generally time-limited, and successful course completion must occur within a set period of time. One way to use mastery goals in the classroom would be to develop specific goals to be completed within particular time periods. Some students might still not have mastered goals in the required time, but there would still be more emphasis on mastery and less on comparison with others.

Principle 2: Consistent feedback regarding goal attainment increases motivation.

Teresita is anxious about her performance. The more she worries, the more she becomes unable to focus on her assignments. She is uncertain about her progress so far and wonders if the quality of her work is up to par. An adviser, a teacher, or a mentor in the program could help with regular meetings to discuss how things are going and help her identify small steps she is taking toward achieving her goals. Too often, students are left wondering about their performance in a course or program. When assessments are limited to two or three times a term, large amounts of time pass with no opportunity for evaluating progress. The more frequently progress is evaluated, the more opportunity students have to make necessary adjustments. Teresita could regularly chart her progress with weekly exams or feedback sessions. This would help her stay encouraged and motivated and give her concrete information she could use to make informed decisions about where to put her efforts.

Principle 3: Individual choice and control over learning activities increases motivation.

Jadwiga is definitely a student who exemplifies the importance of individual choice and control. Her decision to move away from her family and increase time with English-speaking friends is evidence of this. She took personal responsibility for this very difficult decision and increased individual control over her own learning.

In the classroom, much can be done to help students develop control over their learning. By releasing more control to students, the teacher encourages personal responsibility for learning and contributes to enhanced motivation. For example, a menu of assignments can be presented, all of which accomplish a particular objective. In Jadwiga's English class, the objective of completing a descriptive essay could be accomplished by having students choose from a number of different topics or choose a topic of their own. In this way, they are more likely to write on something of personal interest and be more engaged in the assignment.

In almost any subject area, assignments can be provided that involve the opportunity for choice. Sometimes the choice is related to a topic. Other times it may be in the final format. For example, Jadwiga might feel more comfortable at first completing an English assignment with a classmate. This would help increase her confidence at first, until she is more secure. Within limitations, the more opportunity students have to decide for themselves how to reach a goal, the more likely it is that they will be motivated to achieve it.

Principle 4: Achievement motivation is affected when self-worth beliefs are threatened.

Linda's self-worth is threatened as she performs poorly and realizes her goal of going to medical school is in jeopardy. She has begun to doubt her own abilities and is withdrawing. Linda might fit the profile of failure-avoider, as she is excessively worried about being discovered as a poor performer. Even though she spends much time studying, she is plagued by poor study skills, high anxiety, and self-doubt. She ends up spinning her wheels and falling further behind. The overriding concern for Linda is maintaining her image and status. This has become a priority over concern for failure. A caring and supportive counselor, adviser, or faculty member is needed to help Linda develop some effective study strategies and deal with her issues of self-worth. This is not easy or likely to be accomplished very quickly. Feelings of self-worth are developed over time, and reframing self-perceptions is often a slow process. In addition, successful experiences are necessary to combat low self-worth beliefs.

In the classroom, it would be best to provide Linda with assignments that she has a reasonable likelihood of completing successfully. Help from peers or others who could work with her individually would also promote success and, in turn, help her develop more positive beliefs.

Principle 5: Observing peer models promotes self-efficacy and achievement motivation.

Again, Linda is a prime candidate for peer model observation. In a small-group meeting either in or outside class, Linda would profit from observing others successfully complete course assignments. Through observation, she would learn new ways of approaching tasks and receive support and encouragement from others without fear of evaluation. Working in collaboration with other students, she would begin to develop more positive beliefs about her ability to perform and stay motivated to achieve.

Having peers model success in the classroom is a very effective way of enhancing motivation for all students. Through class presentations or student-led discussions, others can see how learning takes place without depending on expert demonstration. With the guided expertise of the teacher, peers can effectively teach each other while becoming more self-confident and motivated to succeed.

Reflections

The following questions can provide a starting point for further reflections on practice.

How much individual choice and control do the students have?

What opportunities exist for students to observe their peers learning?

How is mastery goal attainment encouraged?

What opportunities do students have for personal interaction?

Chapter Seven

Interaction with the Environment

In Chapter Two we presented some theoretical perspectives that center on environmental influence in learning, including the person-environment work of Kurt Lewin (1936) and the reciprocal nature that exists between students and environments. In addition, we related Moos's (1986) work to the various dimensions of environment and to McClusky's (1970) theory of margin. Now we extend the discussion to include research on the relationship of environment to learning and development.

In academic settings, important environmental factors are teaching behaviors, classroom climate, teacher-student interactions, and student-student interactions. In nonacademic settings, student affairs programs, student organizations, and life in the residence halls affect learning and development for all students. The learning environment also has unique effects on special student populations: women, students with disabilities, adult learners, and students of color. Environmental influences include physical features, characteristics of groups and subgroups in the environment, and organizational structures.

Learners in higher education are engaged in transitions between membership in past communities (high school, family, neighborhood) and membership in a number of new communities in the college environment. Tinto (1975) constructed an interaction model by way of examining this transition, as well as the processes of social integration, and explaining factors that account for students persisting or not persisting in higher education. The researchers examined the role of settings outside the classroom.

In our review of research in this chapter, we consider student interactions with the environment in both academic and nonacademic arenas and how these interactions affect behavior.

Academic Interactions

Much research has been conducted on the characteristics of effective teachers in elementary and secondary schools (Dunkin and Biddle, 1974; Brophy and Good, 1986), but research on teacher effectiveness in higher education has been less prevalent. In a review of research on effective teaching behaviors in the college classroom, Murray (1997) presents observational and experimental studies that have implications for the improvement of teaching in postsecondary education. In addition, he discusses the extent to which teacher effectiveness depends on context. Questions were posed to participants on the differences between effective teaching behaviors in large lecture classes and small discussion groups and differences among those in different academic disciplines.

Murray's review begins with the difference between low-inference and high-inference teaching behaviors. Low-inference behaviors are those that are readily apparent and seen with little inference from the observer. Examples include providing outlines of lectures or addressing individual students by name. High-inference behaviors are those requiring a good deal of inference from an observer, including speaking with clarity or being student-centered. When student ratings have been used to evaluate teaching behaviors, most of the behaviors studied have been those indicating high-inference behaviors. Murray's review, however, centers on research investigating low-inference behaviors. According to Murray, the emphasis on low-inference behaviors is important because they are easy to record and manipulate. They are useful in feedback for improving teaching because they are specific and concrete. Low-inference behaviors are also valuable because they involve direct contact between teacher and student and are more likely to affect student learning and development.

Observational studies of low-inference teaching behaviors have produced some interesting findings. Tom and Cushman (1975) asked students to estimate the frequency of forty-five different low-inference teacher behaviors. In addition, the students rated their own progress in achieving course goals. The findings of this study show that certain teaching behaviors are related to particular course outcomes. For example, teacher-student discussion is connected to creative thinking, and organized lecture presentations are connected to increased factual and conceptual knowledge.

Mintzes (1979) found that "using concrete examples" is the teaching behavior most correlated with instructor clarity. The behavior "addresses individual students by name" is connected to instructor rapport, and maintaining student attention is correlated with "speaks expressively or dramatically" (p. 148). Cranton and Hillgartner (1981) found that teachers who rate high as good discussion leaders are more likely to praise students, expand on student answers, and ask students questions.

Low-inference teacher behaviors such as "uses concrete examples" and "suggests practical applications" help learners connect prior knowledge to new information (Mayer, 1987). Mayer also found that teaching behaviors that include humor, vocal variation, and gestures are connected to improved student attention and learning.

Further evidence reveals that many cognitive and affective outcomes are related to low-inference teaching behaviors. For example, "the extent to which a student enjoys the course, studies a lot or a little, does well on the final examination, and enrolls in further courses in the same subject area appears to be determined, at least in part, by specific classroom behaviors of the instructor" (Murray, 1997, p. 186).

Finally, observational studies show that teacher enthusiasm is connected to student attention, teacher clarity promotes information processing and long-term memory, and teacher interaction advances active learning and memory (Murray, 1983). Some teaching behaviors encourage cognitive outcomes, whereas others promote affective outcomes. Findings are inconclusive regarding whether certain teaching behaviors are more facilitative in lecture or discussion environments, and overall, there is no evidence from observational studies that particular teaching behaviors are more effective in some academic disciplines than others (Murray, 1997).

Experimental studies have also contributed to the literature on teaching behaviors. Perry's research (1985) shows that expressive teaching behaviors such as body movement and vocal pitch variation lead to higher levels of student achievement and sometimes promote personal control over learning. The researchers conclude that when students are in settings where they are exposed to expressive teaching behaviors, they tend to feel more positive about the experience and exhibit more control over their own learning. Another study shows that expressive teacher behavior positively affects out-of-class assignments as well (Perry and Penner, 1990). Overall, the research shows that expressive and enthusiastic teaching behaviors positively influence student learning (Murray, 1997).

Last, teaching behaviors that reflect clarity also influence student learning positively. Land (1979) found that when teachers give explicit transition signals, students are assisted in organizing their learning. In contrast, vagueness in presentation results in students losing confidence both in the instructor and themselves. In a study by Hines, Cruickshank, and Kennedy (1985), teacher behaviors characterized by using relevant examples, questioning students, repeating material, and reviewing material contributed to clarity and improved student learning.

In general, research has shown that specific teaching behaviors positively influence student learning and development. These behaviors can be learned and acquired so that they are displayed in greater frequency in the classroom.

In addition, it is important to look more closely at the interactions between students and teachers and among the students themselves. According to Moos (1979), supportive environments are those in which individuals are involved, help each other, and feel comfortable expressing themselves openly and freely. Supportive social climates are not only pleasant ones but they contribute to positive learning outcomes (Moos, 1986). For example, peer teaching enhances the socialization process and provides a means for promoting learning and development.

Peer teaching has value and appeal in higher education for several reasons. First, the peer teacher serves as a role model who helps stimulate enthusiasm and motivation for learning. (In Chapter Six, we emphasized role modeling as a way to address motivational concerns.) Second, students who serve as peer teachers benefit as they experience content again and develop new perspectives. Finally, through peer teaching experiences, students may become interested in pursuing college teaching careers (Whitman, 1988).

Research on peer teaching in higher education is particularly relevant for the discussion of environmental interaction. Studies have shown that one form of peer teaching—supplemental instruction (SI)—has interesting, positive results. SI is a well-known academic support program developed in the 1970s (Blanc, DeBuhr, and Martin, 1983). Students are trained as peer teachers, and they facilitate sessions in which course content is reviewed and clarified through active learning. Research has shown that students who attend SI sessions have higher course grades and higher term grade point averages than those who do not, even when controlled for motivation (Center for Academic Development, 1991).

Peer teaching also takes the form of tutoring. Research has shown that students with relatively high ability and more experience in college achieve better grades as a result of tutoring (Irwin, 1981). Tutoring has also been found to affect student retention. Studies reveal that students who are tutored stay in college longer than those who are not (Carmen, 1975; Koehler, 1987; Vincent, 1983). Reasons for this are unclear, but it could be inferred that tutors serve as mentors who encourage their peers to persist. Another possible reason is that students who seek tutoring are already more motivated to remain in school.

Another researcher found that the closer a student and tutor are in class standing, the greater the degree of problem solving is demonstrated in tutorials (Brown, 1987). This study supports the notion that tutoring by peers close in age and experience is more effective than tutoring by professionals who are more removed from the immediate experiences of the students.

More research needs to be conducted on the effects of tutoring in higher education, but the evidence so far indicates that it is a powerful way to enhance student learning and development.

Nonacademic Interactions

Climate outside the classroom is also important. In the study of residence hall life, Moos (1979) found that all-male residence halls are more likely to be competition-oriented, whereas all-female halls tend to be more socially oriented. Co-ed halls are likely to be independence-oriented and intellectually oriented.

Living in a residence hall on a college campus is a unique form of environmental interaction. Berger (1997) investigated residence hall life and found that social integration and sense of community are connected to persistence in the first year of college. Berger stresses the importance of student interaction with various communities on campus to achieve integration in the college environment. The findings of several researchers (Davis and Daugherty, 1992; Kuh, 1991; Spitzberg and Thorndike, 1992) emphasize the importance of a strong sense of community leading to fuller integration into the larger institutional system. Many have underscored the idea that living in a residence hall on a college campus is connected to a number of positive student outcomes, including persistence at the institution (Astin, 1993; Blimling, 1993; Schroeder, 1994; Tinto, 1975).

Four components have been identified that help define the development of a sense of community: membership, influence, integration and fulfillment of needs, and shared emotional connection (McMillan and Chavis, 1986). *Membership* is the idea that a person has become fully invested in a group and is identified with that group. *Influence* refers to the idea that individual members are affected by norms of their group and that the individual members also affect the group. *Integration and fulfillment of needs* means that the individual and the group are symbiotically connected so that each is satisfied and both individual and collective needs are met. Finally, *shared emotional connection* is when there is sufficient contact between the individual and the group to develop personal attachments.

A survey instrument, the Sense of Community Index (SCI), measures an individual's sense of community based on the four aspects of community described (Chavis, Hogge, McMillan, and Wandersman, 1986). Research using the SCI shows that students who do not have a well-developed sense of community are more likely to exhibit higher levels of physical and emotional exhaustion. Students who develop a strong sense of community are more likely to adjust well and cope with college (McCarthy, Pretty, and Catano, 1990). Another study found that students who live on campus have a better-developed sense of community than those who do not (Lounsbury and DeNuie, 1995).

Berger (1997) discovered that having a sense of community has positive, indirect effects on intent to reenroll in college. In addition, findings indicate that possessing a sense of community in the residence halls is important to persistence and commitment to the institution. Berger found a direct connection between a developed sense of social integration and persistence in college; also, developing a sense of community while living in a residence hall is connected to enhanced social integration overall.

The case study of Linda is particularly relevant to these research findings. She hasn't made a good adjustment to college and is not actively involved in either residence or campus life. Given the connection between social integration and persistence in college, Linda is at risk for leaving. If she were encouraged to join a social organization or become active in a residence hall activity, the likelihood of her remaining in school might improve.

In addition, positive effects have also been found when students are actively involved in student organizations. Pascarella and Terenzini (1991) cite extracurricular activities, including student organization membership, as being connected to the encouragement of educational persistence and enhanced self-concept. Other researchers report that when students are fully and intensively involved in college life, they are more likely to persist to graduation (Carroll, 1988; Dukes and Gaither, 1984). Extracurricular activities are also positively connected to entrance into graduate and professional schools (Stoecker, Pascarella, and Wolfe, 1988) as well as continued enrollment to the doctoral level (Pascarella, Ethington, and Smart, 1988). Finally, studies have shown that when women are involved and have leadership roles in student organizations, they are more likely to pursue careers that have traditionally been dominated by men, including the sciences (Ethington, Smart, and Pascarella, 1986) and law (Braxton, Brier, Herzog, and Pascarella, 1988). Overall, increased involvement in the full range of campus activities, including participation in student organizations, has been found to have a positive effect on student learning and development.

Haworth and Conrad (1997) propose a model of engagement that is relevant to environmental interaction. These researchers based their ideas on a national survey of students in master's-level education. Based on this survey, Haworth and Conrad constructed what they call an "engagement theory of program quality" (p. 16).

The concept of engagement forms five clusters: (1) diverse and engaged participants, (2) participatory cultures, (3) interactive teaching and learning, (4) connected program requirements, and (5) adequate resources. These clusters serve as a framework for the concept of engagement, and each cluster contributes to program quality; contributions include the idea that student learning and development are at the core of higher education and that all program activities must be directed toward this outcome. In addition, program quality is not just the result of students' active learning but the interaction of students with all players in the educational environment, including teachers and administrators. This interaction among all participants takes place in an environment characterized by critical dialogue, integrative learning, and risk taking.

Other studies have supported the idea of engagement. The importance of diversity in the learning environment appears in the work of Astin (1993) and Pascarella and Terenzini (1991). The critical factor of learning communities is supported by the work of Gamson (1984), Spitzberg and Thorndike (1992), and Tinto (1975). The idea of risk taking is upheld by Parker Palmer (1983), who emphasizes the importance of openness to new and creative ideas, and Macrorie (1984), who reports that outstanding teachers are those who construct climates in which students are free to take chances and to make positive use of mistakes. The value of an interactive approach in the learning environment has many supporters, including Boyer (1987), Cross (1987), and McKeachie (1969); critical dialogue between teachers and students has been emphasized in the work of Brookfield (1987), Bruffee (1993), and Gabelnick, MacGregor, Matthews, and Smith (1990), to name a few.

According to Haworth and Conrad (1997), interactive teaching and learning also involve mentoring. Research findings connected to mentoring appear in the work of Astin (1993) and Pascarella (1980), who cite students' greater satisfaction with the college experience after having been mentored. Astin (1993) and Hoyte and Collett (1993) also found increased self-confidence and self-esteem linked to mentoring.

A major review of studies concerning cooperative learning in higher education was conducted by Johnson, Johnson, and Smith (1991), and evidence from these studies shows that cooperative learning has many positive effects, including productivity, more positive relations among students, increased social support, and improved self-esteem. Finally, interactive learning occurs outside the classroom. One major, comprehensive study shows that out-of-class activities in college have a significant positive effect on student development, particularly in the areas of social competence, self-awareness, and self-worth (Kuh, Schuh, Whitt, Andreas, Lyons, Strange, Krehbiel, and MacKay, 1991). Overall, the engagement concept of Haworth and Conrad (1997) is unique in that it combines factors related to student learning and development from a variety of perspectives.

All the students in the case studies could profit from more engagement in learning. For example, Sabina is frustrated with the lack of involvement with her peers, and the distance learning format does not provide sufficient interaction for her needs. Her persistence will be affected unless more opportunities are provided for active engagement. Jadwiga needs consistent interaction with others in her English course in order to advance her language proficiency. Linda would definitely benefit from interactive teaching and learning to move her away from passive study methods.

Special Populations and Environmental Interaction

Specific student populations, including women, students with disabilities, adult learners, and students of color, are uniquely affected by different environments. The literature concerning these groups and environmental effects is quite large, and the discussion of it here is by no means comprehensive. We present the significant aspects of that research so we can discuss some of the findings.

In relation to female students, the phrase "chilly climate" has been used by many who study the effects of learning environments. Research on college outcomes for women has centered on various topics, including self-esteem (Arnold, 1996), identity (Josselson, 1987), intellectual reasoning (Baxter Magolda, 1988), and leadership development (Whitt, 1994). Hafner (1989) found that even though women go to college with higher grades than men, they have lower expectations for their academic performance than men. After reviewing a number of studies on college environments and women, Pascarella and others (1997) propose that many co-educational institutions in higher education may not facilitate

learning for women students. Hall and Sandler (1984) identify negative out-of-class climates for women as well. According to Hall and
Sandler, behaviors such as using sexist humor, discounting or ignoring female students, and using some discriminatory practices
against women made many learning environments chilly for women.

What implications are there for the notion of this chilly climate?
Hall and Sandler (1984) propose that such a climate results in reduced self-confidence for women that, in turn, promotes lower academic and career aspirations. Other researchers put forth the
notion that in addition to lowered aspirations, women in these environments are compromised in their intellectual and personal development (Holland and Eisenhart, 1990; Kuh and others, 1991).

Pascarella and others (1997) set out to test the hypothesis that
women's perceptions of a chilly climate are connected to cognitive
development. Their findings yield only moderate support for the hypothesis. The negative implications are slightly greater for women
in two-year colleges than for those in four-year institutions; however,
there was no direct explanation for this difference. Overall, these researchers conclude that even though a modest negative effect is present for women in two-year colleges, it is important to take an active
stance in reviewing institutional policy as it relates to this issue. They
suggest that policymakers need to better understand the climate
for women and to recognize that gender differences in response
to environmental settings may have implications for women's educational development beginning in the first year of college.

Although women as a group are certainly heterogeneous, research still has a unique application to them as a group. This is also
the case for students with disabilities, who have an ever-increasing
presence in postsecondary education primarily as a result of legislation and advocacy for their rights to equal access and opportunity. The degree to which the environment is comfortable and
promotes learning and development for students with disabilities
is of particular importance. In this discussion, we are concerned
with various kinds of disabilities as defined by law and confirmed
by diagnostic documentation, including physical disabilities involving mobility challenges, mental or emotional disabilities, and
learning disabilities. The focus here is on aspects of the learning
environment and how they can be modified to foster growth and
development for these students.

It is important to address access and accommodation issues for all students with disabilities; however, here the focus is on students with learning disabilities. These students are the most prevalent of those with disabilities in higher education; of particular interest is the kind and degree of accommodation provided. Researchers of support programs for students with learning disabilities have found that services have most frequently included tutors, readers, additional academic advisers, reduced course loads, computer laboratories, and study skills classes (Ostertag, Pearson, and Baker, 1986; Shell, Horn, and Severs, 1988; Strichart and Mangrum, 1986; Vogel, 1982; Wren, Williams, and Kovitz, 1987). Adelman and Vogel (1990) studied the effectiveness of environmental accommodations for students with learning disabilities and found that academic advising, tutoring, use of computer laboratories, and use of test accommodations are positively related to success in students with learning disabilities. Testing accommodations are of particular interest in that care must be taken to maintain the standards of the course. Typical types of testing accommodations include extended or untimed tests, oral exams, different exam formats, and the option of typing or tape-recording answers (Strichart and Mangrum, 1986). Ostertag and others (1986) found that testing accommodations are viewed as almost always essential by the students who use them. Bursuck, Rose, Cowen, and Yahaya (1989) found that 95 percent of the colleges they surveyed provided testing accommodations for students with learning disabilities.

There continues to be a good deal of controversy surrounding the identification of students with learning disabilities and the provision of accommodations for them in postsecondary education. Faculty and others in the institution need to be aware of information and issues surrounding disability accommodation and educated to understand the role of the environment in promoting learning for these students without compromising standards and fairness. Students with disabilities are, first and foremost, students whose basic needs and concerns reflect the research cited for all students. However, because of their disabilities, these students have additional needs that require specific environmental accommodations.

Again, Linda's story is relevant here. She has not shared her learning disability needs and is struggling academically. If she revealed her disability, she might qualify for accommodations that would greatly increase her likelihood for success.

Adult students such as women and students with disabilities have unique characteristics; generalizations can also be applied to them as a group. The literature on adult learners has grown in recent years, and only the surface is skimmed here as the identified needs of adult students are connected to interaction with the environment. The hallmark of the adult learner has been defined as autonomy and individual self-direction (Merriam, 1993). Although self-direction is considered to be a prevalent characteristic of adult learners, it is recognized that adults move toward self-directedness at different rates and do not exhibit the same amount of self-directed behavior in all situations. Recognizing that adult learners, in general, want environments where they have opportunities for self-directed activities, the research of Hammond and Collins (1991) produced a nine-step procedure for introducing self-direction into a formal education setting. Components of this approach include building a cooperative learning climate, analyzing the situation, diagnosing learner needs, and evaluating and validating learning. Critical analysis and reflection is emphasized as an important ingredient throughout the process.

Other adult learner researchers have focused on the importance of learner-centered instruction in which the teacher functions as a facilitator and gradually promotes the move from teacher control to learner control (Candy, 1991). The factors that help determine whether or not self-direction will be exercised include level of technical skills, familiarity with the subject, sense of personal competence as learners, and context of the experience (Brockett and Hiemstra, 1991; Candy, 1991).

Grow (1991) advances the notion of staged self-directed learning (SSDL) and describes four distinct stages of learners. In stage one, learners demonstrate low self-direction and need an authority figure (teacher) to direct them. In stage two, learners have moderate self-direction, are motivated and competent but generally ignorant of the subject matter. In stage three, learners have an intermediate level of self-direction, have the skills and basic knowledge, and see themselves as ready and able to proceed in learning tasks with the help of a guide. Finally, in stage four, learners have a high level of self-direction and are willing and able to plan, execute, and evaluate their own learning, with or without the help of a guide or expert. Grow stresses that teachers have different roles to play, depending on the stage of self-direction for each learner.

Problems arise when there is a mismatch between the teacher's role and the learning stage of the learner. The best-case scenario is when the teacher individualizes instructional approaches to match the stages of each learner. In keeping with the discussion of interaction with the environment, the best teaching is situational in nature and adaptable to varying student needs.

Another view of adult learners involves perspective transformation (Mezirow, 1981). According to Mezirow (1991), perspective transformation is the idea that adult learners critically reflect and become aware of why they connect particular meanings to reality. It is this critical reflection and awareness that helps distinguish adult learners from younger students. Apps (1988) researched the transformation process in adult learners and identifies five phases: (1) developing awareness, (2) exploring alternatives, (3) making a transition, (4) achieving integration, and (5) taking action. According to Apps, the transformation process can involve these phases simultaneously and provides for movement back and forth between the phases.

The work of Knowles (1980) produced the notion of *andragogy* to denote an alternative to *pedagogy*—learning that is particular to younger students. Andragogy is based on two main principles: (1) learning is actively constructed by the learner and not passively received from the environment, and (2) learning involves interaction, interpretation, integration, and the transformation of experiences.

Using the Adult Classroom Environment Scale (ACES), Darkenwald (1987, 1989) researched adult learners in formal settings and identified a number of dimensions that influence learning in the classroom environment, including affiliative relationships among students and teacher support of students. In a study investigating the social climate of adult learning situations, Ennis (1989) found that shared decision making in an atmosphere characterized by mutual trust is important in adult learning experiences.

Overall, the work in adult learning has characterized the adult learner as moving through stages of self-direction: learning in a transformative way rather than in an additive process, using critical reflection and interpretation through the lens of experience, and interacting with the environment in ways determined by the sociocultural context in which learning occurs.

Finally, students from various minority groups are also of interest in the study of interaction with the environment. The retention of these students continues to be a concern in higher education. Recent research has shown that persistence or degree completion rates for black students is about 40 percent and for Hispanic students about 47 percent six years after matriculation (Tinto, 1993). For Native American students the rate of degree completion is estimated at only 25 percent (Wells, 1989). With an increasing number of minority students in the U.S. population, the problem of low retention in higher education is a serious concern (U.S. Bureau of Census, 1993). Students leave college for many reasons (Tinto, 1975), but the focus here is on some of the environmental and institutional factors related to this phenomenon.

In Chapter Five we examined the research on historically black colleges and universities, which shows that institutional type has a relationship to minority student growth and development. Historically black colleges and universities (HBCUs) have a more positive effect on the development of self-concept in black students than predominantly white institutions. Causes for this finding were related to the educational climate at HBCUs as well as increased opportunities there for black students to become involved in campus activities. It is important to learn more about the environments of HBCUs and how they contribute to black student development so that other institutions may strive to achieve the same results.

A classic study of black student development on predominantly white campuses found racism in faculty-student relations and a climate of hostility (Fleming, 1984). According to Fleming, minority students who are in an unsupportive or hostile environment experience isolation, loneliness, and alienation that in turn affects their academic success. For students remaining in these environments, internal dissonance and conflict are often the outcome. There is additional psychological and emotional stress, and premature departure from the institution is likely to occur.

Wright (1987) proposes several ways institutions can change their campus climates to promote minority student development and in turn improve retention. He suggests that mentoring relationships be fostered so that two-way relationships can be developed between faculty and students, with both benefiting. He stresses that traditional mentoring programs have emphasized the expertise of the faculty member who is expected to share with the student. Instead, Wright proposes that students and faculty develop more mutually beneficial relationships, with the sharing going both ways. Overall, Wright stresses the need for changing the total campus climate so that bias toward others is reduced and tolerance for racism and sexism is eliminated. According to Astin (1982), too many minority students perceive college campuses as hostile environments. The need to transform hostility to acceptance is critical.

Stikes (1984) found that black students are less satisfied with college than white students because they do not participate in activities directly related to their own experiences. According to Pounds (1987), black students need to interact with black staff and faculty. In particular, black faculty are crucial as role models, mentors, and advisers. Like Wright, Pounds supports the idea of mentoring activities and recognizes that it is not possible for all black students to have black mentors. The important ingredient in mentoring is that the mentor be vested in the student's academic and personal growth and be willing to invest time and energy with the student to promote it.

Role models and mentoring are seen as important for other minority groups as well. Quevedo-Garcia (1987) recommends that colleges and universities use their Hispanic alumni and currently enrolled students to help new students adjust to the demands of college life. Also, according to Chew and Ogi (1987), Asian American students benefit from making connections with Asian American Studies departments on campus. This networking helps students enhance an understanding of their own cultural backgrounds and fosters self-esteem and self-validation. LaCounte (1987) stresses that Native American students do not want to assimilate with the majority population and are focused on maintaining attachments to their cultural heritage. It is important that educational climates provide opportunities for identification with cultural backgrounds while fostering integration with the prevailing majority culture.

Underrepresented groups in higher education include blacks, Hispanics, and American Indians. Only about 7 percent of blacks, 6 percent of Hispanics, and 6 percent of Native Americans attain a bachelor's degree. This compares with 14 percent of whites and 22 percent of Asian Americans. (*Chronicle of Higher Education Almanac, 1998–99*). If these students are to experience higher education fully, issues in the educational environment that impede success in higher education must be addressed. Affirmative action debates abound in the academy, and legislation banning affirmative action bodes poorly for increased minority access to higher education. Friendly environments, however, are only one piece of the puzzle. Success in higher education is complex. It involves a combination of student preparation and readiness to compete, as well as ways of predicting academic readiness that are not solely dependent on test scores. Flexible environments in which majority cultures reassess their biases and alter their behaviors and beliefs are important, and minority students should be able to evaluate which college environments best support their development.

One final study that is related to minorities and the environment in higher education is of particular interest. Padilla, Trevino, Gonzalez, and Trevino (1997) conducted a study to investigate the strategies that successful minority students use as they strive to overcome barriers to success in college. Using an expertise model of success developed by Padilla (1991, 1994), the researchers identified campus-specific knowledge and actions that successful minority students use; the results show a taxonomy of barriers that successful students must overcome.

In the study, discontinuity barriers (moving from small town to urban area, learning to be independent, having difficulty coming to terms with the value of the job) were overcome when students framed the college experience as different and challenging and prepared themselves to face new challenges. They mentally conditioned themselves before arriving on campus and were determined to overcome challenges because they valued education highly and knew their efforts to overcome barriers would be worthwhile.

Lack of nurturing barriers (lack of family support or understanding, lower expectations of student by faculty or staff, and lack of minority role models) were faced by students nurturing themselves or acquiring nurturing from others. They accessed support groups and sought mentoring resources. They used resources such as faculty advisers and tutors and involved their own families in the college experience.

Lack of presence barriers (lack of minority issues or materials in the curriculum, lack of visibility of minority support programs, cultural isolation, lack of minority role models or mentors, and racial isolation) were overcome by these achieving students as they actively participated in minority student organizations and made themselves known on campus.

Resource barriers (lack of money, financial aid system) were overcome by preparing early for the financial aid process and networking with others who had information about sources of financial assistance.

Overall, Padilla's study suggests that successful minority students try to incorporate their cultural community into the campus community instead of experiencing ongoing separation from their home culture. It is this effort to maintain cultural identity while adjusting to the campus environment that is a significant factor in the success of these students.

In this chapter, we have looked at research. Now we make connections. Using the TRPP model, we link theory and research to principles and practice.

Using the TRPP Model

The research findings and theoretical foundations have led us to construct the following principles.

Principles

1. Teachers who use concrete examples and suggest practical applications help learners connect prior knowledge to new information.
2. Social integration and sense of community are linked to persistence in college.
3. Environments characterized by critical dialogue, integrative learning, and risk taking promote student learning and development.
4. Peer teaching promotes active learning, academic achievement, and retention in college.
5. Adult learners prosper in learning environments that allow for autonomy and self- direction.
6. Students with disabilities benefit when necessary accommodations are provided.
7. Students learn better when their cultural backgrounds are incorporated into their academic lives.

Applying Principles to Case Studies

Principle 1: Teachers who use concrete examples and suggest practical applications help learners connect prior knowledge to new information.

Charles is frustrated with his evening class in computer technology. The teacher leaves directly after class and isn't available for consultation. In the absence of teacher contact, Charles would benefit from a caring tutor who could help by providing more concrete examples of the assignments and showing him how the course work relates to his day job as a data entry clerk. In the class itself, the instructor could help Charles and other students by using more examples to demonstrate the practical application of the course material.

Problem-based learning approaches would also be helpful. For example, the teacher could develop a problem based on a real-life situation and have the students work in small groups to solve it. In problem-based learning, students apply information from their own experiences, analyze new information in the course content, and then synthesize all information to address the problem. This approach demands a reorganization of instructional delivery so that there is less reliance on lecture and more emphasis on student collaboration in the learning process.

Principle 2: Social integration and sense of community are linked to persistence in college.

In Jadwiga's case, the role of cultural heritage and her need to remain connected to it is critical. In order to succeed in learning, however, she found it necessary to move away from her family and become more integrated with her English-speaking friends. The tension mounted between her need to remain connected to her Polish roots yet to separate from them in order to advance her learning in English. Knowing that social integration and sense of community is linked to learning persistence is helpful in understanding Jadwiga's decision to move away from her family. However, it is also important to recognize Jadwiga's need for nurturing her family and culture.

Environmental research suggests that Jadwiga would benefit from connecting to support groups and mentoring activities with Polish friends and teachers. Because her own family is not providing the support she needs for continuing her education, perhaps others connected to her Polish culture could help fill the void. Participating in a Polish student organization could also help her overcome feelings of cultural isolation.

Principle 3: Environments characterized by critical dialogue, integrative learning, and risk taking promote student learning and development.

Sabina is frustrated in her distance learning classroom. She feels like an outsider as her classmates interact with each other while she watches on the monitor miles away. The importance of critical dialogue is evident in this case. In order for Sabina to succeed, she needs to engage in critical thinking with her peers, integrate her own experiences into the educational setting, and take risks with the formation of her concepts. The role of the teacher in this situation is crucial. The course needs to be designed so that Sabina is more actively included in class discussions. For example, questions for reflection could be posed before each class session, with the expectation that each student will pair up with another student and discuss them. Sabina could be paired with a fellow student and begin to become more actively engaged. Prior to having a guest speaker in class, preview questions could be provided so that Sabina would be able to ask questions of the speaker and feel more present in the session.

Principle 4: Peer teaching promotes active learning, academic achievement, and retention in college.

Peer teaching would be a good way to help Linda become more active and succeed academically. Working one-on-one or in small groups with a trained peer helper, Linda could observe how to more actively approach her studies. She could be encouraged to answer questions and summarize content without fear of being evaluated by her instructor. In addition, she would begin to develop some social relationships that would help her adjust in the new environment.

Providing opportunities for help from peers is often not enough. Students facing difficulty are often hesitant to ask for help. Even when given the opportunity, they might not take it. Offering peer teaching activities in the classroom or making them part of the syllabus is one way to overcome this. SI (supplemental instruction) is an excellent example of how this can be accomplished. Weekly sessions led by trained peer teachers can be integrated into the course syllabus. Even though the traditional SI format promotes voluntary attendance, required participation for students in jeopardy can be considered. Linda would be an excellent candidate for an SI session.

Principle 5: Adult learners prosper in learning environments that allow for autonomy and self-direction.

Teresita is striving toward a degree in early childhood education while continuing to work and parent her children. In addition, she has an unsupportive husband who is discouraging her educational pursuit. Findings from environmental research reveal that adult learners seek autonomy and self-direction. Perhaps adjustments in the curriculum and assignments could be made so that Teresita can work more autonomously and be a participant in the design of her own assignments. Timelines could be extended and projects developed so that she can achieve the standards of the course in ways that are more conducive to her situation. As a mother of young children, she might be able to complete assignments at home by observing her own children and connecting these observations to concepts in the course. If these kinds of adjustments are not possible, another suggestion would be to provide opportunities for Teresita to meet with other mothers returning to school. In small-group meetings, Teresita and other student-mothers could talk about their frustrations and find ways to help each other persist toward their learning goals.

Principle 6: Students with disabilities benefit when necessary accommodations are provided.

Linda most definitely needs to reveal her learning disability and seek assistance. It may have been some time since her disability was diagnosed, and now could be a good time to have an updated assessment of her current functioning. The disability coordinator at her school is a good resource and could assist Linda with the necessary steps. Faculty can reach out to students with disabilities and indicate on the course syllabus that any student with a disability or suspecting a disability is encouraged to self-identify. In a private meeting, the instructor can then refer the student to the special services office. With the required disability documentation, accommodations can be made in the classroom to promote successful learning. In Linda's case this could greatly improve her chances for academic success.

Principle 7: Students of color learn better when their cultural backgrounds are incorporated into their academic lives.

How can Charles be helped through the application of this principle? One of his main frustrations is that he must spend many hours away from his family. In Charles's culture, family is of primary importance. The tension mounts as time away from his family increases, and this affects his ability to concentrate and focus on his studies. At first, there seems to be no obvious solution to this problem. On further consideration, however, it might help if some content in his accounting course were more directly applied to his family situation. Even though he can't be with his family and attend class at the same time, he could be using the family budget in some of his accounting course assignments. In this way, he would be connecting content to his own family situation and begin to feel less stressed about spending less time with them.

Reflections

The following questions can provide a starting point for further reflection on practice.

How often are concrete examples used to promote learning?

In what ways are students encouraged to engage in critical dialogue, integrate learning and take risks?

How can peer teaching be incorporated into learning the course content?

Are there opportunities for adult students to pursue self-directed projects?

In what ways are students with disabilities identified and helped?

How is the cultural background of students incorporated into learning?

Chapter Eight

Ways of Knowing

In Chapter Three we reviewed ways of knowing; we discussed the theories related to cognitive development and different ways of understanding the concept of knowledge. The classic work of William Perry (1970), with his hierarchical stage theory and the learner advancing through four major categories of thinking, was included. Belenky, Clinchy, Golberger, and Tarule (1986) used this framework and discovered, through interviewing women, that their stages of cognitive development are somewhat different and not necessarily hierarchical. Baxter Magolda (1998) studied undergraduates and found that there are gender patterns within broader categories of thinking and that they tend to build on one another.

Bruffee's (1993) notion that knowledge is constructed through collaboration led to the concept of students as active participants in the learning process. Paulo Freire's (1970) dualistic teaching strategies contributed to an understanding of banking versus problem solving to describe the difference between passive receivers of knowledge and those who actively seek answers. The concepts of Mezirow (1991) and Cross and Steadman (1996) helped describe systems that affect the learner's organization and storage of information for future use.

We also examined different kinds of intelligence. Howard Gardner's work (1983) indicates seven talents that individuals possess to varying degrees, and Robert Sternberg's theory (1988) produces a triarchic model that he contends could be taught. Another way of looking at intelligence comes from Mayer and Salovey's (1997) ideas regarding emotional intelligence and the developmental nature of the four stages they describe.

Looking back at this framework, we see four common denominators: (1) cognitive development occurs in stages, not necessarily hierarchical ones, that may be related to gender; (2) intelligence is not one generalized factor underlying all learning; (3) learning is an active process in which collaboration plays a significant role; and (4) knowledge is at the very least partially constructed by the learner.

These theories raise as many questions as they provide answers. They have the potential to shake up the practice of teaching and the routine surrounding it. The next step is to engage in reflective inquiry and examine the research to see if these theoretical concepts have been applied in a way that will lead to the construction, or more likely the deconstruction, of some of the principles that have traditionally guided the practice of teaching.

Cognitive Development Occurs in Stages

Much of the research on cognitive development describes various levels of processing. These levels are thought to build on one another but are not locked into a given sequence and can be related to factors such as gender patterns, context, and instructional delivery. For instance, Cross and Steadman (1996) suggest that instructors can induce higher-order processing, not by explaining but by providing an environment that "demands active learning" (p. 189) and introducing cognitive conflict (looking at things through different perspectives) through instructional delivery methods.

In the case of Mike, for instance, if his teacher used case studies of small businesses and groups of students were given the task of cooperating to solve authentic problems, he might be stretched beyond his current dualistic stage (there is a right and wrong) of processing information. The research of Price and Jang (1998), which investigated Vygotsky's zone of proximal development in relationship to calibration (balancing) and stretching cognitive complexity, supports this notion. Price and Jang found in a study of Korean children and their mothers that the more the mothers "stretched" the children's responses to stories being read, the more the children's reading levels increased. Conversely, when a child's current cognitive level was calibrated to the expected response, there was less advancement in reading behavior.

Research dating from the 1970s has indeed shown that course-based interventions and formal education in general have advanced students' cognitive development. The work of Stephenson and Hunt (1977) describes a freshman-year social science course designed to advance students from Perry's dualistic level to the more advanced relativistic one; the results demonstrate a substantial movement toward relativism in the experimental group. According to Pascarella and Terenzini (1991), other research has shown similar advances when the constants include providing challenges to students' cognitive levels and values within a supportive environment.

In Mike's case, authentic problems that include "messy" data and no single, correct solution will likely stretch his current way of thinking if delivered along with a support system that rewards creativity and validates his thought processes while suggesting alternatives.

Much of the research related to levels of cognitive processing in adult learners has been done through the lens of the reflective judgment model (King and Kitchener, 1994). What is reflective judgment, and how does it compare to the levels of cognition that we discussed earlier in Chapter Three? To develop their model, King and Kitchener investigated how individuals make judgments about confusing, complicated problems. In their research, they identified some consistent patterns and found that people justify their beliefs based on their assumptions about knowledge. Their model is based on how individuals work through ill-structured problems that have uncertain solutions, and they describe it as a developmental progression from childhood to adulthood. It was developed through extensive interviews following a problem-solving exercise in which two contradictory views of an intellectual issue were presented. Through their observations, they identified seven stages of thinking that, like Perry's stages, reflect sets of assumptions related to what knowledge is.

They describe stages 1 through 3 as pre-reflective thinking—knowledge is absolute and obtained from an authority; this parallels Perry's dualistic level and Belenky and others' silence. Stages 4 and 5 are characterized by a contextual view of knowledge—interpretation becomes significant; they have labeled it quasi-reflective thinking. Stages 6 and 7 are considered reflective thinking and occur when knowledge is seen as the outcome of "reasonable inquiry." Their research shows significant gender or cross-cultural differences. In general, King and Kitchener found that those engaged in educational activities improved their reasoning ability and that development follows stage-related patterns.

An early study (Shoff, 1979) compared seniors in college with adults entering college for the first time and found that the seniors scored higher on a measure related to the reflective judgment model (King and Kitchener, 1994) than did adult freshmen of the same age or older. This supports the idea that schooling is an intervention that may contribute more than maturation to a person's cognitive level of processing. Other studies (Schmidt, 1985; Glatfelter, 1982) have shown that nontraditional-aged freshmen are no different from traditional-aged freshmen or junior-level students on a measure of reflective judgment. Kitchener, King, Wood, and Davison (1989) conducted a longitudinal study comparing two groups of similar ages; one group attended college and the other did not. The results show greater gains in reflective judgment for those who obtain a B.A. degree than for those who do not.

Kitchener and King (1990) conducted an overview of earlier studies and averaged the scores for nontraditional-aged, first-year students and those of traditional-aged freshmen and seniors. They found that the older returning adults had a level of cognitive processing consistent with the traditional-aged freshmen. It seems that formal schooling definitely has an effect on levels of cognitive processing. Pascarella's work in 1989 supports this, as he looked at individuals who entered college immediately following high school and compared them to those who did not. In that study, those who completed one year of college scored 17 percentage points higher on the Critical Thinking Appraisal (Watson and Glaser, 1980) measure than those who did not.

Research guided by the reflective judgment model also provides support for the findings of Price and Jang (1998) that are related to stretching the learner rather than simply targeting the current level of cognitive functioning. Kitchener and King (1990) report the transitions between levels to be more like waves than steps and plateaus. In fact they describe the stages as "waves across a mixture of stages where the peak of a wave is the most commonly used set of assumptions" (p. 140). Using this metaphor, students are likely to be processing information at more than one level, and educators need to be challenging them at the highest edge of that level within a supportive learning environment (Kroll 1992; King and Kitchener, 1994). Related to Cross's notion of introducing cognitive conflict, King and Kitchener assert that development is stimulated when individuals' experiences don't match the expectations of a situation, and they are forced to abandon their usual assumptions and try something new. This can be facilitated in a classroom through careful design of the learning task and feedback to ensure development. Kitchener, Lynch, Fischer, and Wood (1993) found that students' optimal levels are one stage higher than their functional level.

In Linda's situation, half of this challenge-with-support equation is being met; she is being challenged to think about information in new ways, but very little in the way of support has been constructed. For example, one mechanism to stretch Linda's thinking would be to integrate relevant problems into the science lecture. After providing a mini-lecture, if the instructor would stop and pose a problem to the students that challenges them to apply the information in small groups, Linda would be forced to think at a different level. Following this, a class discussion on the various group applications, with positive feedback from the instructor, would affirm its value.

In Mike's case, the support may need to be more individualized at first. Establishing a personal relationship with the instructor in which they talk informally, outside of class, about applying new information to Mike's business might be a way to break down some of his resistance and challenge him to process information at a higher level.

Kitchener and King (1990) also report that, on average, high school students function at stage 3, whereas traditional-aged college freshmen are likely to be processing information at stages 3 and 4. Pascarella and Terenzini (1991) estimate that college students advance half a stage during their college years, and Kitchener and King assert that although this may seem like a small shift, the significance is a qualitative one: the students have developed from reasoning that is based primarily on personal beliefs to a process that depends on gathering evidence in order to make judgments. In related research, Dings (1989) asked faculty their perceptions of students' processing. He found that they underestimated freshmen and overestimated seniors. (Interestingly, faculty estimated themselves to be at stage 7.)

Another model articulated by Baxter Magolda (1992) examines levels of thinking and relates them to assumptions about the concept of knowledge. Through longitudinal interview studies with traditional-aged college students, she identifies developmental ways of knowing and, as we described in Chapter Three, the levels seem to contain gender patterns. As did Kitchener and King (1990), she discovered that the levels evolve with increasing complexity throughout the college years. At the absolute level, students place the responsibility for learning on the instructor, who has the authority and has all the answers. In Baxter Magolda's study, these students were most prevalent in their first year of school; they represented only 2 percent of the population in their senior year and disappeared completely in the year following graduation. In the next stage, the transitional one, the student began to understand knowledge and saw it as more uncertain. This way of thinking increased dramatically during the first three years of college, from only 32 percent of the population in the first year to 83 percent in the third year. The independent level was not represented at all in the first year and increased to only 16 percent in the fourth year. Baxter Magolda's work shows that the biggest increase in this level occurs in the year following graduation when it represented 57 percent of the learners. At this level, individuals thought for themselves and actually created their own perspectives.

Baxter Magolda's research identifies no college students at the highest level of knowing—the level she calls contextual. In this stage knowledge is contextual and judged on the basis of evidence within a context. She identifies no gender patterns here, and she found that only 12 percent of the students interviewed following graduation were characterized by this stage.

Levels of cognitive development have served as frameworks for various studies seeking to improve instructional delivery and curriculum development. Several relate to the teaching of writing. Mullin (1998) analyzed the strategies of college writers and discovered that by applying theories of intellectual development, the instructor could both develop relevant "strategies to help a writer complicate her thinking process as she practices some writing patterns" (p. 86) and design more appropriate assignments. She found that by increasing the students' metacognition, or self-awareness of how they were approaching various writing tasks, intellectual development is facilitated. She compared the process approach of the writing class where students are guided across levels of thinking to a content course where assignments are frequently made without regard to a student's current development. The content instructor often "presupposes abilities to synthesize, construct or contextualize ideas and evaluate evidence to support competing authoritative claims" (p. 89). Mullin contends that if the student is functioning at Perry's dualistic stage, for example, this type of assignment could create enough stress to cause a regression to the level of comfort and the student, not wanting to take any chances, will produce a paper that appears simplistic.

Nugent (1993) analyzed a community college writing class using Belenky and others' (1986) theory of development and found that it was possible to monitor students' growth throughout the class by utilizing their levels of knowing. Students operating in silence said very little, and those at the next level of received knowledge were still looking for an external authority and did not feel capable of voicing knowledge; their papers often consisted of strings of quotations from accepted "authorities." At the subjective level, student writing consisted of vast generalizations based on personal experiences, whereas at the procedural level it began to demonstrate a recognition of the need to learn procedures. Finally, at the constructed level of thinking the writing showed more synthesis and an application to students' lives.

What Nugent concludes from this study of writing is that there is cognitive development during one term of instruction, but it is slow. She further notes that facilitation of this change could be affected by the teacher scheduling regular in-class conferences with students to challenge them and discuss their levels of thinking. Development could also be enhanced by encouraging student metacognition; one way of doing this is by giving writing assignments in which students are asked to think and then write about what they learned from an assignment.

Other studies have looked specifically at teaching argumentative writing in relationship to Perry's scheme. Henderson (1994) contends that the writing teacher must understand the connections between student levels of intellectual development, views of knowledge, and the skills involved in writing arguments. More specifically, Hays (1988) found that students at the higher end of Perry's scheme produce the most effective argumentative essays and that a score based on this scheme is a better predictor of a quality essay than age, gender, or grade level.

The work of Perry and that of Belenky and others has also been used to design curriculum in which students must interpret meaning and face controversial issues. For instance, Crawford (1989) reports on developing art and art history courses based on Perry's work. Because these are courses in which students are encouraged to accept ambiguities and conflicting perspectives related to evaluating and creating art, it can be uncomfortable for those who are operating at the lower levels of Perry's scheme. For instance, students who are in the stage of dualism and see the teacher as authority and possessor of all knowledge will not want to construct their own perspective nor will they value their peers' thoughts and opinions.

Basing his work on the varying degrees of cognitive levels that students bring into the classroom, Crawford (1989) developed a set of tactics he felt would facilitate development while acknowledging current levels of processing. He suggests having a direct discussion regarding the process of cognitive development so that students understand why certain aspects of the course might be frustrating. He also recommends balancing challenge with safety in order to lessen student discouragement.

He identifies four instructional components that students want in varying degrees, depending on their current ways of knowing: diversity, structure, abstraction, and closeness to the instructor. With the exception of closeness, which all students seem to want, students at higher levels of thinking are able to deal with higher degrees of diversity and abstraction and less structure, whereas students at earlier stages of thinking want more structure and less diversity and abstraction.

Another content area that has been studied is that of social justice classes in which students are expected to challenge stereotypes and accept divergent perspectives. This was examined by Adams and Zhou-McGovern (1994) at a large public institution where students must take a social diversity course. After studying the course goals and the students within the frameworks of Perry and of Belenky and others, the researchers came to several conclusions. First, they decided that first-semester students who often function at Perry's dualistic stage of processing are not ready for a course that encourages listening and learning based on divergent experiences. For this reason, they now discourage first-semester students from enrolling in the social diversity course. Second, they found that the number of issues raised should be limited to accommodate the students' lack of readiness to confront so much uncertainty. They also discovered a need to begin the course with concrete, personal, and experiential themes in order to provide a foundation for the more abstract, uncertain concepts. Equally important was the provision of support and structure for the contradictions that would be introduced as the course progressed. Finally, they recognized the usefulness of the students' perceptions of teacher as authority and used it to provide modeling of new ways of thinking.

Intelligence Has Multiple Facets

For the better part of this century, the construct of intelligence has been defined by what standardized tests measure rather than by a rational analysis of the factors contributing to intelligent behavior in an appropriate environment. Many of these tests were originally designed to predict successful academic performance in a formal educational setting; for college admissions, they do predict grades, but frequently this prediction is only for the first year of study.

Robert Sternberg (1996) developed a more comprehensive view of intelligence with his triarchic theory. He looked at the predictive value of the Graduate Record Examination (GRE) as it relates to doctoral students in psychology. He and his colleagues found that the GRE provides some prediction of first-year grades but not second-year grades. He concludes, "The message of the GRE study is largely negative: for the most part, a conventional test of intellectual abilities did not provide much prediction of interesting aspects of academic performance" (p. 211). Related to this was his finding from interviewing business executives that when they hired top graduates (those who had the best grades) from business schools, they had individuals who could analyze case studies but who were frequently unable to be creative and innovative.

As Sternberg continued to investigate this notion of a broader definition of intelligence, he looked at whether the prediction of academic performance in college would improve if broader tests were administered. He developed a test based on his triarchic theory and offered it to a sample of high school students who had been invited to take a college-level course at Yale. This test measured the analytical, creative, and practical abilities of the students. The findings support the idea that no general factor crosses all areas; in fact, there was little correlation among the subtests. They also indicate that at least two and sometimes three of the abilities measured are significant in predicting academic performance. Additional studies (Sternberg and Lubart, 1991; Davison and Sternberg, 1984) have found support for the relative independence of the analytical, practical and creative abilities of individuals. Creative abilities seem to be domain-specific, and practical abilities have little correlation with analytical abilities across a range of domains although they do predict successful job performance (Sternberg and Williams, 1995).

Related to practical ability is what Sternberg (1988) called tacit knowledge. This component of intelligence combines knowing how to do something and its relevance to the achievement of a valued goal. This ability is acquired with little assistance from any external force. Sternberg (1996) reports that it predicts performance in business management and is correlated with salary, level in a company, and years of experience. In one study, it was the single best predictor of performance on two managerial simulations with a correlation of .61; a traditional I.Q. measure had a correlation of .38 (p. 236). Tacit ability tends to increase with experience; I.Q. does not. According to Sternberg, in "study after study, we have found only trivial correlations between tacit knowledge and I.Q." (p. 242). In work related to a college environment, he found that tacit ability predicts academic achievement as well as the SAT did and additionally is a good predictor of personal adjustment.

Sternberg (1996) describes three case studies of graduate students in psychology that clearly point out the effects of the different components of intelligence as he defines them. In the first case, Alice was admitted to school with an 800 on her verbal SAT and was at the top of her college class. By the time she finished graduate school, 70 percent of the class was outperforming her. In analyzing the reasons for her lack of achievement, Sternberg concludes that she was excellent when it came to remembering and analyzing others' ideas, but she was not as competent in coming up with her own ideas. In other words, she was high in analytical skills but lacked creative intelligence.

In the second case, Barbara was at first denied admission to graduate school due to her low test scores, even though her portfolio indicated a creative individual. She was hired as a research associate, and two years later was admitted to the graduate program; she had demonstrated her highly creative abilities. The last case, Penn, displayed both analytical and creative abilities but had no practical intelligence whatsoever. He continually was sought after during the interview process for jobs after graduation, but due to his arrogance and lack of ability to control it, he only received one job offer and lasted there only two years.

These cases clearly point out that there is more than one component of intelligence necessary for success in the real world. The components may be independent, but a successful individual needs a combination of the three functioning together.

Sternberg (1988) contends that these components can be taught and that our formal system of schooling could be assessing and teaching them. In collaboration with Howard Gardner, he developed a curriculum, "Practical Intelligence for School," to teach practical intelligence in the middle schools, and the results have shown increases in reading and writing achievement and test-taking skills and a decrease in behavioral problems (Gardner, Krechevsky, Sternberg, and Okagaki, 1994).

Sternberg's (1996) research with the broader tests we mentioned earlier also found that students' achievement increases when they are taught according to their pattern of abilities. He concludes from this last finding that teaching needs to focus on more than simply the students whose analytical abilities are strong; other kinds of "smart" need to be recognized. During the study, he also noticed that the students who had scored high on the measure of analytical abilities were much more homogeneous than those who produced high scores on the creative and practical measures. These latter students were more reflective of racial, ethnic, and economic diversity. Yekovich (1994) discusses this too and suggests a need to construct assessment measures that relate to experience more than to any predetermined, innate capacity. He stresses that teachers are facing a wider range of students than in the past and that this diversity represents many "expressible abilities" that need to be acknowledged.

Looking back at Linda and Mike from Chapter One, we see that Sternberg's (1988) triarchic concept can be easily applied. Linda has arrived at the university with a solid high school record and acceptable test scores; thus, she seems to be fairly analytical but has trouble when it comes to the practical and creative components related to intelligence. If she were skilled in the practical realm, she would be trying to figure out how to adjust to her new environment. Also in the area of creativity, she needs assistance in processing lecture and text information beyond the literal level.

Mike, however, exhibits a great deal of practical and creative intelligence at work but has a difficult time with the more analytical component that is expected at school. In both of these situations, the teacher could make a difference, according to Sternberg. In Linda's case, to promote the practical side, there could be direct references made to events on campus and how to manage time and activities along with integrating strategies for studying into the content of the classes. In addition, making the class time more interactive would provide models and rewards for student creativity. For Mike, making connections to the real world as often as possible would ease his transition into the analytical component that needs to be strengthened. Assignments that are problem-based, requiring data collection first and rewarding a variety of solutions, is one way to build his weaknesses through his strengths.

Howard Gardner (1990) has also studied multiple intelligences. He contends that our formal schooling system focuses exclusively on the analytical and logical-mathematical abilities of learners while ignoring the other five (spatial, musical, bodily-kinesthetic, interpersonal, and intrapersonal). Much of his work revolves around assessment, which he believes should be a "part of an individual learner's natural engagement in a learning situation (with) no need to teach for the assessment"(p. 42). Related to this, according to Gardner, the schools need to identify the learners' dominant talents, construct tasks to encourage them, and then construct relevant assessment measures rather than using standardized tests that drive the tasks and subsequent values.

Much of Gardner's work has been applied in the schools where curriculum has been developed around his various intelligences, and assessments have come to be known as domain projects. Gardner believes that assessment should be conducted within specific domains and that it must be based on true performance within that domain. For instance in his study, Project Zero (Gardner, 1994), students were assessed within a musical domain through a process of learning to critique their own ongoing performances. The instructor initially taught them how to critique and gave them criteria by which to evaluate their own performance. Each time they rehearsed, they evaluated themselves immediately afterward from memory, and then they listened to a tape recording of the same performance in order to evaluate again and to compare the two sets of evaluations. Gradually throughout the term, they learned to take on more of the responsibility for assessing as well as directing the learning experience. This procedure contains all the ingredients that Gardner suggests are necessary for assessing learners in authentic situations. It is a direct measure; there is no need to infer from a multiple choice question whether the student can actually perform music. Its scope is wide enough to look at more than one intelligence within the specified domain (for example, linguistic, musical, or intrapersonal), and it is "transparent," that is, the criteria are not hidden away to be guessed at by the learner.

Smagorinsky (1991) uses Gardner's work as a basis for talking about cultural differences that foster various types of intelligence. He emphasizes that the first two of Gardner's intelligences (analytical and logical-mathematical) are dominant in Eurocentric cultures, whereas students coming from diverse backgrounds "perform roles which are essential to the perpetuation of their cultures and they are among their people's most highly valued members. Yet they might not appear intelligent according to measures used in American schools" (p. 2). His work examines cultural symbol systems and how they differ. For instance, a learner's system of encoding can vary from using language to using music. Similarly, one's dominant manner of expression could range from dancing to drawing. Rather than devaluing alternative ways of performance and achievement, ways must be found to structure learning experiences that will take advantage of them and at the same time create environments that encourage students' strengths and consequently increase achievement.

One example of the differences between cultural communities and formal schooling as they relate to perceived intelligences comes from the research of Moll (1990). She worked with Mexican American households in which problem-finding and problem-solving skills were central and were used regularly but did not represent the skills valued in the schools. She relates how important the social network was within this particular community; yet, "schools isolate students for formal evaluation of remote knowledge, denying them opportunities to construct meaning by using knowledge from their own worlds in diverse activities" (p. 3). Another study by Okagaki and Sternberg (1993) found that the more parents from different ethnic groups emphasize social competency skills like getting along with others and helping out, the less intelligent the children seem by school standards.

Sternberg (1988) strongly suggests that intelligence cannot be understood outside its cultural context. He describes a study done with the Kpelle tribe in Africa in which the adults were asked to sort items into categories. The adults sorted by function, as we would expect children to do in American culture, and the researchers were ready to conclude that individuals in this particular African community were not able to sort taxonomically. They had to change their conclusion when they asked the subjects to sort in a way they thought stupid people would; with that direction, the Kpelles easily demonstrated a sort by taxonomy!

Within the culture of work and everyday experiences, intelligence has been demonstrated in different ways as well. In a study done by Scribner (1984), workers in a milk processing plant whose job it was to fill orders and who were the least educated in the plant were using mental calculations that required an understanding of different base number systems. When white collar workers were brought in as substitutes, their performance was not as effective, even though they probably had more formal training in various mathematical operations. In another series of studies related to everyday math, shoppers in California who effectively used mathematical shortcuts to determine the cost per unit of items were given the MIT mental arithmetic test. No correlation was found between the test results and the shoppers' proficiency in the actual shopping situations (Lave, Murtaugh, and de la Roche, 1984).

Emotional intelligence is another aspect of intelligent behavior that is relevant to the big picture but has only recently been studied. LeDoux (1996) describes the neurological branching in the brain that allows the connections between emotional and rational thought. The amygdala is that part of the brain responsible for emotional thought and emotional memory. It reviews a person's experiences from an emotional perspective and compares them to the current situation before a decision to act is made. According to the work of Damasio (1994), "the emotional brain is as involved in reasoning as is the thinking brain" (p. 130) partly because it helps to narrow one's choices by looking at the results of prior experiences. His research on the circuit between the working memory area of the brain and the amygdala shows that when it is not fully functioning, decision making is flawed, even though the individual's I.Q. and cognitive ability are not deteriorated. He concludes that because the individual has no access to prior emotional learning, the associations are lost and everything becomes neutral, making it difficult to make an effective decision.

Mayer and Salovey (1997) discuss how individuals prioritize cognition through their emotions. They suggest that by interrupting cognitive processing, emotional reactions have the capability to direct attention to what might be significant in a given situation. By using emotions as one basis for thinking, Mayer and Salovey relate emotional intelligence to social competencies and adaptive behavior. This sounds very much like Sternberg's (1988) notion of adapting to one's environment as a significant component of intelligence and Gardner's (1983) concept of intra- and interpersonal intelligences.

Mayer and Salovey insist that emotional intelligence is a mental skill and not simply a trait or way of behaving. At the beginning level, individuals recognize their emotions; as they progress through subsequent stages, they use these emotions to assist them in their general intellectual processing. With maturity, emotions help to direct attention to areas that need to be highlighted for learners. For instance as individuals develop, they learn to worry about tasks that need to be completed for successful achievement. At a subsequent level, they will be able to generate emotions "on demand" and anticipate how a particular action will make them feel, for instance, going back to school while working full time. According to Mayer and Salovey, this kind of anticipation contributes to more effective decision making.

Sabina is a good example of a learner who recognized her emotional state and used it to make a decision. She was enrolled in the distance learning class, and even though she was learning and earning good grades, she realized the experience was not satisfying. Her emotional intelligence led her to make a change. Teresita is at a different level of emotional development and currently is not able to sort through her emotional needs in order to use them for decision making. She doesn't seem able to prioritize her various needs at the moment; both family and personal needs compete for her attention, and she is unable to use her emotions, as Sabina did, to direct her attention to the significant variables in the situation.

Mayer and Geher (1996) predict that the ability to know another's emotions is related to intelligence. In their research, they gave subjects transcripts of others' thoughts and asked them to infer what emotions were being utilized. They found a positive correlation between ability to successfully predict emotions and SAT scores. Additional correlations were indicated for empathy and emotional openness. From these findings, the researchers suggest that this ability probably leads to a social advantage as well as to more successful employment experiences. They also surmise that those high in this ability probably tend to engage in certain professions more than others. Also, like Sternberg and like Gardner, they believe that this intelligence can be taught and should be incorporated into school curricula.

Collaboration Enhances Active Involvement

It is deceptive to talk about student collaboration as one generalized format for learning. Various models and characteristics of group structures reflect important differences. One way to begin the discussion on collaboration is to look at three models proposed by Hamilton (1994). These models represent distinctive formats used for group learning, and they are distinguished mainly by the source of authority and the type of task.

The first type of collaborative activity—the *postindustrial model*—is the most easily adapted to a traditional delivery mode. The instructor develops problems and gives them to small groups to solve.

There is a right answer, and the group's task is to work together to find it. The instructor is the source of authority, and the expectation is that each group will arrive at similar solutions. Weiner (1992) would contend that this is not really collaboration. According to him, "students put into groups are only students grouped and are not collaborators unless a task that demands consensual learning unifies the group activity" (p. 91). Some experts would say this first model represents cooperative learning rather than collaborative learning because the teacher is still the primary authority; collaboration implies more of a shift in authority to the group (Flannery, 1994).

The second type of collaboration Hamilton describes represents more of a shared decision-making process between instructor and students. Under this *social constructivist model,* groups of learners are expected to construct their own meaning with regard to a problem—one they may have generated themselves. Each group processes information in a way that reflects the perspectives of its members and most likely tries to build consensus as the group integrates individual ideas. For this to be successful, the instructor may have to "reacculturate" students who are used to more traditional experiences with teachers as the sole authorities. Bruffee (1993) warns that students must learn, "sometimes against considerable resistance to grant authority to a peer" (p. 47). To counteract this resistance, students coming from earlier, more competitive models of learning must develop a new set of skills. Bosworth (1994) suggests a taxonomy for groups that includes interpersonal skills, group-building and management skills, inquiry skills, conflict-processing skills, and presentation skills. Many of these skills have already been learned implicitly from social experience, but the instructor needs to facilitate making them explicit as students learn to draw from their "reservoir of tacit knowledge" (p. 29).

The third model for collaborative activity is referred to as the *popular democratic format,* and it focuses more on the differences within the group than the similarities. This type of activity has the least amount of external authority and uses the group to bring out differences as it gets at underlying assumptions of a problem. The group's goal is not necessarily to reach consensus but to understand the process itself and break down traditional thinking. Cooper's (1995) research indicates that when students experience such conflict in a heterogeneous learning group and work to resolve it, conflict contributes in a positive way to their intellectual development. In a study conducted with learners enrolled in a biology course where small-group problem-solving activities replaced lectures, group performance was highly dependent on a mixture of cognitive styles. As the cognitive diversity of individuals in a group increased, there was more group conflict and less satisfaction, but the overall performance improved (Miller, Trimbur, and Wilkes, 1994).

In Chapter Three we discussed Bruffee's ideas of increased opportunities for development when a group's zone of proximal development is wide. Pascarella and Terenzini (1992) also found that cognitive and attitudinal changes result when students hear different perspectives in small-group settings. This may be the first time students recognize that their perspective is not the only one in a world that is much larger than they realized.

Williams and Sternberg (1988) studied the workings of groups and found that the work produced by groups reflects a higher quality than that produced by individuals alone and that both cognitive and social-cognitive skills are related to the effectiveness of the group. They define a group as "an interdependent, dynamic system whose behavior we term 'group intelligence'" (p. 356). The collaboration of all the members constructs a system that is unlike any one individual. According to the researchers, high group intelligence develops when each member understands and operates within appropriate behavioral norms, has a sense of self-awareness, and contributes an average amount of talkativeness and dominance.

Clinchy's interviews with women (1994) relate to the significance of individual behavior within the group. She asked women what classes had helped them develop the most, and they answered, those that had "connected conversations" (p. 193). The women contrasted this format to that of debate and affirmed that within the effective groups each individual served as a midwife "building together a truth none could have achieved alone" (p. 41). Tobias's work with seniors at the University of Michigan (1990) affirms that women often find college science classes to be "unfriendly" places. The emphasis on competition rather than collaboration makes them uncomfortable, and Tobias concludes that there is an absence of community in these classrooms.

It may be this sense of competition that is helping to drive Linda away from the university. In such a climate, it can be more difficult to seek support because it signals a weakness, an inability to compete. If only her classes could be restructured to reflect more of a learning community where peers depend on one another to solve problems, study for exams, or simply talk through the new information, Linda might feel more comfortable.

Much of the research on group structures in learning does not distinguish among the three models that Hamilton has discussed nor does it examine differences between cooperative and collaborative learning. What it does tell us, however, is that generally the effects of student-centered instruction versus instructor-dominated environments are positive. McKeachie, Pintrich, Lin, and Smith (1986) reviewed studies comparing student-centered methods to those in which the instructor maintained dominance; they found that the more student-centered instruction leads to a higher application of concepts, increased abilities to solve problems, more positive attitudes, increased motivation toward group membership, and more effective leadership skills. It even seems that the students themselves are aware of the effectiveness of working in groups. Brennan and McGeever (1988) found that college graduates are critical of higher education when it tends to emphasize individual work and competition at the expense of collaborative experiences and teamwork.

Some studies do provide a definition of what they mean by collaborative or cooperative learning. For instance, Johnson, Johnson, and Smith (1991) reviewed 137 studies on cooperative learning instruction at the college level. Prior to their review, they defined what they meant by cooperative learning. Their definition includes an approach to group learning that is characterized by five elements: positive interdependence, face-to-face interaction, personal responsibility, collaborative skills, and group processing of information. They found that when the learning environment is structured around these criteria, there is increased productivity, increased self-esteem among the individual learners, increased social support for learning, and a committed and positive relationship among the group members.

More recent research by Geary (1998) indicates three essential components to successful cooperative learning. First, a positive learning environment must be created in order to reduce fear and to increase students' willingness to take a risk. Second, social skills must be developed so that group interaction can be facilitated. Finally, there needs to be some type of structure to give the groups guidance as they proceed.

A case study describes a developmental math classroom where the instructor confessed that he had run out of ideas for engaging the students' attention (Emerson, Phillips, Hunt, and Bowman, 1994). Following the integration of collaborative learning into the classroom, the instructor reflected, "Teaching collaboratively has enabled me to get through more material, and students have achieved a deeper understanding, worked harder and enjoyed it" (p. 83). He outlined the instructional components that he felt contributed most significantly to the effectiveness of the method.

First, he recommends doing away with the traditional textbook and generating one together with the students. He feels that with any textbook, the instructor is forced into the old lecture format because an explanation is always provided before the students have the opportunity to work out a problem for themselves. With collaboration, explanations are best provided as they become necessary during the process of solving problems.

The next strategy he recommends is that of requiring student learning logs during the last five minutes of each class session. His method is to ask three standard questions plus one question that changes on a regular basis. The three standard questions everyone answers each time are, What did you do today?, How are the groups working for you?, and Is there anything I should know about? He also keeps a teacher's log before, during, and following each session to ensure a record of what he is learning himself about the change from lecture to collaboration.

In addition, he suggests that the groups be changed approximately two times per term and be composed of three to five members. Last, he provides mini-lectures at each session that serve two purposes: to introduce new material and to provide assistance with potentially difficult areas.

This instructor kept a record of the results of the collaborative activity over a period of several terms and found that out of 240 students, only 5 preferred a lecture format. He also found that he was able to cover more material at a more difficult conceptual level without "overrunning" the students. Additionally, the students became more engaged with the material, and their attitude toward math changed. These findings probably had an effect on another result: an increased ability to conceptualize and articulate mathematical ideas.

In related research, a group of biology instructors shifted their teaching formats from lecture-driven classes to small-group, problem-solving workshops and found that there was a higher overall completion rate for the courses, increased student achievement, and increased excitement on their part toward teaching (Smith and MacGregor, 1992).

The work of Uri Treisman (1986) at Berkeley reinforces the notion that working together in small study groups can result in higher achievement in math for students who have not previously been exposed to learning in groups. He first looked at a calculus class and found that 60 percent of rural whites and ethnic minorities—students who were "socially marginal"—had lower grades than other students in the class. He discovered they had been taught in high school to believe that only weaker students studied together and that working in groups was related to cheating. Also studying in high school had a negative social prestige for these students, so they most often chose to study alone. Asian students in the class, however, easily formed study groups, and their social status increased with their ability to teach others.

Treisman's study focuses on decreasing the isolation of the socially marginal students by inviting them to discussion sessions that he labels "honors discussions" and by requiring peer checking of all homework assignments, using collaborative, small groups during class (Fullilove and Treisman, 1990), and organizing social activities outside of class. The results of this research indicate a decrease in the number of D, F, I, and W grades from an earlier 60 percent to only 4 percent. The difference between average grades for the socially marginal students and all others disappeared.

Another study of community in the classroom was conducted by Sheila Tobias (1990). She worked with individuals that she labeled the "second tier"—college graduates who had avoided science in college but who had gone on to become high achievers in their chosen fields. She asked them to "seriously audit" an introductory course in physics or chemistry. What she discovered through the students' journaling of their experiences was that they were often critical of the "classroom culture." They commented on the need for "more discussion, more dissent, and more community in the classroom" (p. 31). The culture of the classroom did not seem to value sharing, and their best learning came outside of class when they studied together and did what could not be done in the class: they taught the material to each other through a question-tryout-question format.

Tinto and Riemer (1998) took the notion of community beyond the traditional classroom and applied it across the university as they looked at learning communities at La Guardia Community College where counselors and faculty collaborated to make a difference. Here, entering groups of students in the New Student House program were required to enroll in four out of six courses, depending on their assessed need. The courses included reading, writing, speech, and a new-student seminar. The students went through the courses in groups, and collaborative learning was emphasized throughout the program. Results in three areas indicate the positive effects of building community. There was an increase in the creation of supportive peer groups, which influenced the students to persist in college. As these peer networks developed, there was increased academic engagement on the part of all students, and they spent more time studying. They also achieved higher passing rates than students in a comparison group, and they were more satisfied with their experiences which most likely led to the high persistence rate of 69.8 percent.

Active Involvement Leads to the Construction of Knowledge

Bruffee (1993) provides an effective connection from the concept of collaboration to the construction of knowledge when he asserts that collaboration "challenges our traditional view of the nature and source of the knowledge itself. Collaboration takes a toll on the cognitive understanding of knowledge that most of us assume unquestioningly"(p. 47). Is knowledge an entity that is simply transferred from one individual (the instructor) to another (the student)? If so, it would reflect the banking concept that Freire (1970) articulated when he discussed making deposits into empty vessels. Or is it more fluid? Is it instead sets of assumptions that are continuously being challenged and interpreted within different, often social, frameworks?

The research on collaboration validates the effectiveness of learners being actively involved in constructing knowledge. Williams and Sternberg's (1988) notion of group intelligence suggests that task completion is often of higher quality when carried out with others rather than alone. Clinchy's (1994) concept of connected conversations describes how women believe collaboration has a positive effect on their development. And too, the work of Emerson and others (1994) demonstrates that students have an increased ability to conceptualize and articulate mathematical ideas when given the opportunity to construct problem solutions collaboratively.

In the earlier section on cognitive development, we suggested that the way learners view knowledge depends partly on the level from which they are processing information. This level can be related to a variety of factors, including age, level of schooling, gender, and instructional delivery methods. Many theorists consider these levels to be hierarchical, starting with a view of knowledge that is mostly dualistic: someone else possesses the knowledge that an individual needs to have. The assumption here is that individuals are not active participants in the process of constructing the knowledge; rather, they simply take what they need to know from someone in authority. As the hierarchy of cognitive development progresses, however, individuals become increasingly aware of the need to be active learners and take part in the construction of knowledge so that it becomes more meaningful to them.

In Perry's scheme, for example, once learners think within the level of relativism, their beliefs about what constitutes knowledge are completely different from their beliefs when they operated at the dualistic stage. Within relativism, learners see knowledge as contextualized, and they have learned to make judgments based on their own perspectives. This implies a belief in their personal contribution to learning. When Belenky and others (1986) interviewed women, they determined that the highest level of processing was that of construction of knowledge. Likewise, Baxter Magolda's (1992) work describes the independent level of thinking as the highest represented by the typical college student.

Baxter Magolda (1997) conducted research with a college biology class where it was evident that the instructor and the students had very different meaning-making systems, or views of what knowledge was. The instructor expected students to take an active part in the construction of meaning for the class, but the students had difficulty understanding their roles. They had enrolled expecting to be given the knowledge they needed from the instructor. The instructor had to find a way to bridge these two very distinct ways of knowing before active collaboration could take place. Three principles emerged from this study that describe how to create such a bridge. The instructor must (1) validate the students as knowers, (2) situate learning in student experiences, and (3) regularly engage in mutually constructive activities.

In a related study, Springer, Miller, and Wright (1997) designed a chemistry course that seems to incorporate these principles. The instructor developed activities that forced the students to become active participants in the learning process. His lecture classes were formatted around pairs of students who regularly interacted with the instructor during lectures. He also added open-ended lab sessions and established a peer board of directors made up of students who took an active role in the direction of the class sessions. The outcomes indicate an increased level of student competence when compared to other more traditional classes and an ability on the part of the students to relate abstract concepts from the class seven months after the class ended.

Vygotsky (1965) is often discussed within the framework of constructivism, and his zone of proximal development is similar to the bridge in Baxter Magolda's study. Vygotsky describes learners' abilities through two lenses. The first shows what they can accomplish independently; the second highlights their potential or what they will be able do following assistance. The zone of proximal development is the distance between these two levels and the area where learning occurs. According to Hausfather (1996), it is imperative that activities within the zone are shared experiences with interpersonal engagement. He further states that "joint construction must exist for cognitive change to occur" (p. 7). This is referred to as intersubjectivity—the teacher and learner have a shared purpose and focus. In other words, the teacher's role within Vygotsky's zone is that of a collaborator and co-constructor of meaning rather than a transmitter of knowledge. This was found to be true in a study by Moll and Greenberg (1990). They looked at the ways in which knowledge and skills were transmitted in Hispanic households, and they found that zones of proximal development were continuously being generated. Within these zones, however, knowledge was not imposed; it was obtained by the children through reciprocal social relationships that "allowed children jointly to construct knowledge within social contexts" (p. 4).

Kegan talks about an "evolutionary bridge" (1994, p. 43) that is similar to Vygotsky's zone in that the assistance provided there simultaneously values and acknowledges where the learner is while facilitating more complex ways of thinking. In order to effect a change, teachers must connect to the student side of the bridge by understanding how they currently make meaning and understand the world. Once they have made this connection, a support system can be developed that facilitates their crossing in a collaborative, negotiated way.

An example of this comes from the work of Tharp and Gallimore (1988) who constructed "activity settings" where students could share with the instructor on a daily basis their personal experiences as they connected to the text assignments. In addition to facilitating a collaborative, cooperative spirit, these activities enabled the instructor to assess how the students constructed meaning systems and also to confirm for the student that the instructor valued their perspectives. In another setting, a "zone" was established in a math class where groups of students shared different problem-solving techniques with the teacher in an open dialogue. By encouraging this, the teacher allowed students to see the value of constructing their own approaches with peers and at the same time blending them with teacher input if that added meaning. (Peterson, Fennama, and Carpenter, 1989).

Hewson and Hewson(1988) took this approach one step further in a science class by initially eliciting conceptions the students had regarding science. They were then encouraged to collaborate with peers to solve problems using their personal and group-constructed ideas. Based on these, the instructor developed a set of problems that challenged students by creating a conceptual conflict for them. This gave the students the opportunity to reconstruct cooperatively their previous understandings. The teacher then was not imposing knowledge on the class but allowing them to actively integrate new ideas with their previously held concepts. Hewson stresses the importance of being sensitive to student viewpoints when negotiating their acquisition of new knowledge. He also emphasizes the use of instructional conversations in which teachers and students explore problems together as a community of learners.

Yakimovicz and Murphy (1995) describe a class based on similar principles of constructivism that was delivered over the Internet. It was a graduate class in which the students were learning about distance education via distance education; all communication was computer-based. They found that it was successful due to the active engagement of all students who were constructing their knowledge of distance learning through interactions and discussions. Students were conditioned at the start not to expect too much structure or direction. As they found information on their own and with others in their discussion group, grades became less of an incentive and the construction of new understandings took precedence. The authors conclude that the students "constructed the meaning of CMC for themselves, grounding it in their individual and group experiences" (p. 209). In addition, the authors comment on how appropriate the constructivist framework seems for adult learners who have decades of experience with both the development of socially negotiated meaning and personal schemata.

Scheurman (1996) describes another adult learning experience in which constructivist principles were applied in an educational psychology classroom. The goal of the instructor, in addition to facilitating an understanding of content, was to advance the students' level of critical thinking. Activities were designed to provide (1) open-ended inquiry to first elicit students' prior conceptions related to a topic, (2) provocative, authentic contexts, and (3) a regular consideration of multiple perspectives.

The shift toward the joint construction of meaning has been quite visible in the area of mathematics, as there has been increased emphasis on problem solving and inquiry and less emphasis on rote memorization and mastery of computational methods. Students are being encouraged to "recognize when problems or statements that purport to be mathematical are, in truth, still quite ill-posed or fuzzy; becoming comfortable with and skilled with bringing mathematical meaning to problems and statements through definition, systematization, abstraction or logical connection making; and seeking and developing new ways of describing situations"

(Cuoco, Goldenberg, and Mark, 1996, p. 376). This has been furthered by the NCTM (National Council of Teachers of Mathematics) standards, developed in 1989, which include the following reforms: development of classrooms as mathematical communities; movement toward logic and mathematical evidence as verification rather than relying solely on the teacher as authority; emphasis on reasoning and problem solving over memorization and mechanistic solutions; and connecting mathematics to other areas rather than continuing to see it as a separate body of isolated procedures.

In addition to the NCTM standards, the National Council of Teachers of English has sponsored research reports to gather information through observations, experimental studies, and detailed case studies about the nature of writing instruction. One of these reports (Langer and Applebee, 1987) concludes, "Rather than providing information and evaluating what students have learned, effective writing instruction provides carefully structured support or scaffolding as students undertake new and more difficult tasks. In the process of completing those tasks, students internalize information and strategies relevant to the tasks, learning the concepts and skills they will need in order eventually to undertake similar tasks on their own . . ." (p. 139). The authors acknowledge the influence of Vygotsky on their findings.

Notwithstanding a few earlier examples, many of these reforms are taking place more frequently in elementary schools than they are in postsecondary education. This is partly due to the growth of constructivist principles being incorporated into teacher education programs. At the University of California-Berkeley, a developmental-constructivist model for pre-service teachers has been designed. It takes into consideration what the research there has shown (Black and Ammon,1992): the students in the program evolve through several stages of professional development. They enter with a behaviorist pedagogy, that is, they assume that transmittal of information in their future classrooms is the goal. By the time they leave, their understanding is more constructivist with a new goal: to help their students develop reflective ways to better construct meanings.

Rainer and Guyton (1998) report the effects of another teacher training program that has been developed around the principles of constructivism. The basic elements of this program include regular dialogues, negotiated curriculum, constructivist roles, and authentic assessment. The students are expected to initiate and direct the content of their study so that it has relevance for them; their roles are collaborative with their faculty and peers. Outcomes of this program include a heightened consciousness of practice, a deeper level of thinking, and an increased tendency to collaborate, inquire, and reflect.

How does such training transfer to the classroom? Pressley and others (1994) observed and interviewed teachers who were teaching reading comprehension through strategy instruction at the elementary school level. The approaches they observed emphasized the use of individual interpretation of strategies and engaged the students in interactive dialogue 88 percent of the time. Teacher commentary was not evaluative; rather, it encouraged individual elaboration. The researchers conclude that good strategy instruction "invites" students to be creative and flexible in their own application.

In one of the observed programs, the teachers who were interviewed articulated many strengths of this approach for their students. Following strategy instruction, the students seemed to understand that comprehension is under their control, not someone else's such as the author or the teacher. Also, the students exhibited a higher level of thinking than before the instruction. In addition, the students seemed more excited, and their academic self-concepts increased.

In their argument for how such instruction fits into a contructivist framework, the researchers describe three of its significant characteristics. First, the instruction did not break tasks into parts where skills were practiced in isolated, short passages. Students were always working with whole text and were encouraged to apply a developing repertoire of procedures, not a series of discrete, memorized skills. Second, errors were an important part of the instruction. Errors were considered a natural part of the process. Rather than elements to be extinguished or ignored, they allowed the instructors to better understand the students' conceptions. Finally, instructors were aware of the importance of the students' prior experiences and understandings and how they contributed to new applications. Pressley and others conclude that good strategy instruction does fit into a constructivist framework, as it allows students to fill in gaps in information, adapt the strategies to their own style, and apply them to new tasks.

The constructivist framework has been reviewed through instructional approaches, but another significant lens is provided by Ramsden (1992) as he describes how students approach learning. What is expected from students within this constructivist context? Ramsden calls the traditional process "imitation learning"—the student gains factual knowledge that might be useful in a limited setting but makes no real connections to the world. He describes studies in which students were asked to read academic texts and respond to questions. After categorizing student responses, he found that they applied two basic approaches to the task: a surface approach and deep approach. Within the surface approach, the students never really intended to understand the text. They saw their role "as if they were empty vessels into which the words on the page would be poured" (p. 41). They were not personally involved and felt as if the task were simply an "external imposition." Those who applied a deep approach defined the task more constructively as one in which they had to actively make sense of the text.

In other studies related to students' approaches to learning, Prosser and Millar (1989) looked at first-year physics students and found that their development through the course was related to which approach they applied. Those who functioned with a deep approach exhibited a greater development of higher-order understandings than those using the surface approach. Biggs (1987) found that a deep approach is related to student satisfaction and that, conversely, students feel a dissatisfaction with achievement that results from a surface approach. Ramsden also found that students experience more personal fulfillment and pleasure when they use the deep approach. Those using the surface approach experience more tedium, tend to procrastinate more frequently, and have a more negative attitude toward studying.

In an earlier study Biggs (1987) discovered that students define learning differently depending on which approach they apply. Those with a more surface approach conceive of learning as "paying attention, doing assigned work, and memorizing" (p. 37) whereas those using a deep approach believe that learning depends on thinking and understanding. Ramsden contends that the approach a student selects is not skill-based, but that it is "inseparable from both the content and the context of student learning, both as previously experienced and as currently experienced" (p. 69). The approach can vary with any individual, as it is an adaptive response to the environment, which is defined in part by the teacher and the course itself. He also feels that students may select an approach based on their perceptions of the quality of interaction with the teacher and also the overall ethos of the classroom. (See Chapter Seven for a discussion of classroom environment.) If this is the case, it seems as if teachers have the ability to influence significantly the approach to learning that students take. If it is deep processing that one is expecting from students, then the constructivist approach to instruction seems most appropriate.

In this chapter, we have looked at research. Now we make connections. Using the TRPP model, we link theory and research to principles and practice.

✐

Using the TRPP Model

The research findings and the theoretical foundations have led us to construct the following principles.

Principles

1. Learners move through different levels of cognitive development that influence their understanding of knowledge and their roles as learners.
2. An effective learning environment provides challenges within a climate of support.
3. Working in groups enhances learning outcomes.
4. The concept of intelligence has many facets that need to be nurtured and valued in the learning environment.
5. In an effective learning environment, the teacher-student relationship is a collaborative one.

Applying the Principles to Case Studies

(It seems artificial to separate these two principles; there is much overlap when applying them to practice.)

Principle 1: Learners move through different levels of cognitive development that influence their understandings of knowledge and their roles as learners.

Principle 2: An effective learning environment provides challenges within a climate of support.

Frequently, instructors express dismay at the passivity of the learners they encounter in their classrooms. They expect them to ask questions and even debate with them from the first day. When this doesn't happen, they conclude that the students simply do not care or are underprepared. They decide to provide no challenges because few could meet them; the lecture continues.

The majority of recent high school graduates, however, who are either beginning college or entering the workforce are thinking and reasoning at levels that differ considerably from those of their instructors. They also hold different views of what knowledge is. For many of the learners, knowledge is still something to "get" from someone else—someone who is an expert and can simply hand it over. For these learners, going to class or work, taking notes from someone more experienced, and then attempting to memorize the expert's words constitutes learning. They do not see themselves as active participants in the meaning-making process; they see no value in interpreting or adapting a perspective based on their own experiences or knowledge because they do not see the personal connection. Consequently, their approach is fairly passive and, as Ramsden describes, on a surface level.

If these learners are given the opportunity to connect their understandings and prior experiences to the new material right from the beginning, they will begin to understand the significant role they have in the process. The instructor can then gradually lead them into higher levels of reasoning as they start to depend on their own abilities to interpret meaning and eventually to construct it. In the process, their approach to learning will go beyond the surface, to the deep level, where they assume the responsibility for understanding and constructing meaning.

In the case of Linda, she feels isolated at school and is falling behind in her assignments; she is hopeful that her lecture notes will save her, but her anxiety is increasing rapidly as exams approach. Suppose that in her chemistry lecture class the instructor had started the term by grouping students into small groups and presenting them with problems to solve collaboratively. A portion of a class session during the first week could have been structured around the various groups sharing their knowledge to solve problems. The problems could have been constructed to lead into some of the concepts to be discussed in class. Following the group activity, the instructor could either have elicited responses from a sample of the groups or asked each group to write out a summary of their discussion and turn it in.

This type of activity would accomplish several goals at once. First the students would immediately receive the message that the instructor values their perspectives. They would then have the beginnings of study groups, which would connect them to others throughout the term. Also, the activity would allow the instructor to assess the levels of thinking and the knowledge base represented in the class. At a following session, the instructor could create some conceptual conflict by introducing variables to the earlier problem that would force the students to think it through it from a new perspective, perhaps one that stretched their original thinking. A significant component of this follow-up would be an acknowledgment of the value of the students' earlier processing and how it was helping to further develop the course. The instructor could at that point discuss some of the group solutions along with the processing she had gone through to work on the problems herself. This would confirm the value of students' thinking and allow students to see an "expert's" way of thinking.

This would be a very different and probably intimidating experience for Linda, who is used to simply being the passive recipient of information. A key element would be the positive and supportive environment in which it is delivered. The instructor's acknowledgment of the value placed on the students' thinking and ways of understanding would need to be stated regularly and directly as she leads them through more difficult ways of thinking.

In the case of Mike, who is looking for relevant information that can help him in a very practical way, a similar strategy would be effective. He is a student who is easily turned off by formal schooling and often displays an attitude that can be a barrier to building a positive relationship with teachers. One thing that does excite him though is his auto body business and in his evening continuing education classes, he is probably not unique in his need to apply what he is learning to something "real."

As we discussed in an earlier chapter, Mike probably reasons at a much higher level when he is at work in an environment where he feels comfortable. Most likely, he does think independently in his shop, as he depends on his past experiences to solve new problems that arise. In school, however, he hasn't been able to connect his personal knowledge with the more abstract concepts that are presented. One way to reach out to Mike would be to acknowledge his wealth of knowledge and ability to reason with it and facilitate a connection to the new information that he needs.

For example, a class in business management could start out by asking the students to discuss a case study of a small business in trouble. The students, working in teams, could be asked to assume various roles in this business and come up with solutions based on their own experiences. Working together, the students would hear different perspectives from their peers, and they would also have the opportunity to present their own ideas to other teams. Throughout the term, these teams could remain intact and continue to apply new principles from the class to the problems in the case study. Additional class activities could include bringing in owners of businesses to act as consultants to the student teams as they try out various solutions and also having panels of team representatives debate different perspectives on keeping the businesses solvent.

As with Linda, this type of class would be intimidating at first to students who are attending class after long days at work and who think they want to simply take notes and "get through." Once they realize, however, that their experiences are considered valuable and that they are working on problems that seem real, their level of comfort and engagement would increase and their processing would be at a deeper level as they synthesize information and apply it for a meaningful purpose.

Principle 3: Working in groups enhances learning outcomes.

This is closely related to principles 1 and 2, as the examples of effective practice demonstrate. The significant components of instruction for the earlier principles included active collaboration for the learners and implied a co-construction of meaning between teacher and learner. The collaboration that was described in the activities for both Linda and Mike would serve multiple purposes beyond developing their levels of reasoning. It would connect them to a network of learners who most likely share some of their own fears and anxieties. By helping them connect, the message is sent that they are not alone and that learning in groups is valued and encouraged. For Linda, this may help her overcome the isolation and homesickness she feels. The in-class groups might extend into her personal life and help her participate in other institutional organizations. In addition, for Linda especially, the discussions generated by the groups in class would supplement her weakness in reading. This could help her get through the readings, but it would also let her know that reading is only one way to process information. It would validate for her that discussion and oral expression are also valuable ways to learn.

In Mike's case, he has always felt confident of his talent and ability to succeed in the auto body business. Along with this, he has resented the imposition of seemingly irrelevant tasks designed by teachers who are not coming from his world of reality. By working in the type of group described earlier, he would be thinking right along with his teacher as the case study continued to develop throughout the term based on new principles and student-led solutions. This, in addition to being a member of a team of peers who is coming from the "real" world, would foster his active engagement.

Collaborative activity would be very helpful to Teresita, who feels overburdened with personal responsibilities and the lack of family support. In her program of early childhood education, projects could be developed to enable the students to carry them out at job sites. Classes would not need to meet every week as students became engaged in the application of theory on the job. They could be responsible within groups of peers for developing reports for class based on their observations. For instance, Teresita could be part of a group assigned to investigate the play habits of boys compared to girls in her day-care environment. Rather than meeting every week at a scheduled time, the instructor and groups could stay in contact through a listserve set-up on the school's computer network or through the regular mail. With this process, Teresita would be collaborating with peers both at work and from her class. The various perspectives would inevitably stretch her own perceptions and enable her to connect theory to practice directly. Her time would also be more flexible as she and her peers could arrange conversations via the telephone, the computer listserve, or face-to-face meetings at times and locations convenient to everyone. This would make her feel more in control of her life as she combines work and school at times that suit her schedule. In addition, the peer network would give her the personal support she lacks from family.

In this type of delivery format, regular, encouraging feedback from the instructor is particularly important. With fewer face-to-face class meetings, the instructor needs to respond to the groups often to affirm their experiences and reports and let them know how they are directly contributing to the overall meaning of early childhood for this class. The instructor would continue to help them understand how the theory fits their experiences but would also make it clear that it is through the students' own personal experiences that meaning is being made for this class. Rather than telling them what she expects from their activities, she will let them discover the meaning through ongoing dialogue.

Principle 4: The concept of intelligence has many facets that need to be nurtured and valued in the learning environment.

Once again, by linking this principle to the others the connections are clear. With principles 1 and 2, instruction began with an awareness of the students' entering levels of thinking and content knowledge. There would most likely be a range of strengths evident throughout the class. The instructor's use of small groups to look at chemistry problems with no set solutions highlighted the fact that no one perspective was expected. In the continuing education class, the instructor acknowledged a range of talents by forming teams that subsequently assigned roles to their members, presumably based on their individual strengths.

An instructor was described who demonstrated such a respect for the individual learners and their strengths that she gave them the freedom and guidance to master the material primarily in their own environments. She encouraged them to use the strengths of their peers by forming collaborative groups in which discussions took place and ideas were synthesized into reports for the whole class. Rather than setting an expectation that the class would simply adopt her way of understanding, she guided them through a process in which they could integrate her ideas with their own in order to build a new way of knowing the concepts in the field of early childhood.

To develop strategies that emphasize principle 4, we only need to further extend the ideas from the other three principles. For instance, when using small groups to personalize a large lecture or encourage more active learning, the instructor could be proactive in assigning individuals to the groups. In smaller classes, once the individual students are better known, they could be placed into groups based on their strengths. Mike might be teamed with others who, functioning together, have what it takes to work on the case study. Mike's business success seems at least partially dependent on his ability to meet the needs of his customers. He may have good interpersonal skills and could assume the role of negotiator in a small group. Another member of the team might be identified as having excellent skills relating theory to practice, an apparent weakness of Mike's, and her role could be to facilitate the group discussions. Someone else may have demonstrated good writing and could be the team's recorder. The more the instructor can identify various strengths across the class, the more easily groups can be constructed to make the best use of them.

In a larger class in which this personal relationship is more difficult, the instructor can at least ensure that the composition of groups changes regularly. Rather than constructing groups based simply on established seating patterns, the instructor can develop more creative criteria. For instance when grading a particular paper, a number system could be created in which various types of approaches to the topic are categorized by number. Then either the instructor or a graduate assistant could add the appropriate number to the paper and ask students in class to group themselves with those having a different number. The instructor, of course, would discuss the meaning of the categories and the strengths and weaknesses of each approach. By mixing up the groups, the students would be forced to interact with different perspectives, which would contribute positively to their own development. If this is too cumbersome, at least the instructor could lead a discussion based on the variety of approaches taken in the student papers so that a range of perspectives is acknowledged and affirmed.

Another way to acknowledge the variety of strengths and perspectives in a group is to have options available for ongoing assignments and for methods of assessment. In Teresita's class, for instance, there are alternative communication systems built into the class. The students, depending on their proficiency with computers, can use the listserve as their primary means of communicating with both peers and instructor. If this doesn't work for them, however, there are additional means for connecting: face-to-face conferences can be scheduled with the instructor, phone calls can be arranged, and the more traditional mail can be used.

In Teresita's class, although identical assignments are given regularly to the small groups, there are not prescribed formulas for completing them. One group may document their observations by creating a videotape that covers the required concepts. Another group may bring in a panel of experts from various work environments to discuss the same concepts; another may interview children and present a summary of their responses to the class.

These alternatives demonstrate the variety of strengths and talents within each group. They also exemplify how assessment regularly intersects with instruction. The instructor is evaluating throughout the term how each group is developing its understanding of the course content. The interviews with children, for instance, were a natural way for one group of students to better understand the theoretical concepts from their readings. For another group, creating a videotape necessitated applying new understandings as they edited and connected realistic scenes from their work environments. In other words, both of these projects grew out of the needs of the learners and were not artificially imposed by the instructor. They allowed the individual talents of each group to be highlighted while enabling the instructor to continuously evaluate development.

In Mike's class, it would not make sense to require an individual, written exam at the end of the class if the entire course had been structured around group experiences designed to make the learning more relevant. Because managing a business is rarely an individual endeavor, assessment related to the group processes would seem more appropriate. An effective assessment process would begin with the first group report and occur regularly throughout the course, with input from the groups regarding format. Perhaps a student "board of directors" could be formed with a representative from each group. This group could work with the instructor to set guidelines for continuous assessment and to provide peer input regarding various projects. In addition to facilitating a variety of formats, this would allow the students to see the direct link between assessment and learning.

Principle 5: In an effective learning environment, the teacher-student relationship is a collaborative one.

Each principle leading up to this one has implied a collegial, personal relationship between teachers and students. At the core of each one is the idea of the classroom as a community where everyone is genuinely valued and expected to contribute actively. The expectation for this climate needs to originate from the teacher, and it needs to be established from the beginning. It will be a new concept for most students, so a rationale and clear procedure should be outlined.

Students don't expect to be asked for input; they arrive for class with their notebooks and are ready to take one more set of notes from another expert. But if the class is to be a community of learners, the teacher will, instead, on the first day ask them for their ideas and experiences related to the subject matter. This could then lead into an "instructional conversation," as Hewson suggests and we discussed earlier in this chapter, where everyone is actively engaged. Teresita would become immediately involved, as she could add her day-care activities to a discussion of child development. Charles, too, might begin to see the relevance of his coursework beyond a salary increase if he were asked to connect it to his experiences.

Using the experiences provided by the students, the teacher can facilitate a conversation in which new information is provided but is linked to them personally. This type of activity sends the message to the students that their backgrounds are valued and connected to the subject matter. If the teacher links the content to her own experiences as well, the beginnings of a community have been established.

This culture of shared experiences also implies that everyone is responsible for learning. Within this framework, the teacher needs to decide what might be negotiable in the course. Perhaps the students are given the task of constructing at least one of the assessments for the class; they can decide if it will be a traditional test or some other measure. If it is a test, they are then responsible for preparing the questions and possibly evaluating them. With alternative measures such as presentations or projects, perhaps the students and teacher both construct the criteria for evaluation. Self-assessment can be another component, and students could be responsible for creating portfolios of their best work and suggesting a grade based on the development they document. These strategies not only release the responsibility for learning to the students but they create an enthusiasm that comes from involvement, and they allow the teacher to have a broader overview of the learning that is going on.

Within this type of learning community, options need to be provided that allow for different learning styles and approaches. For instance, students can be given a topic to investigate and asked for input on how to complete the task. They can choose to work alone or form small groups. They can decide to write a paper or make an oral presentation. With the small group, perhaps it decides to role play the results of its investigation or produce a videotape. Students will need assistance in this kind of decision making, as it is most likely new for them, and the teacher will also have parameters. But what is important is that choices are possible and the students have a voice in making them.

Regular feedback from students is important in any learning environment, but in this classroom learning community, not only is it solicited but it is shared with them directly and built into the instruction. For instance if students are asked to summarize a session or write any confusions they may have, it needs to be clear that the information gathered will affect subsequent sessions. Too often, feedback is gathered but never used. Students don't take it seriously, and consequently they don't put much thought into it. Here, the feedback could be used to begin the next class session. The teacher could either directly answer questions that were posed or construct problems around them and have the students work out the confusions themselves in class.

Reflections

The following questions can provide a starting point for further reflection on practice.

How can students' levels of thinking best be assessed?

What support can a teacher provide to help students meet the challenges in a classroom?

How can a teacher demonstrate to students an understanding of the value of their various strengths?

How does a teacher acknowledge different perspectives and encourage students to broaden and deepen their understandings?

How can a true collaboration be facilitated in which activities and assessments are negotiated with students?

How can students and teachers engage in a mutual dialogue in which both are learners?

Chapter Nine

Learning Styles and Preferences

The concept of learning styles and preferences is closely related to ways of knowing. In Chapter Three, we explored ways of knowing through four areas: cultural, physiological, personality-based, and instructional preferences. We stressed the importance of understanding these factors as they overlap and influence one another rather than as discrete components of the learning process.

We considered the cultural factors first and asserted that they provide the overall context for thinking about learning styles. We used Brookfield's (1990) concept of cultural suicide to demonstrate the significant consequences to students when moving from their community culture to that of the university. We considered systems of communication for their effect on classroom behavior. Bruffee's (1993) ideas about collaboration provided a focus on how family relationships can influence a student's behavior in groups. The work of Pai and Adler (1997) extended this to teacher expectations regarding student engagement and instructional delivery and how often they may conflict with students' experiences at home. We noted that Fordham and Ogbu (1986) and Branch-Simpson (1984) specifically examined the culture of African American students and how it may affect their expectations as well as performance in school. Their suggestion that African Americans frequently refer to the importance of personal connections at school was also discussed in the work of Baxter Magolda (1992).

The section on culture concluded by taking a look at the model proposed by Wlodkowski and Ginsberg (1995) that addressed culturally responsive teaching. They conclude that when teaching is sensitive to various backgrounds, everyone is able to maintain their integrity and student motivation increases.

Following the discussion of cultural factors, we briefly reviewed theory related to the physiological aspect of learning styles through the work of Kitchens, Barber, and Barber (1991) on left-brain–right-brain differences. We noted personality-based styles, described by Bonham and Boylan (1993) as the most stable of learning styles and those that influence a student's approach to learning. Related to this was Witkin's (1949) concept of field dependence and field independence that accounts for learners' various needs for working alone or with others. This section on personality-based styles concluded by looking at the Myers-Briggs Type Inventory (Myers and Briggs, 1985), which can help determine how learners prefer to take in information and make decisions.

The final area reviewed was that of instructional preferences—an area most open to change. It is less deeply embedded in the learner than the cultural, physiological, and personality-based factors because it is more frequently dependent on circumstances in the immediate learning environment. We described Canfield's inventory (1988) as a framework for examining this component through four lenses: conditions for learning, content preference, mode preference, and expectation for grade.

It became evident as we reviewed the theories related to learning styles and preferences that there is a lack of agreement regarding not only terminology but how the various components intersect. Much is written about learning styles; the topic is a popular one and is discussed from multiple perspectives. It is also organized in a variety of frameworks that are different from the structure chosen here. After reviewing much of the literature, however, we decided that three of the four components introduced in Chapter Three provide a practical window for study: the cultural, physiological, and personality-based areas. As this chapter connects theory to current research, it will be creating a unique framework for reflecting on learning styles and preferences.

The Cultural Framework

As we suggested earlier, culture provides the filter through which much meaning is constructed. If the individual's home community is built around a culture that differs significantly from that of the school, it will clearly be more difficult for that individual to adjust. Pai and Adler (1997) describe this as "two divergent social structures with fundamentally different sets of rules" (p. 212). They also stress that the "degree of discontinuity" affects how successful the learning experience will be.

Researchers differ in the labels they apply to learners who come to a formal educational setting with a different cultural framework than that of the school. Some have described them as bicultural (Goldberger, 1996; LaFromboise, Coleman, and Gerton, 1993); others describe them as shared function groups (Pai and Adler, 1997). Whatever the label, the learners are faced with new expectations that Wlodkowski and Ginsberg (1995) describe as "alienating, exhausting (the relentless anxiety of determining how to behave appropriately) and unfair" (p. 146). Different groups of learners tend to respond to the new expectations with a variety of styles.

Fordham (1988) studied African American adolescents as they responded to the educational environment in a high school that was 99 percent black students. She discovered through her case study analysis that those who were most successful academically adopted an identity of "racelessness." In other words, they rejected the values of their home communities in order to meet the standards of the school culture. They tried to become inconspicuous to their peers while appearing raceless to their teachers. This caused great stress and anxiety although it did lead to high achievement. In one case, Fordham describes an academically successful student who was asked by her teachers to compete for an academic team by taking a test. The black student agreed to do it only if the test results would not be publicized. As it turned out, she received the highest score but, per the agreement, was not chosen as a team member, as that would have made her too visible to her peers. Fordham concludes that the student's strategy validated her capabilities to her teachers while keeping her invisible as a high-achiever to her peers. In all the cases that Fordham studied, racelessness was used as a strategy by students who assimilated into the school culture and internalized its values. It was not done, however, without a great deal of ambivalence and a high level of stress.

Other approaches to learning are used by individuals from the same ethnic background. Instead of internalizing the values of the school, some students create their own environment within the school setting to better reflect that of their home community. For some African American students, school is viewed as an institution that rejects their culture and, as they attempt to hold on to that culture exclusively, they are often regarded as having an "attitude" by teachers. These students are frequently less successful academically than those who adopt the raceless strategy.

Another response to the educational expectations of the dominant culture appears in the research of Thomas and Chess (1989), who describe the behavior of some Hispanic students when taking standardized intelligence tests. In their study, the students approached the test in a very relaxed manner and saw it as a game rather than a serious challenge. The researchers suggest that this could be due to child-rearing practices in which Hispanic mothers often encourage children to explore words and experiences playfully rather than in a "precisely intellectual" way that is more characteristic of the middle-class white culture as well as that of the American schools.

According to the work of LaFromboise and others (1993), several models are useful to the understanding of learners making the transition between cultures. One of them, assimilation, was demonstrated in an extreme way through a case study of high-achieving black adolescents who gave up the values of their own community in order to succeed academically. This approach can be risky; the learner may be rejected by both the culture of origin and the dominant culture and suffer stress in the process. LaFromboise suggests an alternative model—bicultural competence—in which learners understand both cultures and are able to adjust their behavior depending on the situation.

Schiller's research (1987) examines the impact of bicultural competence on Native American college students. He found that students operating within a bicultural framework were better adjusted academically and culturally than those who were nonbicultural. They had higher GPAs and more effective study habits. In addition, they perceived their Indian heritage to be more advantageous than their nonbicultural peers did. This last factor is important with bicultural competence; the learner holds positive attitudes toward both cultural groups. Golden (1987), studying Korean American high school students, also found that those operating within a bicultural context had higher educational outcomes as well as better self-concepts.

When discussing the bicultural approach to learning, the issue of language is significant; in fact, LaFromboise suggests that it may be the most important factor. In a study done with Chinese Canadians, Young and Gardner (1990) discovered just how closely ethnic identity is tied to second-language acquisition. Those who had a greater fear of losing their cultural identity also had a more negative attitude toward the study of language and achieved at lower levels in their second-language acquisition. The individuals with a more positive attitude toward both cultures were more interested in improving their second-language skills.

Another significant factor related to bicultural competence is that of "groundedness." LaFromboise suggests that those who maintain sound social networks in both cultures will be better adapted than those who feel the need to reject one culture, as the raceless black adolescents do, for example. This is supported by the research of Baker (1987), who found that African Americans able to use the resources of their extended families, in addition to those of the dominant culture, experienced fewer problems.

Jadwiga provides a good example of a student operating within the framework of bicultural competence. She is eager to participate in the dominant culture and for that reason has worked hard to improve her English. At the same time, most of her new friends are Polish, which allows her to maintain and perpetuate a network grounded in the Polish community. Although they have all chosen to move away from home, they still value the culture of their families and return regularly to stay connected.

Although becoming competent in two cultures may lead to high achievement, as LaFromboise suggests, individuals who belong to bicultural groups experience much confusion and conflict. Goldberger (1996) interviewed sixty such individuals and describes their "double consciousness" as they reconciled the ways of their home culture and those of the more dominant one. Her work makes it clear that culture is more than a "series of facts, physical elements or exotic characteristics" (Wlodkowski and Ginsberg, 1995); rather, it includes a complex set of behaviors related to community values. For instance, Goldberger (1996) discovered when interviewing Native American women that silence is modeled throughout their lives through tribal meetings. It is considered a waste of time to talk when it isn't necessary, and learning when *not* to talk is a basic cultural value. The whole notion of silence is so "wrapped up in identity and racism" that one interviewee who was considered a big talker within her native community was labeled "quiet" in the external community. A teacher in the U.S. system of education is apt to consider such a nonverbal individual as non-analytical as well; U.S. schools expect their learners to articulate ideas and take issue when they disagree. To many Native Americans, this goes against every cultural norm with which they are familiar. One of Goldberger's interviewees stated, "I listen to anyone who is talking to me and I respect someone who is talking to me whether I like what I am hearing or not. If a person is an expert, I have to agree with them" (p. 349).

LaCounte (1987) found that Native Americans frequently are afraid of losing their unique cultural foundation and consequently may resist assimilating into American culture. Within an educational setting, this often leads to a mistrust of the faculty and the institution, as they both represent the dominant culture.

Within cultural groups there is a wide range of learning styles, but there are also statistically significant clusters of styles (Dunn, 1993). When they are treated as "deficits" and not integrated into the culture of the classroom, they can contribute to higher dropout rates from kindergarten through college (Wlodkowski and Ginsberg, 1995). However, when these different learning styles are addressed in the learning environment, scores on standardized achievement and attitude tests improve. In a study conducted with elementary school students in a low-socioeconomic district, California Achievement Test scores rose from the 30th percentile to the 89th percentile by introducing instruction related to the students' learning styles (Dunn, 1993). Wlodkowski and Ginsberg refer to this teaching approach as a culturally responsive one and suggest that it include linking students' experiences to the content matter, providing a holistic perspective, establishing social contexts for learning experiences, and appreciating humor and emotion as it occurs in the learning process. This supports the earlier notion that teaching begins where the student is and facilitates growth from that point.

Dean (1989) discusses the need to help students mediate between cultures. In his own classrooms, he has observed that 85 percent of the freshmen don't believe they must give up their own culture and home values to succeed at the university. By the time they are juniors and seniors, however, they feel they have lost more than they have gained in terms of their "lost" cultures. He feels this may affect dropout rates, as students leave in order to "protect their cultural identity." He describes writing strategies that help to bridge the transition between cultures for students. In peer response groups, for example, the home and university cultures can be linked. By giving students culturally sensitive issues to write about and then share in small peer groups, they develop support groups and an increased sense of confidence. Through the Puente Project (Jaffe, 1997) in the California community colleges, strategies like this turned a 50 to 60 percent dropout rate into a 70 to 80 percent rate of retention. This project involved Chicano and Latino students who had graduated from high school with D averages and with little self-confidence in writing.

By providing writing topics that students can relate to through their prior experience and well-established schemata, the instructor contextualizes the learning environment so that it is
not only relevant for the students but is one in which they can feel more comfortable and expert. When learning has no relevant framework, students become frustrated and often leave.

One example of an adult education class in which the instructor did not provide such a context shows how much the learners need this relevancy in order to make sense of the material. Hvitfeldt (1986) observed a class with a Hmong student population; the teacher continuously decontextualized instruction by talking abstractly and making no personal connections for the class. The students, however, regularly interrupted to talk in small groups in order to provide personal contexts for the content. They gave names to abstract examples the teacher had introduced and discussed situations in terms that related to their own experiences.

Tharp (1989) describes research done with children of different cultures that contributes to an understanding of how to alter more traditional classrooms. He first looked at social organization and describes the typical North American classroom as one that is designed around a group of students led by the teacher. When this clashes with the learners' cultures, teachers often interpret student behavior incorrectly. For instance, in his work with Hawaiian schools,

Tharp found this structure to be contradictory to the children's home culture. They had been raised in an environment in which collaboration and assisted performance were more common than solitary work. When they exhibited a low attention span and "inappropriate" behavior in school, it was most likely not due to a low level of motivation but rather to the imposition of an "alien social organization" (p. 350).

In order to integrate these values of the Hawaiian culture into the classroom, a curriculum was introduced at the elementary school that included more emphasis on working in independent groups, with a great deal of peer teaching and learning. The teacher took a back seat and facilitated the overall experience. Along the same lines, when a similar curriculum was introduced to a Navajo classroom, it was adjusted again to accommodate a different value system. Navajo students are more accustomed to working independently with little feedback; their home culture values individualism and self-sufficiency more than a collaborative group effort, so more individual projects were embedded in the curriculum. Both examples show how skills that students bring with them can be activated in order to encourage their further growth and development.

In the area of sociolinguistics, Tharp describes differences that can also be accommodated once they are understood. One example that all teachers experience is that of appropriate "wait time," that is, the amount of time that teachers wait for an answer after asking a question or wait to respond after hearing a student talk. The length of wait time is culturally dependent. A study of the different wait times between Anglo and Navajo teachers showed that the Navajos waited longer to respond than did the Anglos (White and Tharp, 1988). When the Anglo teachers thought the student was finished, they often interrupted a thought by responding too soon. The researchers also found that Pueblo children in science classes participated twice as frequently when the teacher increased the wait time. In contrast to the Native American populations that were studied, Tharp found that Native Hawaiians actually prefer a negative wait time, that is, overlapping speech as students all talk at once. In some groups this could be interpreted as rude behavior, but in Hawaiian culture it demonstrates involvement and strong relationships.

Learners who have experienced participation structures that are different from those within traditional classrooms are frequently considered nonverbal. In one example, Tharp describes Hawaiian students who often did not respond when the teacher directly asked for an answer. In order to explore this apparent nonpartici- pation further, a study was conducted in which the students were required to co-narrate stories with their peers, with the teacher's role becoming nondirective. This format resembled a structure from their home culture called talk-story, in which adults partici- pate regularly in similar activities. The students became highly en- gaged verbally, and it led to "higher rates of academic productive behavior" (p. 352).

This finding is supported by the work of McCarty and others (1991), who note that observed passivity in students of different cul- tures is more the result of teaching style than of the students them- selves. In their work with Navajos, they found that students responded eagerly when the discussions were shared among peers and a social environment was constructed in which everyone was encouraged to use their own experiences. It was significant with the inquiry cur- riculum they developed that teachers build on the prior socializa- tion experiences of the students and the learning styles they brought to school with them.

It is evident that teachers can adapt learning environments to incorporate the cultural differences shared by their students. By getting to know the backgrounds of the students and understand- ing their behaviors within the greater context of their home cul- tures, teachers can contribute to increased retention rates and academic success rates. Although it is important to understand that different cultures have varying frameworks for levels of participa- tion, social organization, personal relationships, and linguistic rules, it is also important that students be treated as individuals. Within all cultures there are, of course, individual differences re- lated to physiological and personality-based styles of learning.

Physiological and Personality-Based Styles of Learning

The physiological component of learning styles we discuss in this section comes from research related to "hemispheric dominance" (Zenhauseon, 1978).

The Physiological Lens

This research examines distinctions between left-brain and right-brain processing and how the differences relate to learning styles. Most important, the research addresses how to best structure environments to ensure attention to varied approaches to learning.

We used two metaphors earlier to describe the differences in left- and right-brain processing: computers and kaleidoscopes. Individuals who seem to be left-brain-dominated tend to process information in a linear, analytic manner, similar to a computer, whereas those who seem more right-brain-dominated process in a more holistic, visual manner, similar to a kaleidoscope. Dunn and others (1990) add to the understanding of these approaches by listing descriptors for the two hemispheres. They describe left-brain tendencies as analytic, successive, and inductive and right-brain approaches as global, simultaneous, and deductive. They contend that both sides of the brain are involved with reasoning but they reason differently. Others concur by viewing processing along a continuum rather than a dichotomy and describing the two sides of the brain as interdependent sources of capacity (Creswell, Gifford, and Huffman, 1988).

The work of Creswell and others in the area of mathematics education provides examples for Dunn's descriptors. These researchers suggest three ways the two sides differ: (1) each is more sensitive to different stimuli, (2) each processes the same stimuli differently, and (3) "typical" responses differ. Examples from the field of mathematics help clarify these distinctions. First, students who process from a left-brain approach in geometry will understand a theorem after studying definitions and proofs from related theorems, whereas the right-brain student will understand more readily by studying related geometric pictures. Second, when asked to solve a problem, the left-brain learner will most likely outline each step carefully to come up with a solution; the right-brain learner will probably read the problem several times, look at notes, appear to be idle while mulling over the possibilities, and then reach a solution. Third, the left-brain learners will tend to explain how they reached a solution, whereas the right-brain learners will probably draw a picture to show their processing.

Most research has concluded that American schools favor a left-brain approach to teaching and learning. Browne (1986) connects this to the general values of the Euro-American majority culture and claims that minority cultures are frequently disadvantaged in the American system when their preference is different. She believes that cultures encourage the development of one hemisphere over the other and cites Native American students whose culture is based more on a right-brain framework. This fits with the earlier section on culture where we described a significant means of communication in Native American communities as one of story telling and of holistic perspectives.

It seems clear that Linda's primary approach to learning is a left-brain one. She has always been more comfortable with following a sequence of steps in order to process information. She likes the structure of analyzing components piece by piece in order to understand the whole. Because this approach can be reinforced through objective testing and the ability to answer straightforward questions in class, her previous school performance was fairly successful.

Basing their work on the assessment of over five thousand teachers, Dunn and Dunn (1988) conclude that 65 percent are analytic, whereas at least 50 percent of the students at the secondary level approach learning from a global perspective. This can lead to an ineffective fit between teachers and some students and a definite lack of communication in the learning environment. The work of Croker, Bobell, and Wilson (1993) exemplifies this. They surveyed adult female prison inmates, of whom more than 50 percent were considered to have right-brain preferences regarding their preferred learning activities. These women rank ordered the learning activities they considered to be most effective: on-the-job training, field trips, demonstrations, experiments, and role playing. (These seem compatible with our earlier description of right-brain preferences.) They also rank ordered the instructional delivery methods they had most often experienced in formal learning situations: textbook assignments, readings, chalkboard exercises, worksheets, and handouts. It is easy to see how this disparity between preference and actual experiences could lead to a lack of communication and success in school.

Indeed, Hodges (1994) contends that 88 percent of all school dropouts exhibit strong tactile abilities, and 99 percent have strong kinesthetic tendencies. This dropout rate could be related to the lack of attention given to right-brain approaches to learning in the school systems. In related research, Marshall and Johns (1992) found that the following groups of students often have more well-developed right-brain and tactile-kinesthetic tendencies: at-risk students, poor achievers, dropouts, alternative school students, and incarcerated learning-disabled adults.

Browne (1986) details two areas in which hemispheric preferences directly influence school behavior: language style and interpersonal interaction. In the area of language style, left-brain learners tend to be more successful with abstractions and vocabulary development, as they use words to give meaning to abstract concepts. Those who tend to use their right brain are more apt to construct meaning through visuals and by relating concepts to a personal context. Meanings for these learners are stored in memory with no verbal labels, so there is often a delay in answering when they are asked to respond quickly as they are first translating the stored picture into words. While completing this process, it may seem to the instructor that they are talking around the answer when they are actually processing the question in an unanticipated way.

In the second area—interpersonal interaction—students with a left-brain disposition more often relate to a teacher impersonally, work more independently, and seem very task-oriented as they strive for personal recognition. Those with a right-brain preference seek out a more personal relationship with the teacher and prefer to avoid competition. Overall, the social environment in the learning setting is more important to these learners.

Looking back at some of Mike's approaches to learning, it seems that they are probably more right-brain-dominated. Much of his success at the auto body shop is due to his ability to visualize a problem and then fix it. In school he found it difficult to understand a concept without first envisioning the whole; he often became impatient at having to list the steps necessary to arrive at solutions for math problems. It was much more interesting for him to simply illustrate the solution. Although this approach is very effective on the job in his case, it often led to failure in school when he had to translate his mental images into words both orally during class and on written tests.

Much of the work on hemispheric dominance examines the relationship between teaching style and students' preferences for approaching the task of learning. Dunn and others (1990) found a significant positive relationship between hemispheric preference and achievement when teaching was tailored to complement the students' styles. Working with seven hundred developmental math students in a technical college, they discovered that when instruction was delivered in a global format (including visuals and personalized associations) to simultaneous (right-brain-dominant) learners, their test scores following instruction improved significantly. When analytic (left-brain-dominant) learners experienced instruction delivered in a successive or sequential format, their test scores also went up. This instruction was delivered in a step-by-step manner, with details leading up to general concepts. The researchers conclude that all instruction should be delivered using a combination of both formats in order to reach as many learners as possible.

Another study examined hemispheric dominance and final course grades across four business courses at the college level (Carthy, 1993). Carthy wanted to see if relationships existed that would be helpful to teachers as they advised students regarding study strategies. He found that students who were assessed with the McCarthy Hemispheric Mode Indicator as being left- or whole-brain-dominant received a significantly higher percentage of A grades than those diagnosed with a preference for right-brain activities who had the highest percentage of B through F grades. The tests in these courses were primarily objective problem-solving and multiple-choice questions, which fit the profile of left-brain preferences. Carthy recommends that business instructors assign more cases, practice sets, and problems to help students integrate concepts and get the big picture more easily.

Other researchers have suggested general instructional strategies to meet the needs of right-brain learners. They have concentrated on this population because so much formal schooling already engages the left-brain learner. Browne (1986) recommends that specific skills not be presented in isolation but rather as part of a "continuous flow of experiences" (p. 17). Pieces of information leading up to abstract concepts need to be presented together so that the right-brain students can see connections and get the whole picture. She also suggests personalizing the learning environment, having the students relate personal experiences to content *before* assigning any readings, and using as many visuals as possible (for example, charts, time lines, or graphs).

Creswell and others (1988) discuss how frustrating it is to right-brain mathematics students when they are required to master small pieces of the whole without being shown how the pieces fit into the overall concept. They contend that these students need time to synthesize without being interrupted and asked to write out steps in the process. Often the students can already see the end result due to "insights (that) enable them to make intuitive leaps that may lead to accusations of cheating" (p. 122). Creswell and his colleagues suggest facilitating more emotional closeness in the classroom and providing alternatives for students to demonstrate proficiency: physical or verbal demonstrations, drawing graphs or charts, or writing paragraphs. They also recommend, even at the high school level and beyond, using manipulatives and demonstrating principles through physical representations such as cutting out squares of paper. These researchers contend that if the curriculum were supplemented with such right-brain activities, all learners would develop a more integrated approach to learning.

Christensen (1991) suggests a method of instruction that would "accommodate all types of learners while inherently encourage(ing) stretching of less preferred styles" (p. 22). This method is the 4MAT system developed by McCarthy (1980), and it is based on her research involving both brain hemisphericity and the ways learners perceive and then process information. Because ways of perceiving and processing are often considered to be related to personality factors, this work provides a good transition between physiological factors and the next section that examines personality-based factors.

Using the 4MAT system, McCarthy began by describing learners through Kolb's learning style dimensions. This resulted in four types—those who (1) perceive concretely and process reflectively, (2) perceive abstractly and process reflectively, (3) perceive abstractly and process directly, and (4) perceive concretely and process actively. To gain a more complete understanding of the learner, she then overlaid research from right- and left-brained functioning onto these typologies. In the resulting 4MAT model for instruction, McCarthy suggests that the general characteristics of these four types of learners represent a sequential process that can be applied in all learning situations.

The following example shows both ends of the process. The first type of learners—those who perceive concretely and process reflectively—often need answers to "why" questions. Their right hemisphere leads them to look for personal experiences in order to construct meaning while their left hemisphere has them analyzing these experiences. They are interested most in how new information will affect them and their belief systems. For McCarthy, instruction needs to begin here and continue by incorporating characteristics from all four modes until it reaches the final stage which includes the predominant style of the fourth type of learners—those who perceive concretely and process actively. These individuals are looking for relationships between learning and its application to the real world. Their right hemisphere leads them to find applications, and the left hemisphere is directing them to analyze the learning for its significance. Ultimately, these learners are synthesizing information in order to create new meanings. In McCarthy's model, this represents the highest end of the learning process and one that all instruction needs to include.

Studies have shown the positive effects on learners when instruction incorporates all four quadrants or modes. Learners have shown more positive attitudes toward a subject area and achieved higher scores on critical thinking and objective tests following such a delivery format (Wilkerson, 1992). When faculty have incorporated it into their teaching, their attitudes are generally positive, but they run into the "usual" problems of designing right-brain activities to fit into the quadrants (Scott, 1993).

Because learners generally process information in a variety of styles, it is important not to look at individual styles too rigidly. The more difficult the task, however, the more apt learners are to choose a style that works best for them (Williams, 1997). The significance here is the importance of integrating different approaches, as McCarthy suggests, to ensure that teaching reaches out to all styles of learning and doesn't favor one simply because it is the most familiar or reflects the teacher's own style.

Personality-Based Lens

Moving into personality-based factors, it is important to point out again that these styles are not ways of learning; rather, they are preferences that influence a person's approach to learning. Using these descriptors to discuss individuals should not lead to the creation of rigid labels but to seeing patterns of preferences located along a continuum—patterns that can be used to expand ranges of teaching strategies. In fact, one useful approach to reading this section would be for readers to apply the concepts to their own learning preferences and then examine them to see how much they influence their own instructional strategies.

Several theorists have proposed models to describe learning styles. McCarthy used Kolb's (1984) work as a framework for research of left-brain–right-brain hemisphericity. In Chapter Three, we discussed how the results of the Myers-Briggs Inventory can be applied to the better understanding of Jadwiga. A great deal of research relating to adult learners has been conducted based on Witkin's (1950) concept of field dependence–field independence. The research seems particularly significant to the area of postsecondary education and thus forms the framework for most of this section. We discuss some of the more interesting findings, as they relate to field dependent–independent learners within two broad categories: learning strategies and instructional delivery.

As we noted in Chapter Three, the concept of field dependence–field independence is based on the work of Witkin (1949, 1950), who developed a test of visual perception—the Grounded Embedded Figures Test (GEFT)—to see how well learners could distinguish figures from the background in which they were represented. From this initial framework, the theory has been applied to describe learners on a continuum that ranges from high (field independent) to low (field dependent). Field-independent learners generally are more apt to separate the figure from the background as they analyze its attributes, whereas field-dependent learners are less likely to be able to separate the figure from its background. This very generalized description, along with the universal use of the GEFT to determine learner approach, forms the foundation for much of the research described here.

Several studies have looked at education majors and preprofessional teachers in terms of their fit along Witkin's continuum. One result that has been affirmed across several studies is that these students tend to change over their course of study. Simpson, Portis, Snyder, and Mills (1995) found, from a study of over two hundred education majors, that these students became more field independent by the end of their internships. They also discovered more males to be field independent. In a related study, Portis and others (1993) discovered similar results: those education students who were field dependent in their first course had become more field independent by the end of their internships. They also found a significant difference between females and males at the beginning, with males being more field independent, but there were no significant gender differences by the end of their course of study. Most of the studies reported here emphasize the value of field-independent over field-dependent learning. As we examine the results, it is important to remember that both approaches have value; however, field-independent preferences are typically more likely to be rewarded in formal educational settings.

Wieseman, Portis, and Simpson (1992) looked more specifically at course grades for education majors and found a correlation between FDI (field dependence-independence) and course grades. Students who were more field dependent had lower grades than field-independent students: those with high scores on the GEFT earned more A grades and those with the lowest GEFT scores earned more D grades.

In the study conducted by Portis, Simpson, and Wieseman (1993) the researchers outlined sets of characteristics related to both field-dependent and field-independent learners. By looking at these descriptors, it becomes clear how Witkin's original concept is being applied today. Field-dependent learners, according to Portis and others, tend to depend on the following components in a learning environment: social interaction, external structure, and teacher direction and feedback. They also are most affected by criticism and tend to benefit from instruction in problem-solving strategies. These learners, who are least likely to separate a figure from its background, appear to have difficulty providing structure to a learning task. They need external direction (from a teacher) to help them see the significant aspects of a problem. Because it is difficult for them to separate the significant from the insignificant details of a task, they are more apt to examine something uncritically and simply accept it as it is presented to them.

Field-independent learners, however, tend to exhibit the following approaches to learning: orientation to task, self-regulation of goals, organization and analysis independent of the teacher, less need for guidance in problem solving, and ease in working individually; they are also less affected by criticism than the field-dependent learners. Once again returning to Witkin's original test, the distinctions seem clear. Field-independent students are able to separate the figure from its background. They are able to distinguish significant from insignificant details and, in doing so, provide more structure to a problem. Consequently, they rely less on external sources (teachers) for direction and support.

A look at two of the case studies from Chapter One underscores the importance of considering these approaches along a continuum rather than as dichotomous and discrete. Charles, for example, is extremely task-oriented and inclined to monitor his own progress and assess whether or not he is succeeding. He has no trouble working alone; in fact, he prefers it when it comes to completing a project. He is very dependent, however, on initially processing information through interaction with his peers. Charles was always one of the most verbal students in high school because debating and articulating his thoughts was a crucial first step for him before engaging in the subsequent quiet, independent synthesis of ideas.

Linda does not seem to need the social interaction often associated with field-dependent approaches, but she is very dependent on external structures for directions and also for teacher feedback. She is not able to effectively monitor her own progress during the intervals between graded tests and papers. She depends on grades to evaluate her performance. These needs, along with her independent, very task-oriented approaches place her, along with Charles, somewhere in the middle of the continuum between field dependency and field independency.

Fritz (1992) looked at these differences in terms of gender and students' conscious tendencies to act a certain way. In his research with secondary marketing education students, he administered the Educational Style Preference Inventory and found twelve differences between approaches favored by males and females. In general, the males had a more analytical approach to learning, whereas the females preferred social interaction and wanted the input of their peers to help organize experiences and make decisions. Related to their sensitivity to the learning environment, the female students also relied more on cultural codes, for example, positive communication and punctuality than their male counterparts. The females also scored higher on abstractions that involved a dependence on external referents such as reading and hearing words and reading numbers.

Fritz analyzed these preferences in terms of field independence and field dependence; he related the former to an internal frame of reference and the latter to an external frame. This seems to fit with the earlier studies that showed a significant difference between the two styles in how much individuals relied on external sources for direction and structure. In this analysis, field independence represents a more active discovery type of strategy that includes an active reasoning pattern and the skill of cognitive structuring. The field-dependent student is characterized as more passive in approach, tending to "take it as it is" and using a chain link reasoning process, which is also more people-oriented.

As Fritz examined the females' high scores on abstractions, he concluded that this may represent a reliance on external information sources, which could then suggest that they paid more attention to the environment itself to create meaning; the males' scores could suggest that they operated more independently from presented facts and details. In addition, Fritz found that females in the study preferred to work with information that was organized in the form of rules and in a comparison-contrast style, and that was presented with many examples. He was careful to state that these differences did not represent abilities to perform tasks; rather, they were simply distinctive ways in which individuals approached learning.

These approaches are most apt to be significant to the learner who is confronted with a new task. In such a situation, the field-independent learner probably constructs meaning independently, whereas the more field-dependent individual looks for support in the environment. Based on these tendencies, Fritz recommends that when presenting new learning tasks, teachers should make a conscious effort to provide structure. Students who tend toward more field independence will not suffer from the structure (they may simply ignore it), but those who are more field dependent will seek it and rely on it for successful processing.

Farr and Moon (1988) looked at student performance in various subjects, including math and reading, and related it to distinctive tendencies for structuring information. They discuss "mathematically capable students" and experts and suggest that both groups have more highly organized the knowledge stored in their memories than have those who are less capable or who are novices as problem solvers. In math, they argue, it is also important for the learner to select information that is relevant to solving a problem and to ignore what is extraneous. This clearly relates to the ability to bring an appropriate structure to a task.

They analyzed reading skills in a similar manner and assert that "it seems plausible that field-independent persons are better readers because of their ability to access material in their long term memory that is more highly structured" (p. 27). They then applied this to identifying vocabulary in context and drawing inferences, both of which assume that the successful reader is able to separate significant data from that which is not, another example of structuring information. This background provided a framework for their study of adult achievement; they show that FDI correlates significantly with traditional indicators of academic success such as the Graduate Record Examination and the test of Adult Basic Education.

Additional studies related to the skill of structuring have shown that this is an area of significant differences. Frank and Keene (1993) asked undergraduates in a psychology class to recall lists of words that had more or less inherent organization and to report the strategy they used as a memory device. The results show that field-independent students recall more words than those considered field dependent and that they also use strategies more related to the active organization of word categories. Field-dependent students reported using a rehearsal strategy (memorization), whereas those considered field independent more frequently used a categorization strategy. The researchers describe the categorization strategy use as more "cognitively mature" and assert that it is less passive than the rehearsal strategy, as it requires a restructuring of the words.

In this same study, when the groups were provided with strategy instruction explaining how to use categorization, all students were able to recall more words. The researchers conclude that training did make a difference in this situation and that it should be provided to encourage students who may have field-dependent tendencies to use more active processing strategies They also recommend that cooperative learning groups composed of learners with differing approaches would be helpful, as field-dependent learners would be exposed to more field-independent approaches to processing information. Rush and Moore (1991) also looked at the effects of training students to use new strategies. They suggest that it may be more beneficial to provide instruction and practice in how to restructure information for field-dependent students than simply to provide the structure itself. This training would then be "reusable or adaptable" (p. 310) across coursework.

Thinking back to Linda's unsuccessful attempts to memorize the increasing mounds of information in her lecture classes lends support to the idea of teachers providing direct instruction on how to organize their content. Her history teacher, for instance, could model the structure of selecting significant events and constructing a time line. Perhaps small groups could collaborate on these and from there begin to look for trends within certain time periods. The trends could then be analyzed in terms of cause-effect or comparison-contrast. These activities would provide Linda with a more effective system for processing information beyond the literal level of memorization, and she might begin to look for appropriate organizational patterns in her other coursework.

Kardash, Lukowski, and Bentmann (1988) describe different approaches to taking lecture notes. In their research, they used a self-report survey following a videotaped lecture. They found that while both types of learners use similar strategies, field-independent students use certain ones more often, including underlining important points in their notes, mentally reorganizing and rewriting information so that it makes sense to them, looking away from their notes and asking themselves questions, and rereading portions of their notes that didn't make sense. There is an emphasis here on interacting with the information until it is restructured to fit the needs of the learner.

Fehrenbach (1994) studied over three hundred students and their approaches to reading comprehension. In establishing her framework, she cited the work of Blohm and Colwell (1984) showing that field-independent high school students are more able to learn material that is not highly structured, whereas field-dependent students have a very difficult time with such material. Fehrenbach found a significant difference in reading strategies between the two types of learners: the field-independent learners summarize accurately, use rereading when confused, and analyze the structure or content. The field-dependent learners, by contrast, summarize but do it inaccurately. Her recommendations include providing structural organizers for students and instruction on how to summarize.

Another study related to reading strategies examined differences in textbook note-taking techniques (Lipsky, 1989). The researcher looked at a small sample of community college students in a reading and study skills course to assess their successful use of mapping and outlining when taking notes from textbooks. She found field-independent students more apt to use mapping successfully and field-dependent students more comfortable with outlining. She adds that most of the students in the study were field dependent and preferred outlining over mapping. Although this is a small study, it is interesting to note that outlining is a better fit with the field-dependent tendencies we have been discussing. It is a more linear approach and, depending on the structure of the text, is probably an easier one, as it may follow the author's organization sequentially through headings and subheadings; mapping requires a more individualized restructuring of material.

This leads to the research on teaching styles as they relate to this same concept. Field-dependent teachers, as described by Simpson, Portis, and Mills (1995), tend to use discussion and also to integrate democratic principles into their classrooms, whereas those who are more field independent tend to use lecture as their primary delivery format and are more direct in their instruction. The earlier research of Guild and Garger (1985) provides a foundation for these recent findings. They established that field-dependent learners who become teachers establish warm, personal learning environments and are less likely to provide negative feedback and evaluation to their students. Also, field-independent teachers are more subject-centered and emphasize the cognitive component of learning; they are also more likely to use an inquiry or problem-solving approach in their classrooms.

These few examples alert teachers to the significance of knowing their own preferred approaches to learning and how they probably influence their instructional preferences. For instance, if they have learned from a field-dependent perspective, they are more apt to establish an environment for students that includes cooperative learning activities, considerable feedback, a good deal of structure, and a personal relationship that may extend beyond the classroom door. However, if they have always approached learning from a more field-independent view, they may have very different expectations for their students, including more individual responsibility, less structure, and little personal interaction. In order to connect with a wider range of learners, natural tendencies may need to be broadened to include instructional styles that may be difficult for them. An example of this comes from research related to math teachers (Smith and Easterday, 1994). The researchers looked at math teachers and found that teachers in their sample were highly field independent and had a very difficult time modifying their existing methods to meet the needs of more divergent students. They tended to present principles holistically and less analytically, thus putting at a disadvantage those students who needed support in analyzing problems and seeing the steps leading up to the whole. The authors suggest that a better match between math teachers and students is needed.

Several studies have examined various expectations of students related to reading comprehension and how student performance may be linked to their differing approaches rather than to their ability to understand. Davey (1989) wanted to know whether field-dependent students are affected negatively by postreading tasks that involve reliance on memory and the need to restructure information. She found that when given comprehension questions for a series of passages, field-independent students outperform those who were identified as field dependent on tasks that included those criteria of memory and restructuring. When the task allowed students in the study to look back at the text, however, responses were comparable. This may be related to the field-dependent person's less developed tendency to structure material for storage in memory which makes it more difficult to access material without looking back at the original source.

Related to this is the work of Kardash, Lukowski, and Bentmann (1988), who found that by giving an immediate test to students following a lecture, then a delayed test one week later, the performance of field-dependent students increased. The researchers contend that the advantage of the immediate test for these students is to provide them with a structure that helps them focus their review for the delayed test. The field-independent students in the study were more successful on the immediate test, but there was no significant difference in performance on the test given one week later. This seems to lend support to the idea that students restructure information independently, whereas the field-dependent students require additional assistance in this area.

Meng and Patty (1991) looked at the effect of different types of reading organizers used with social studies content in a computer-assisted instructional setting. They developed written pre- and post-organizers as well as illustrative pre- and post-organizers and predicted that the field-dependent learners would prefer the most highly structured and concrete ones. The results support these predictions. The pre-organizers that were illustrated rather than simply narrated were most effective for the students who were field dependent. The type of organizer appeared to neither support nor hurt the performance of those who were more field independent.

The investigation of learning through computer use has been going on for some time. Hahn (1983–84) found that field-independent learners perform equally well with different instructional methods but that field-dependent learners may benefit from computer-assisted instruction. More recently, MacGregor, Shapiro, and Niemic (1988) looked at students in a developmental algebra class and found that achievement increased for the field-dependent students who were exposed to computer instruction. The researchers surmise that this may be related to the consistent, highly structured nature of this computer setting, with its linear, drill, and practice format. Students in the study received immediate feedback, and they may have felt they were in a personalized, safe environment.

Clearly, the type of computer delivery format has an impact on performance for different styles. In a study with community college business students, Lyons-Lawrence (1994) analyzed students' tendencies through a framework of visual perception. She looked at those who were field independent as more visually perceptive than the field-dependent students who, she theorized, would be less able to perceive visual images. In her research, the field-independent students scored significantly higher on a posttest in a computer-based office systems course, and she concludes that computers may not be the best learning tool for the more field-dependent students.

With more course work being offered through the technology of computers, it will be increasingly important to conduct research in this area. It seems as if the use of computers may be related to learning preferences but exactly how isn't clear. In these two studies, the instructional formats were obviously different. In the first, a drill and practice, personalized experience apparently worked well for field-dependent students. This structure also seems to work well for them within a more traditional setting. The authors describe a preference for a safe environment which should be further explored because field-dependent people tend to prefer a more social setting. There may be something in the individualized, immediate feedback structure of a programmed course that replaces that need. The second study focuses on the visual perception tendencies of both types of learners and raises an interesting feature of computers that may be significant here. How information is displayed to the learner may be a key factor in compatibility with learning style. Given the field-dependent students' general difficulty of separating images from their background, it may be that computer courses designed with a maximum amount of visual stimulation are too overwhelming for them. Rather than providing an appealing graphic display, the computer screen may contain stimuli that get in the way of processing the significant information.

Dwyer and Moore (1992) also looked at the relationship between visual perception and learning style and investigated the effect of color versus black and white on student achievement. They worked with college students and found that color coding instructional materials maximizes the ability of field-dependent students to acquire information for tests that are visually oriented. They discuss how field-dependent learners don't tend to modify information that is presented to them visually; rather, they accept it as it is presented. In other words, they are unable to see the various components independently, whereas, field-independent students analyze the information, select the appropriate cues, and restructure them to fit their needs. The authors assumed that by using colored materials rather than black and white, they would be providing more structure for the field-dependent students, which would lead to deeper information processing and higher achievement levels. The results demonstrate that color coding does assist these students.

Burwell (1991) investigated the interaction of learning styles with the amount of learner control in a computer tutorial. There were two treatment groups, each of which allowed for varying amounts of learner control during the instructional process. The researchers predicted that the field-independent students, who are generally considered to be more assertive in learning new concepts, would prefer the program that allowed more student options for control. What they found was that these students actually performed best in the program that was structured with no control options, and the field-dependent students preferred the more interactive program that allowed for more options. They took longer to complete the program. The authors suggest that this may have been due to their heightened sensitivity to all the cues that caused them to study the options longer than the field-independent students. They conclude that those who are considered field dependent will "thrive on personal control of learning when aided with appropriate instructional advice" (p. 42).

Once again, this study forces readers to break open the neat little boxes they may have constructed for particular learners and look at ways to create learning environments that provide support in order for students to broaden their natural tendencies. Based on what we have discussed so far, field-dependent learners may not have been expected to perform well on tasks in which they are put in control because the literature frequently describes them as passive and in need of direction. It seems, however, that with appropriate amounts of external structure and guidance, they can succeed in an environment that expects them to be more actively involved.

In this chapter we have looked at research. Now we make connections. By using the TRPP model, we link theory and research to principle and practice.

Using the TRPP Model

The research findings and the theoretical foundations have led us to construct the following principles.

Principles

1. Cultural transitions can be created for students by providing opportunities for them to link their personal experiences to the learning environment.

2. Learning will be most successful when there is a recognition of and respect for different cultural styles of communication in the learning environment.
3. Sensitivity to cultural differences is just as important as the recognition that all learners from particular cultures are individuals and do not necessarily share similar patterns of expectations or behavior.
4. Different approaches to learning and processing information do not imply different abilities to learn.
5. A range of instructional styles is necessary to facilitate learning for the wide range of student learning styles.
6. Approaches to learning can be modified through strategy instruction in order to increase the learners' repertoires and consequently their opportunities to succeed across a range of environments.

Applying Principles to Case Studies

Principle 1: Cultural transitions can be created for students by providing opportunities for them to link their personal experiences to the learning environment.

Creating a relevant environment is important for all students; they will be more motivated and feel more valued as learners if they are allowed to link what they already know to what they are expected to learn. Schema theory suggests that when students are able to access prior knowledge and apply it to what is new, the new material has a "hook" and makes more sense. This is particularly true when the learner is entering an environment that represents a culture distinctively different from home. It may not feel very safe because it is so different, and the learner may have difficulty understanding how to become actively involved and how to make sense of the expectations. In addition, the learner from a different culture may feel very alone, cut off from family and friends, and uncomfortable sharing feelings of confusion.

One way to create a bridge from the student's culture to that of the school and facilitate mutual understandings is to facilitate the integration of personal experiences to the new environment. In a writing class, for instance, if students are asked to write about something with which they are familiar, such as a traditional holiday or special celebration, they will be less intimidated by the assignment. Following the writing, if small groups are formed to allow the students to share ideas, their comfort level will begin to rise and their feelings of isolation will decrease. Small-group work may also provide a more immediately relevant reason to edit their own papers: to help others understand something they know well and wish to communicate.

This same approach to reading assignments will bring similar results. Before the reading, facilitating a sharing of student experiences related to the topic will increase involvement and consequently will provide students with a real purpose for reading: to discover similarities and differences with their own experiences. If the topic is political science, for instance, raising a question like, How is leadership determined in your native country? will elicit far more involvement than simply starting with a textbook explanation.

When Jadwiga began taking English classes, the instruction regularly included conversation and writing assignments that linked her experiences to the topic of discussion. This was, in fact, how she overcame her overwhelming reticence to talk in class. During the first class session, the students were all asked to talk about their arrival in the United States. This provided a topic that everyone could relate to, and it became a common reference point for the friendships that soon began outside of class. It also made the new environment seem safer because their experiences were being valued. It was then applied to new learning, as the students were asked to form groups and make a written list of their experiences. Once again, this provided them with a real purpose for writing; they wanted to preserve the stories they had shared.

Just as it is important to think of cultural transitions for nonnative speakers, they need to be considered also for students like Mike. For Mike, going to school includes a significant cultural transition. He is not used to sitting and listening to someone talk about something that he would rather be practicing in the real world. Mike is probably not alone in his anxiety and perception of the irrelevancy of the classroom. If the instructor regularly asked the students to talk about this and to share their experiences, both in school and in the world of work, they would become more involved. By allowing them to talk about past failures and how they feel the formal school setting has not met their needs, the instructor will gain insight into how to meet their needs better. Also, by starting each session with a student-led discussion that links the topic of the day with a personal experience, the instructors encourage students to feel more connected to the learning environment.

Principle 2: Learning will be most successful when there is a recognition of and respect for different cultural styles of communication.

Communication is clearly at the foundation of any successful learning experience. When the system and the instructor have expectations that differ significantly from the experiences the students bring with them, instructors need to carefully reflect on how to be effective. Those who have traditionally depended on collaborative activities as their primary delivery format must first recognize the experiences of their students. Rather than simply imposing this format on the group, they should first discuss their rationale and expectations. If they know some of the students may find this type of activity threatening or personally uncomfortable, this should be openly addressed as well. They can talk about how it fits into an overall plan for learning and how there are different roles for students to assume within it. For instance, they can assign roles within the groups that will ease the students' participation; a person who is afraid to express herself orally, for example, can be a recorder for the group until she becomes more comfortable. Over the course of the term, students can be encouraged to rotate and assume different roles.

Closely related to modes of communication is assessment. Is student participation evaluated solely on oral contribution to class discussion? This may be unfair to those whose backgrounds have taught them to listen carefully to everyone's ideas before coming to any conclusions. Creating ways for students to participate through other modes is important. For instance, students could be given a topic before a class discussion takes place and asked to write their reflections. These reflections could be read by the instructor to start off the discussion, or students could share them in small groups, which may be less intimidating to some. This would be helpful for Teresita, who is always afraid to speak up in class. She is an excellent student, but she was brought up to listen quietly to others and refrain from entering into a discussion unless she is absolutely sure she has something significant to add. It becomes even more difficult for her when the class has male students because at home the male members of her family frequently make the important decisions; she has learned not to disagree.

Charles comes from a different background. He has been taught to discuss issues from all perspectives before coming to any conclusions. Oral participation is no problem for him. In fact, he feels that those who do not speak up are not learning and to demonstrate that he often dominates a discussion. Being sensitive to backgrounds such as his, the instructor can lead the class into establishing ground rules at the very start. The group might establish rules that include the following guideline: no one will speak more than two times on the same topic without allowing someone new to participate. By having such a framework up front, students like Charles will understand his limits in a group and will not take it personally if they are reminded to step out of the discussion.

Principle 3: Sensitivity to cultural differences is just as important as the recognition that all learners from particular cultures are individuals and do not necessarily share similar patterns of expectations or behavior.

When Jadwiga returned to school to learn English, she quickly found that her instructors expected her to behave in a certain way. After all she was from the Polish community, and she should act like the majority of her classmates who were Polish. At first this provided a level of comfort to her; it gave her an immediate group with which to identify. After several terms of study, however, she began to resent that her individual needs were not being addressed. She was unable to have individual conferences with her instructors without feeling a total lack of communication based on their expectations of her as a Pole.

She needed to be treated like the individual she was, but when she looked for advice regarding the medical technology program she wished to pursue, advisers referred to her family and asked if they supported her goals. They often referred to the need in the Polish community for this type of professional and how proud she would feel going back into her community with her education.

Rather than advise her on appropriate academic assistance to help learn the new terminology, which she requested, they more frequently suggested that if she could learn Polish she could learn any language and this should not be difficult. She did, in fact, have a difficult time learning Polish as a child and often received additional help in elementary school in Poland, where her teachers even suggested she might have a specific learning disability. When she mentioned this to her adviser, she was simply told not to worry; once she had learned English well enough, everything would fall into place for her.

Principle 4: Different approaches to learning and processing information do not imply different abilities to learn.

Linda has always been a very analytical learner. She has succeeded especially well in math by applying a linear approach to examining problems one step at a time. She has always been able to identify the significant aspects of the problem on her own and enjoys figuring them out independently. In fact, in classrooms where she has been forced into collaborative groups, she becomes frustrated listening to others process the information differently. Because most of the math courses she took in high school emphasized her more individual, analytical approach, she earned high grades routinely.

Charles, however, has learned to avoid math because it causes him such high anxiety. He tends to approach problem solving from a more global view than Linda. He needs to understand the whole problem before he can engage in any step-by-step approach. His best experiences have always been those in which he was able to work with others and talk through possible solutions. Because this instructional approach was rare in his early math classes, he came to believe that he was less capable in this area and started avoiding it.

Clearly, these two students connect their successes and failures to their abilities to learn. Linda has become very comfortable with an instructional delivery mode that is frequently found in math classes; it fits with her preferred approach to learning. When she encounters a different style, for instance, a lecture class where topics are presented globally and students are expected to synthesize ideas, she feels less capable. Because her tendency is to work independently, she doesn't really know how to participate in a small, collaborative study group that might make a difference in this new situation. She avoids it, and her anxiety continues to rise as her self-confidence dwindles.

Charles has experienced success in learning situations when he could bounce ideas off others and listen to different perspectives. The discussions alone help him identify the salient features in a problem; he looks to others for that guidance and regular feedback. Without it, he feels incapable of working through any assignment. In his current environment, he finds himself alone and pressured for time. He cannot access the support that his peers could provide because no one has extra time. He is very close to dropping out of his evening classes, as he feels unable to meet his own expectations and those of his company.

Principle 5: A range of instructional styles is necessary to facilitate learning for the wide range of student learning styles.

Instructors don't necessarily need to teach to the style of their students. Indeed, that would be impossible and not necessarily beneficial, and students need to learn to adapt to different teaching styles. What teachers can do is broaden the concept of what good teaching includes. One way they can do that is to begin considering their own approaches to learning; then they could analyze the situations in which they learn best. Undoubtedly they will discover that their teaching style reflects their learning preferences. If they have always learned best by listening to a lecture and independently restructuring their notes to make sense, they probably expect their students to approach learning the same way. If, however, they are more like Charles and need the external support of peers, they probably structure their classes within a more social framework.

Once teachers recognize why they teach the way they do, perhaps talking to colleagues and observing their classes will help to open up old delivery styles to new methods. Without changing completely, new components can be integrated that will facilitate different approaches. For instance, with lectures, learners like Charles can be accommodated by stopping at regular intervals and having the students interact with the student next to them. They could be asked to figure out a problem together, raise questions regarding the topic, or share a personal experience that applies to the lecture material. Following this, perhaps one or two pairs of students could share the results of their discussion with the class. Another strategy is to stop class early on a regular basis to allow students a designated time to raise questions or to meet with the instructor personally in small groups. For instance with a large lecture class, Monday could be the day when students with last names beginning with A through D stay and get to know the instructor better through some type of discussion.

If the instructor is convinced that her course content is better learned through collaborative teams and creative syntheses than through lecture, she may have to start off with a combination of styles for students like Linda. She has not experienced success with collaborative learning and has been frustrated with it in the past. By teaching the students how to be part of a team and to set guidelines at the beginning for how the process works, individual frustrations will be minimized. It will also stretch student approaches to learning if they can experience success with a new style.

Principle 6: Approaches to learning can be modified through strategy instruction in order to increase the learners' repertoires and consequently their opportunities to succeed across a range of environments.

This principle relates to principle 5 in which we suggested "stretching" student approaches to learning. Rather than simply teaching to as many styles as possible, isn't it a component of the teacher's responsibility to broaden the repertoire of strategies for all students? They can and should accommodate a variety of styles, but they should also gradually expose students to new approaches to learning. This may involve direct instruction and sensitivity to their resistance, but it will serve them better as learners in general.

In the case of Linda, it would be more comfortable for her to keep enrolling in classes where she could expect lectures and figuring things out on her own. It might be comfortable, but it wouldn't prepare her for the inevitable learning environment in which she will be required to work in groups and approach a problem from a different perspective. Rather than simply assuming that she can make such a transfer on her own, why not teach her, along with others, how to work in groups? Guidelines can be provided for working together, and teachers can assist by giving the students roles to facilitate the group dynamics.

Charles might prefer working with others, but in some environments he will have to feel confident solving a problem independently. By receiving guided practice in this mode and a great deal of positive reinforcement when it seems frustrating, he will leave with greater opportunities to succeed in a variety of environments. Teresita would benefit by being encouraged to participate in class discussions. Her involvement should be gradual, and a safe environment must be established first. For students timid about discussion to begin sharing, they must feel that taking such a risk is safe, that is, they will not be judged harshly. To facilitate this type of environment, ground rules need to be set up at the start. The whole class, including Teresita, can get involved by creating the rules, which should include ways to show mutual respect, not interrupt, not make personal judgments, and tolerate diverse points of views. Perhaps once discussions start, there could be a rule that requires participation from everyone. This way students like Teresita understand that their participation, like everyone else's, is valued and expected.

Reflections

The following questions can provide a starting point for further reflection on practice.

How does a teacher demonstrate that she values the personal experiences of her students, and how can she provide opportunities for them to find connections to the content through these experiences?

How does a teacher handle students who never participate in class and are reluctant to answer directly when asked a question?

How does a teacher respond to a student from another culture who comes to her for assistance? Should she make assumptions about the student based on his cultural background?

How does a teacher assist a student who approaches learning from a different perspective than the expected one for a particular content area?

How many different approaches to teaching are realistic to incorporate into a teacher's overall instructional delivery? What criteria are used to determine when to utilize a particular approach?

Whose responsibility is it to teach students strategies for learning?

Chapter Ten

Self-Regulation and Goal Setting

We explored the topic of self-regulated learning in Chapter Three and established a direct connection between monitoring learning and setting goals. The theory suggests that without goals it would be difficult for a person to monitor his or her performance. Goals provide the standards by which learners can more easily evaluate their progress and decide what strategies to employ to regulate it.

Self-regulated learning happens when learners are actively in control and aware of how they process information. Garner (1987) talks about it in terms of comprehension and describes it as an interaction among three variables: the individual, the task, and the repertoire of strategies available to the individual. Weinstein and Mayer (1986) also discuss comprehension monitoring as a management strategy and list it as one of eight categories of learning. They emphasize connecting it to goal setting in order for it to be effective.

Pintrich (1995) describes self-regulated learning as an active process that is goal-directed. He adds that in order to regulate behavior, learners must have control over resources, which could mean having the repertoire of strategies that Garner references. Zimmerman and Paulsen (1995) outline four specific steps for becoming proficient at self-regulated learning—steps that begin with establishing a baseline of expectations from which to set goals and end with generalizing across course content.

In the area of goals, theorists have discussed two general types: mastery and performance. Hagen and Weinstein (1995) link mastery goals to the process of learning and suggest that they are more associated with regulation and self-monitoring, whereas performance goals are linked to outcomes. Cross and Steadman (1996) agree with these distinctions and add that performance goals are often grade-oriented.

As we explored self-regulated learning further, we found that the research is broad-based and focuses primarily on three areas: cognition, metacognition, and motivation. This helps to establish that the concept is a multivariate one; it also forces a limited scope here. Because we discuss goals in relation to motivation in Chapter Six, here we will look at goal setting only as it directly relates to self-regulated learning. We will primarily concentrate on establishing a clear definition of self-regulated learning and on determining the instructional factors and conditions that promote it.

Establishing the Construct

Zimmerman (1990) describes self-regulated learners as those who are "metacognitively, motivationally and behaviorally active participants in their own learning" (p. 4). He clarifies these three universal aspects of the process: (1) *metacognition* is the component that directs planning, organizing, self-monitoring, and self-evaluating; (2) *motivation* relates to high self-efficacy and attribution, as well as to an intrinsic interest in the learning task; and (3) *behavior* is the process for selecting, structuring, and creating an environment that is optimal for learning. These three factors are basic to the process of self-regulated learning.

Zimmerman asserts that although everyone uses some regulatory processes, true self-regulated learning occurs when learners are able to see the relationship between particular strategy use and outcome and then use that knowledge to work toward their goals. In his summary of the research in this area, he determines that this awareness of outcomes is critical to the continued use of self-regulated strategies. As we look back at Linda's case, it seems clear that she does not connect the study strategies she is using to her academic outcomes. Instead, she believes if she simply tries harder in a vague, generalized manner, she will eventually succeed.

In related research, Trawick (1992) discovered a significant positive correlation between student self-reports of self-regulatory strategy use and performance expectations and attributional patterns. The community college students in her study had a history of academic failure and, although their performance expectations were high, there was no relationship between those expectations and the students' subsequent performance. The students indicated that they believed effort to be related to academic success; they had not stopped trying, but their expectation and the ultimate outcome did not match. Based on this finding, Trawick recommends that these students could most likely benefit from instruction in how to "assess the relationship between their own efforts and academic outcomes, including how to engineer the outcomes of choice" (p. 17).

It seems once again that Linda's behavior fits with these findings. She does believe that she is making an effort; she puts considerable time into her studying and has high expectations for success. As she continues to apply strategies that may have worked in high school, she does not analyze the different expectations inherent in college tasks. Linda could benefit from instruction that would force her to revisit the connections and change her approach. Mike could benefit from such instruction as well, but for a different reason. He does not seem to connect personal effort with outcomes in school. He may have higher expectations for success this time around because he has experienced it outside the formal educational setting, but he most likely has no experience with the relationship between effort in school and academic outcomes. Instruction for Mike should include helping him see connections between the effort he makes on the job and subsequent success after he makes such an effort in school.

Warkentin and Bol (1997) used an effort management hierarchy to analyze the differences between high- and low-achieving students in terms of self-regulatory behavior. They interviewed students regarding their study activity for a final exam and analyzed their responses within the four levels of the hierarchy: monitoring, regulating, planning, and evaluating. What they found were few overall differences between groups; most students, in fact, experienced difficulties in monitoring their efforts. There were some reported distinctions, however, in the areas of planning and evaluation, and there were some interesting descriptions of the usefulness of particular behaviors.

All students reported that regulation served a variety of functions for them, including breaking the study session into smaller time segments, which created intermediate goals and subsequently greater persistence. Also the use of a study strategy such as taking notes helped maintain their attention. In the planning area, the researchers found a difference between the high-and low-achievers in two categories. First, although both groups developed self-instructional sequences to structure their efforts leading up to the test, those of the high-achievers had characteristics that set them apart from the others. Ninety-one percent of these students designed study sequences that were selective; they looked at what was likely to be important and paid attention to a review of prior learning, for example, by referring to significant points in earlier notes. Only 44 percent of the low-achievers reported any pattern to their planning, and 22 percent did not engage in planning activities at all.

Distinctions in planning were also found in the nature of goals and purposes that students established for studying. The biggest difference here was that 55 percent of the low-achievers had "remembering goals," that is, memorizing information for the test, whereas only 9 percent of the high-achievers had such goals. The goals of high-achievers related more to understanding and remembering for future needs.

In the area of evaluation, and related to the earlier description of the importance of recognizing the connection between outcomes and strategies, most students did reflect on their efforts following studying. The researchers found qualitative differences here also, however; the low-achievers reported vague, general reflective activity, and the high-achievers looked more specifically at what may have worked for them.

Barnett (1997) suggests that perhaps researchers are idealizing strategic learners who are rarely found in the classroom. Although he describes these "experts" in a similar fashion to Zimmerman, his approach to the study of self-regulated learning is from a different angle—one that may help explain the students in the Trawick study. He lists reasons for using "less-than-optimal" strategies when engaged in learning. Citing Winne (1995), he suggests that for novices the "cost of self-regulation . . . in the early phases of learning, may be too high" (p. 4). In other words, learners may need to attend so completely to simply acquiring information that they have no time left for monitoring their progress. Also on his list are a lack of prior knowledge in the particular domain, competing demands on time, and the creation of personal goals that may differ from those someone else establishes.

These factors very likely affect Charles's behavior. He is so busy simply trying to learn material that he does not have adequate time to evaluate his progress appropriately. In addition, he has a limited amount of time to devote to this, and he has not really prioritized his goals. Currently, he is experiencing tension between his personal, family-related goals and those related to his professional activity.

Barnett conducted his research under conditions that he felt should have been optimal for the use of self-regulatory strategies. He looked at the studying process and subsequent test performance of college students across two different courses. In these courses, student motivation was assumed to be high because the tests made up a substantial portion of their grade. Tests were also scheduled far in advance, so external factors should not have interfered too much. In addition, the students had received explicit feedback from prior tests and expected a similar test format. Barnett was looking for evidence that students adjusted their efforts and strategies across the semester based on feedback on the early tests used that as a guide for preparation.

The results of Barnett's work are interesting because they demonstrate a distinction between self-regulation at an advanced level of study and at a less advanced level. The students who were more advanced and taking a course in their major area of study showed increased effort across the term, minor adjustments in their strategies, and higher test scores. Test scores in the other course, an entry-level course, had a low correlation with effort and quality of studying, which did not vary across the semester. Barnett concludes that perhaps for self-regulation to be used effectively, students need a certain amount of background knowledge in the subject matter.

Alexander (1995) expands on this as she discusses the potency of subject matter knowledge and the individual interest level of the learner in the process of self-regulation. In the domain model of learning, she describes three stages: acclimation, competence, and proficiency. At the acclimation stage, learners have a low knowledge of the subject matter, and their motivation is often restricted to the task at hand. For students enrolled in entry-level coursework, the acclimation stage places high demands on their general cognitive processing, and the required tasks may seem overwhelming rather than stimulating. Alexander stresses that while students may attempt self-regulation at this stage, it will be less frequent and less rewarding. She adds that instructors should not hold them to unattainable standards.

At the competence level, learners become more independent as they are able to organize information around significant concepts. Their efforts begin to relate to realistic goals, and their processing strategies become more appropriate for the subject matter. Finally, at the proficiency stage tasks are frequently self-determined, and the learner is contributing new knowledge to the field. Goals become internally constructed, and self-regulatory behavior operates at an optimal level. Alexander is careful to clarify that these stages are content-specific and that one may be at different levels simultaneously in different areas of study.

Winne (1995) questions the point at which learners should be putting forth the effort required to self-regulate. He suggests that such monitoring "levies charges" against their working memory capacity and may act as a barrier if they are trying to acquire new information. He goes on to say that students who are less knowledgeable are "charged more for monitoring," as it leads to more errors in their processing, and it has not become automated for them in a particular domain. Winne states that "only after the declarative stage of skill learning—the point at which skills are ready to be proceduralized—can costs charged for monitoring fit into the learners' cognitive budgets" (p. 178).

The research of Kanfer and Ackerman (1989) supports this, as it shows self-regulatory behavior to be very effortful. The researchers discovered that when students who are still in the stage of skill acquisition become engaged in monitoring activities, their performance can be affected negatively, especially if they are low-ability learners. In that study, students who were in the early stages of learning to do algorithms were asked to monitor their performance. The students' self-regulatory behavior became "animated," but their performance declined. Kanfer and Ackerman conclude that mental resources are reassigned to monitoring but still are needed for acquiring new skills. They suggest that regulating at this point only complicates study patterns and that students may decide it doesn't lead to higher levels of achievement.

Lindner and Harris (1992) suggest that this ability to self- regulate is not beyond the basics of learning; rather it is "the basic skill underlying successful learning" (p. 3). They developed a model of self-regulated learning that includes five dimensions very similar to those outlined by Zimmerman (1990). They describe them interactively and place motivation in the center as the mediator between the internal processes of monitoring and the external factors related to managing the environment. Using this model, they tried to determine the extent to which self-regulated learning is related to academic performance in college students. They found a significant relationship between the GPAs of the 160 education students in their study and the amount of self-regulated learning they engaged in. Another finding was that the level of self-regulated learning seems to increase with age and academic experience, as the graduate students in the study scored the highest on their measure of self-regulation.

Perhaps it is unrealistic to expect anyone relatively new to a field of study to use self- regulatory strategies routinely. Pressley (1995) suggests that self-regulatory strategies are complex, develop over a long period of time, and unlikely to be used with any real expertise in undergraduate students. He cites the research of Wyatt and others (1993) in which social science professors were asked to read aloud from professional articles that were important for them to understand. The researchers found self-regulated strategies being applied throughout the readings and felt that it was enabled by "extensive strategic knowledge of reading, deep and connected conceptual knowledge in their domains of expertise, well developed metacognitive knowledge and active monitoring" (p. 208).

The activity they observed seemed to be unconscious; the experts weren't thinking about how to process the information. It seemed to be a natural activity for them. Wyatt and others (1993) conclude that such sophisticated strategic learning needs years of experience and development. In addition, they surmise that students who may have recently learned regulatory strategies are not likely to transfer them for a variety of reasons. First, they have to compete with older strategies that require less effort; second, they may have learned how a strategy works but not how to adapt it to different areas; third, they may not understand when and where to apply it; and last, they may not understand the utility of the strategy at all.

Paris and Newman (1990) explore this area through a developmental lens and suggest that self-regulated learning is a process that evolves as students become aware of themselves as learners and is influenced by theories they construct from their experiences in school. They look at their self-constructed theories and continue to relate them to academic self-perceptions, knowledge of tasks, and social cognition.

These theories begin in the early grades where self-perception is often related to external evaluations such as grades and ability groupings. These can become very specific in the areas of math and reading and frequently form the basis for long-lasting perceptions of the self as a learner. As students get older, their perceptions change and are accompanied by changes in their feelings of self-efficacy and sense of control. They may begin to see that high effort acts as compensation for low ability and that success related to hard work may be valued less than success that comes with minimal effort. Related to this may be the perception that assistance is provided to those who are less able to complete the work. These student "theories" can lead to a reduction of effort and an unwillingness to ask for help in order to avoid looking less capable. It is quite likely that Mike's theories related to schooling were formed at an early stage and that they have not developed as he has gone through the system. He does not seem to have a sense of control or positive self-efficacy, and at the same time he probably is unwilling to seek help because it makes him appear less able.

The second area Paris and Newman explored is related to a knowledge of tasks. Students often have only a vague understanding of the structure of the tasks they are expected to complete, and this influences their orientation toward goal setting. Whether the student chooses goals related to learning the material or to simply gaining a particular grade also relates to their emerging theory of abilities. The researchers suggest that by the ages of ten to twelve, goals emerge as part of students' coping strategies. For the underachieving student, "task involvement, persistence, mastery and higher order thinking may simply require too much effort and yield too little success in traditional settings to enhance self perceptions of ability" (p. 91).

As the underachievers begin to make choices related to learning, they may demonstrate a high degree of self-regulation but in a manner that is "debilitating" to their academic performance. For instance, they may be learning strategies for "avoiding thinking, minimizing effort and dodging responsibility for their own learning" (p. 91). Paris and Newman assert that these tactics are important pieces of self-regulatory behavior as they are selected to meet goals that are often counterproductive. Once again, Mike's behavior seems to be an appropriate application of this theory. In high school, he was very likely regulating his activity but applying his efforts to goals that were not productive.

The last area Paris and Newman discuss in the evolution of students' perceptions is in the realm of social cognition. The authors believe that this area, which includes knowing when to access outside support, is a significant aspect of self-regulation and that high-achievers are more likely to seek academic assistance than are low-achievers. Again, they assert that this is developmental and that with age, students are more likely to view outside assistance as a strategy that is beneficial. Those who self-regulate have in their repertoires ways of identifying helpers, taking the initiative to seek help, and knowing when it is necessary. Both Teresita and Linda should seek external support. Linda does not seem to think she needs help, and she still believes that she should succeed on her own—a belief she connects to individual effort. Teresita also believes that her problems are those that only she can solve and does not understand how assistance could benefit her current situation.

Paris and Newman also suggest that in an appropriate learning environment, instructional intervention can make a difference for those learners whose theories about themselves as learners have evolved from negative experiences. This notion forms the basis for the next section in which we discuss instructional factors related to the facilitation of self-regulated learning.

Instructional Intervention

Winne (1995) contends that self-regulated learning is "malleable," depending on environmental influences, and that it develops incrementally through instruction that provides appropriate resources for students. He suggests that, based on the research he reviewed, effective interventions share four basic ingredients. First, they provide the conditional knowledge that helps learners determine when a strategy has been appropriately engaged and affected their progress. Second, they must provide the action knowledge that includes the metacognitive, cognitive, and behavioral skills related to engaging in self-regulated learning. Third, they must make learners motivated to use these first ingredients because they consider them effective and because they value effective learning. Finally, they assume a certain level of prerequisite knowledge in a particular domain as well as an understanding of the tasks involved. It seems clear that effective intervention may take time and is linked to specific domains of knowledge. Instruction must begin by taking into account the prior knowledge of the learner and be applied in relevant settings.

Pressley (1995) supports this framework, as he contends that instruction should first be matched to the learners' zones of proximal development and then proceed with teacher modeling, explanation, and massed practice with authentic tasks. He adds that teacher and peer support are two significant resources that need to be provided. Even though he believes it unlikely that undergraduates would develop a real expertise in this process, he does suggest several instructional factors to facilitate its development.

According to Pressley, teachers need to address students' beliefs about learning and encourage them to understand that knowledge is not absolute and that learning is hard. Teachers must also establish a foundation for students to believe that self-regulatory strategies have utility. Students should be encouraged to practice more than one procedure at a time. Even though this may slow progress, Pressley asserts that it would increase their durability. Also to promote student use, teachers should ensure that the first time a strategy is practiced, it is fairly easy to apply.

Closely related to Pressley's ideas are those of Paris and Newman (1990). They encouraged teachers to address those theories that students construct about school and their own abilities. Just as Pressley talks about students' beliefs, Paris and Newman are concerned with the beliefs students develop about their own sense of control and self-efficacy. They assert that while teacher-directed instruction can be powerful and have an immediate effect on performance, change will not last unless students "make personal commitments . . . otherwise, the change in performance reflects obedience and not enduring new beliefs about what ought to be done in the situation" (p. 97). In other words, the instruction must include methodology that facilitates the students buying into the whole concept because they feel it is valuable and linked to the outcomes they desire. This would be particularly beneficial in Mike's situation. He does not want someone else deciding what is important for him. If an instructor could only engage Mike in a process of self-evaluation in which he comes to the conclusion that certain activities are in his best interest and would give him some control, then he would feel some ownership and commitment.

In a study that facilitated students' increased internalization of the processes that are effective for studying, Butler (1997) worked with postsecondary, learning-disabled students. She used a model of self-regulation called the strategic content learning approach, and her objective was to facilitate students' ability to "engage recursively in a full set of activities central to self regulation" (p. 1). The students met individually with an instructor two or three times a week and worked on real assignments chosen by the student. The sessions focused alternatively on the task and the process of accomplishing that task. Students were continuously asked to articulate their understanding of how the processes in which they were engaging would help them in the future.

Butler expected to find that students would experience an increase in their self-efficacy beliefs, revise their metacognitive knowledge and strategic processing related to academic tasks, individualize strategies, and learn how to select, monitor, and adapt strategies that worked for them. These expectations were articulated in part within instructional guidelines that "built from what students already knew, were founded on their processing preferences, capitalized on their strengths, circumvented their weaknesses, and were described in the students' own words" (p. 8). After working with students across four studies, she found positive changes in students' knowledge and beliefs regarding effective self-regulation.

Butler relied on a scaffolded support system, but instructional modeling is another approach Paris and Newman suggest. Rarely do students get to hear what is inside an instructor's head as he or she processes information. Through modeling, teachers can externalize the internal dialogue that often occurs with self-regulated learning. Another component that Paris and Newman consider significant and that can be linked to modeling is to make thinking public. All students need to articulate their frustrations with given tasks, and when such a discussion is facilitated a range of ideas becomes accessible to everyone.

A third condition recommended by Paris and Newman includes active participation and collaboration on the part of the students. One way to facilitate this comes through peer tutoring. When students are teaching each other, they develop more of a personal commitment to the strategies they are teaching. This may be the perfect solution for some of Mike's behavior. If he could be convinced to use his talents and strengths to teach others, he might better understand the relevancy of the demands in his classroom. There would likely be an increase in his own sense of control in the learning environment, and his feelings of self-efficacy may also increase.

Closely linked to Paris and Newman's suggestion that instruction cannot be teacher-driven is the recommendation of Talbot (1996), who claims that instructors cannot "teach" self-regulation; rather, they act as "mediators." Behavior must be elicited from students who experience an ownership of the process which then becomes meaningful to them because of their personal involvement. The teacher's role is to increase student awareness of the connections between their intentions and the actions they take.

Talbot framed his work around students who are learning-oriented or goal-oriented. The learning-oriented students are intrinsically motivated, independent learners who are curious about learning and meeting their own objectives, whereas goal-oriented students are more bound by external expectations, class requirements, and assigned tasks. Clearly, the learning-oriented approach is more related to a self-regulatory process, but teachers often unintentionally reinforce the goal-oriented students by unilaterally setting all the standards and expectations for the class, including punishing late papers and exams. Perhaps sharing some of the control within the instructional setting, making it clear that knowledge can be generated collaboratively with the students, and reinforcing the enjoyment of learning and setting of personal goals within that framework would help mediate toward students feeling more in charge of their own learning.

In earlier research, Talbot (1996) discovered that providing assistance in self-regulatory strategies to learning-oriented and goal-oriented learners had very different results. Whereas the learning-oriented learners made use of a variety of instructional resources, including peer counselors, workshops, ungraded formative feedback, and re-attributional training to assess their approaches, the goal-oriented students were not interested in evaluating their strategies and making adjustments. These results led him to look at instruction that might "empower students, especially the GO's, (goal oriented students) to engage in purposeful effort" (p. 2).

He found that because these students often have a dichotomous theory about effort and learning (either you have it or you don't), they were not attracted to workshops or outside assistance. They considered these futile and only a reminder of their inability to achieve. Instead, he implies that assistance occurring within regular coursework may be more effective. He recommends that teachers avoid unnecessary references to learning related to external standards, deadlines, and grades; instead, they should focus on ways to help students build an internal locus of control. As an example, he suggests returning papers with a "no grade possible" notation and then engaging in a negotiated session with the student to re-do the work based on mutually agreed-on expectations. Also related to the format of effective intervention is the research of Donley (1992), who looked at college students enrolled in a reading/learning strategies course. She hypothesizes that when students are taught to apply strategies to more authentic materials such as their content area textbooks, the utility of the strategies is more apparent; this then may lead to an increase in their sense of self-efficacy and control over the outcomes, which would probably increase the likelihood of their future utilization.

Donley found that those who were taught to apply strategies directly to their college texts were more likely to use a self-regulating learning strategy following the course than were those who were taught from a study skills book. Although both groups had a positive attitude toward the strategy and demonstrated gains in their learning skills, the course-based group used the strategy more frequently in other courses. Another interesting outcome of this study, however, was that in a delayed survey, the researcher found that students from both groups were using components of the strategy in their other classes. This suggests that, to varying extents, they were all able to adapt and refine the strategy to different tasks and goals—significant components of self-regulated learning.

This study was small and although the results slightly favored the course-based approach, research is needed to further investigate this area of instruction. Studies to date indicate a lack of transfer between reading and study skills courses and content coursework. More investigation is needed to find out whether this is because these students often have attributions and self-concepts that act as barriers to strategy use (Garner, 1990). Perhaps related to Mealey's assertion (1990) is that underprepared college students are not motivated to take responsibility for their learning and need to learn how to attribute their successes to their own efforts. Does course-based instruction foster these necessary prerequisites to independent strategy use?

Lan, Bradley, and Parr (1994) looked at the effectiveness of self-monitoring in an authentic environment—a graduate statistics class. The researchers framed their study by asserting that instruction needs to systematically inspire students to monitor their learning. They suggest that teachers convince students of its effectiveness, facilitate its application, and motivate them to apply such strategies.

In their research, they established three conditions: self-monitoring, instructor monitoring, and a control group. The self-monitoring students were asked to record the time spent and the number of times they engaged in various learning activities for each concept that was presented in the course. This protocol acted as a cue for them to enhance their self-monitoring. The students initially thought this would be a distraction but by the end of the study expressed their interest in having it in all of their classes. The results indicate that students who are encouraged to self-monitor their learning activities outperform the others. In addition, they tend to be more intrinsically motivated and to have a somewhat stronger sense of self-control.

A different kind of intervention was applied in a pilot study for an upper-level college accounting course for underachieving students considered to be at risk. Gaddis and Elliott (1997) wanted to enhance learning for this population by increasing its opportunities for self-regulated learning and self-efficacy. Their assumption was that students would experience self-regulation if they came into a monitored session following an exam and were allowed to attempt to solve problems they had missed on the exam—and they could do this as many times as necessary. Students who were dissatisfied with their exam scores were offered extra credit by attending such a session and working on problems that had been taught in class; they would work without notes or annotated textbooks.

The results show that students who did participate in these "self-regulatory" sessions showed significant improvement on their second exam compared to those who did not (and who showed an average decline in scores). This was a small study, but it does indicate the promise of using a more indirect but content-integrated approach to self-regulation. As the authors assert, the individual quality most affecting this process is a sense of self-efficacy; perhaps this is effectively enhanced through a voluntary format that has a direct link—extra credit first and then raised exam grades—to the content course.

Doring, Bingham, and Bramwell-Viol (1997) argue for a more proactive, comprehensive approach. They believe that the university as an institution must view self-regulation as an inherent component of the transitional process that students experience when they move into postsecondary education and that the university must take an active role in promoting the skills needed by the incoming students. They assert that there is a "real need to integrate and embed self-regulatory skills in academic units rather than as stand alone courses" (p. 9). Students experience a decrease in external support at the same time they enter the university to find an increased demand that they become independent learners.

In order to foster successful learning, the university must help students learn how to set appropriate goals, which then form the foundation for self-regulatory learning. This involves deliberate teaching that is related to goal setting. Students must learn how to develop personal standards and levels of achievement. This may involve a redefinition of earlier goals in order to direct their new learning activities. According to Doring and others, once students begin to develop satisfactory self-regulated strategies, their feelings of self-efficacy will also be strengthened and lead to higher levels of achievement. This, they contend, is a valid objective for the value-added component of a university education.

In this chapter we have looked at research. Now we make connections. Using the TRPP model, we link theory and research to principles and practice.

Using the TRPP Model

The research findings and the theoretical foundations have led us to construct the following principles.

Principles

1. Self-regulated learning enables learners to actively control their learning.
2. Self-regulated learning is enhanced when learners make a direct connection between their use of strategies and outcomes.
3. Self-regulated learning requires the learner to set learning goals that enhance motivation.
4. Self-regulated learning requires a minimal level of prior knowledge in a given domain.
5. Self-regulated learning develops over time as learners increase their sense of self-efficacy.
6. Effective instruction to develop self-regulated learning includes practice with authentic materials.
7. Effective instruction to develop self-regulated learning allows learners to build an internal commitment to the process.

Applying Principles to Case Studies

Principle 1: Self-regulated learning enables learners to actively control their learning.

Jadwiga is an excellent example of a learner who has engaged in self-regulated activities to control her learning process. She certainly began with a metacognitive understanding of what she would have to do in order to meet her goals of becoming proficient in English and independent. She knew that she did not have family support and that she would need to create a different environment for herself that would be a better fit. As she analyzed her needs, she carefully constructed a plan that would allow her to gradually move away from what she considered to be a restrictive environment. That plan included living at home as long as necessary while simultaneously developing new friendships and English skills.

She had a strong belief in her ability to make this dream come true and, because she also believed that her efforts would lead her to achievement, she was able to succeed. The goals she set were personal; no one else imposed them on her, and they were structured for intermediate successes. For instance, each time she completed another level of English proficiency, she rewarded herself, and when she finished all five levels of instruction, she rewarded herself once again with a move into the city.

In contrast, Linda seems to have very little control over her learning. She is unable to distinguish between expectations at the college level and those in high school where she was able to succeed. She has not yet been able to understand the real nature of the learning tasks that are being presented, and consequently has not realized the need to evaluate the strategies she is applying. Once she makes the connection between the outcomes she is experiencing and her own inappropriate strategies, she will be able to take control again. Until then she will continue to put forth effort and continue to have high expectations but experience little success.

Another significant component of self-regulated learning for Linda is that of creating an environment that is optimal for her learning. This includes her need to reach out for assistance and restructure her perceptions of her own role as a learner. Instead of escaping her new environment and continuing to believe that assistance implies less ability, Linda needs to adapt to the new environment and find the social resources that are available, through peers, teachers, and counselors.

Principle 2: Self-regulated learning is enhanced when learners make a direct connection between their use of strategies and outcomes.

Looking back at Linda's case, it is evident that when there is no direct connection between strategies and outcomes, achievement is adversely affected. In her case, she has high expectations and honestly believes that her time-consuming efforts, inappropriate as they may seem to an outsider, will result in success. At least she does understand that personal effort is related to achievement. What she does not understand is the need to evaluate particular strategies and their effectiveness.

Linda's self-regulation could be enhanced if a teacher would suggest study techniques for organizing the material to be learned. The teacher might talk through how to chart the principles for the next chemistry exam and actually lead the class through a practice model. In addition, the class could review notes and highlight significant ideas together which would provide a model for the importance of going over notes selectively. Another model that would help students like Linda is one that suggests ways to read a chapter in the text. The teacher could invite a learning specialist into class to lead this exercise. All of this would give students ideas on how to select strategies appropriate for academic achievement in a particular course.

Sabina has noted that certain strategies are not working for her. She has analyzed her efforts at learning without much social interaction. She has decided that her rapidly decreasing motivation and lower-than-expected grades are the result of not being able to brainstorm and receive feedback from peers. Sabina has come to realize that the current environment is not optimal for the strategies necessary to achieve in this course. The course-related tasks realistically demand a continuous sharing of ideas and peer feedback. Even though she has tried alternate strategies to compensate for the distance she feels from her peers, she found they have not led to the expected outcomes. She is about to take back control of her learning by changing the environment so that she can engage in the particular strategies she knows are related to the results she wants.

Principle 3: Self-regulated learning requires the learner to set learning goals that enhance motivation.

Even though Charles seems highly motivated, his goals may actually be getting in his way. For one, they have not been developed out of a desire to learn a particular content area; rather, they have come from a need to advance at work and increase his long-term professional potential. They are thus related to performance and if, in fact, he does not attain a high enough grade, he will not be reimbursed for the course and will not advance in his job. This external motivation has caused him a great deal of anxiety and has created a barrier to true learning. In addition, Charles has personal goals related to his family role. He wants to be a good father and husband, yet his performance goals in school seem to be in direct conflict with them. His goals at home are more immediate and may be more significant at this time. He may need to stop school at this point and attend to what he sees as a priority—being a part of his children's lives.

Mike has very immediate goals that relate to content he feels he must learn for the success of his business. He is internally motivated to learn but needs help articulating his goals and connecting them to content that may not always seem relevant. If he would discuss this with his instructor, he could receive assistance in developing goals that would help him get past these feelings of irrelevancy. Mike does not have experience constructing goals for his formal education, which has always seemed irrelevant to him. If he could see the relationship between the goals he has established for his business and educational goals, he could enhance his motivation.

Principle 4: Self-regulated learning requires a minimal level of prior knowledge in a given domain.

Teachers who expect self-regulation in the early levels of content instruction may be unrealistic in their demands on students. As the research makes clear, the effort that it takes to engage in self-regulation might be too much for learners who are acquiring unfamiliar skills. In these instances, the teacher should probably do as much modeling as possible to help the students become familiar with the ways of thinking and organizing that are appropriate to a particular field of study. Providing study aids through graphs, time lines, and summaries can facilitate students' attempts at self-regulation.

In other courses, it seems significant to remind students of their prior knowledge and demonstrate how to make connections to new material. In the case of Teresita, who has a background in early childhood education, she may not automatically see the connections because she is so anxious in her new four-year university environment. She may feel that she is starting all over again and that what she learned earlier is a discrete segment of the whole process. For Mike, any connections that he can make to his actual work and course content will enable him to spend more time in strategy application and less time thinking the material is completely new. Linda too needs to understand that it may not be new content (she has a good background in science and math); rather, there are simply new expectations for the way the content is organized and analyzed. Once she sees this, she may make more connections to her prior knowledge and be able to use more appropriate strategies.

Principle 5: Self-regulated learning develops over time as learners increase their sense of self-efficacy.

Looking back at Mike and his lack of articulated goals, we might suspect that his reluctance to set goals is related to his overall low self-efficacy. He has no experience with success in formal educational settings. His self-concept related to his role as a learner in school was probably formed in the early grades and was most likely based on negative experiences. Since then his self-regulation has focused on getting out of responsibilities and decreasing efforts in order to avoid feelings of failure. This has all contributed to his lack of belief that he can meet expectations, whatever they are, if they relate to school. Mike has a strong sense of self-efficacy in the workplace and needs help in transferring this to the educational setting. Helping him to articulate meaningful and attainable goals would be a good first step. The teacher working with him needs to provide opportunities for Mike to succeed and to help him make the connection between that success and his own efforts.

Teresita has experienced success in school and until recently had a strong sense of self-efficacy related to academic achievement. Before she had demanding family responsibilities, she knew what it took to succeed with her schoolwork. Her confidence is now being shaken, as is her belief that she can complete her current level of coursework. She clearly needs to make some changes. Perhaps this means finding assistance with her family responsibilities, or it may mean stopping for a while to rethink her goals. A strong adviser could provide help here and help Teresita construct an overall program of study that might slow down her progress but allow her to succeed and feel better about herself. There may be course formats that would allow her to enroll as an independent learner. There could also be different course sequences that would allow her to first take courses where she has more knowledge and could re-experience the success that would help her regain the level of self-efficacy she once knew.

Principle 6: Effective instruction to develop self-regulated learning includes practice with authentic materials.

As was suggested earlier with Linda, providing opportunities for learners to practice self- regulation with materials that are directly relevant to their goals and immediate needs will lead to greater success. In Linda's chemistry class, assistance with organizing the content and reading the textbook could be given during certain portions of the class at regular intervals during the term. Additionally, giving the students a grade for their early attempts at organizational strategies might let them see the value attached to it by the instructor.

A student with Mike's needs is very unlikely to take anything seriously that is not directly connected to the reason he is in school. If he were assigned to a study skills class, for instance, that taught study skills apart from any relevant context, his attendance would be sporadic at best. But if an instructor teaching the business content that he values were to suggest strategies for learning the material and if the instructor also provided opportunities for the students to feel successful with them, then Mike might actually try them.

Related to this is the instructor's modeling aloud the thinking process used in a particular content area as it relates to self-regulation. By making it clear that teachers also engage in this process, students might be willing to try it themselves. Once the teacher has provided some initial modeling, asking the students to try it out in pairs or small groups with the course content would be an effective method for facilitating its use.

Principle 7: Effective instruction to develop self-regulated learning allows learners to build an internal commitment to the process.

Although we suggested in principle 6 that students be given a grade for their initial attempts to use self-regulating strategies, this practice should only be used at the beginning to provide positive feedback and validation of its significance. To build an internal commitment and encourage transference across the curriculum, students must feel an intrinsic motivation to use the strategies. In order for this to happen, teachers cannot simply provide direct instruction; they must provide opportunities for students to experience success with various self-regulated learning strategies and to make the connections with desired outcomes.

One way for students to build such a commitment is for them to teach one another from their own successes. Facilitating small-group discussions in class that focus on which strategies worked and which ones didn't work following a test is a good example of allowing the students themselves to make connections. If students with needs similar to Charles and Teresita heard the struggles other students were encountering and were able to freely discuss strategies, their anxieties might be lowered. For them the strategies would most likely relate to goal orientation and time management. Linda might discover that discussing ideas with others leads to a better, less effortful understanding of complicated new principles. Mike's self-concept and sense of efficacy might be drastically increased if he were to become a discussion leader and facilitate others' understandings.

Reflections

The following questions can provide a starting point for further reflection on practice.

How can teachers become aware of their own self-regulation strategies?

What would it take to model the thought processes related to their self-regulatory processes for students?

How can authentic materials be integrated with strategy instruction?

What needs to happen for students to internalize self-regulation strategies?

What types of activities would facilitate students teaching each other how to self-regulate their learning?

Part Three

New Teaching Perspectives

In this final section, the discussion moves away from the primary ingredients of the TRPP model: theory, research, principles and practice to the driving force beyond it, critical reflection. This may actually be the most difficult component as it forces the reader to bring everything into focus and use it to analyze practice. It is one thing to read theoretical models and the research of others; it is quite another to risk changing the habits of practice that have become comfortable and have been "effective enough."

In this chapter a model is described that will facilitate the critical reflection advocated throughout the book. The model, RE-CREATE, provides a framework through which communities, or units, of teachers can begin the process of transformation. There are several assumptions underlying the model that need careful consideration. Probably the most significant assumption is that this is not an individual undertaking; to be most effective it must be collaborative and include colleagues.

Moving into Chapter Eleven, there are two lenses for further reflection. The first is a look back at the research that was summarized earlier in Part Two. Highlighted is what is missing in that research base as it applies to teaching and learning in postsecondary learning environments. Applied research relating to older students and those who are culturally and ethnically diverse is lacking in many areas. In addition, there is a lack of longitudinal studies to follow up on initial outcomes. Secondly, an outline of the responsibilities teachers all share to contribute to and strengthen the current, relevant research base is provided. In many cases the data that is needed for such research is already available. Teachers simply need to look at it more systematically and organize it for formal dissemination.

Chapter Eleven

Critical Reflection on Practice

In this chapter we suggest a process for looking at the practice of teaching from a new perspective. We go back to the principles articulated in Chapters Five through Ten and use them as a framework for thinking about how to work with students. Before talking about this process of critical reflection, however, we examine the assumptions at its foundation.

First, in order for any meaningful change to take place, individuals must be ready to take the risk of engaging in a process that could lead to discovering weaknesses in what they do. This is difficult, especially if they are comfortable with their work and it seems to be fairly effective overall. It can be difficult too if it challenges the practices of those around them. Raising the questions that are inevitable from such reflection can be threatening and may sometimes contribute to a loss of community with peers.

This leads to a second assumption: the process of critical reflection needs to be a collaborative one that involves colleagues. The conversations and brainstorming sessions that will occur affect not only the individuals directly involved but their entire unit, and naturally if everyone is involved in the conversation the implicit threats that surround any forthcoming changes are diminished. Collaboration also provides a wider range of perspectives and insights, which strengthens the whole process. In addition, it contributes to the momentum that is necessary not only to implement but to sustain any meaningful change, which leads to the third and final assumption—one about time. We are talking about processes of reflection and subsequent change that will be in development over a period of time. There will be few epiphanies. Changes will more than likely be gradual and may involve many false starts, but it is the process itself that is so vital to the eventual transformation.

One final word about students is in order before we describe the process: students do not directly participate in the change process we describe, but that doesn't mean their input is insignificant. We have chosen to develop a model and a procedure focused on collaboration among colleagues. Another model or an extension of this one that involves students in the process must be considered for any overall change to be complete.

ReCreate: A Change Model

Although the process of change is somewhat different for everyone, there are basic components that can facilitate its effectiveness. The model outlined here includes five basic components or steps; we describe these sequentially, but they can be connected and applied in a variety of ways, depending on a particular environment and the level of change that is desired.

Step 1: Review Principles to Establish Focus

To begin, it helps to focus on one area of practice when exploring new avenues or integrating novel ideas. It could be accommodating the range of learning styles students bring to class each term or perhaps how students' levels of self-esteem affect their ability to learn. Whatever the area chosen, it is important to articulate it in a positive way. For instance rather than saying, "These students don't respond to my methods; what's wrong with them?," a better focus is, "My style of communicating with these students doesn't seem to be working; maybe I can try to understand how they approach learning and adapt my style to meet more of their needs." Not only does this create a more positive focus, but it places the responsibility for change on the practitioner. It makes the teacher's behavior the focus rather than that of the students. Although the students' needs act as the driving force behind the change, the teacher (not students) makes a conscious decision to transform an aspect of practice.

Using learning styles as an example of an area on which to focus, a review of principles such as those in Chapter Nine might provide a convenient starting place. Also, the examples of how the principles were applied to Chapter One case studies provide a framework for reflecting on one's current strategies and effectiveness with students. Reading additional literature on learning styles and seeking out experts in the field to interview would also help enhance a thoughtful review of the possibilities for change.

Throughout this process, it is important talk to colleagues about the reflections and readings in order to gather their ideas too. It can be energizing to add a professional development component to regularly scheduled unit meetings. Spending some time discussing a topic, such as learning styles, that affects the entire unit and encouraging everyone to share how they deal with it in their work is a worthwhile endeavor. This could develop into a regular feature of the meeting, or it could lead to smaller and more focused groups in which readings are discussed and strategies shared. Collaboration like this will create a wider lens through which to view one's work and facilitate the further development of ideas.

Once a focus and a system for collaboration are established, there is a framework for the critical examination of an aspect of practice. Having such a focus will facilitate the likelihood that behaviors will change. If thinking is limited to generalities and abstract terms about change, the process becomes overwhelming and one may give up before really beginning a critical examination. A concrete place to start will enhance the process of critical reflection. This does not mean that change is isolated; rather, it simply needs a place to begin. Once it begins, it certainly will affect other aspects of practice, which eventually must be reviewed with a critical eye as well.

Step 2: Critically Reflect on Practice

To critically reflect on any one aspect of practice, it is necessary to continue digging. The next step after establishing a focus is to examine the assumptions that underlie the belief systems at the heart of anyone's practice. This is more difficult because how individuals behave reflects how they see and present themselves to the outside world. Individuals need to be willing at this stage to deconstruct long-held habits of behavior by looking beyond the behavior itself to their own self-image and examining why they do what they do.

For instance, if material is automatically presented to students in a lecture format, it is not enough to simply decide to incorporate more small-group activities into the learning environment. Teachers must think through why they decided to rely on lectures in the first place. Was it because that is how they were taught? Or was it because they think there is so much material that it is the only efficient way to get it out to students? Or is it really a lack of trust in the students to understand it independently? Is the image they have of themselves as a teacher wrapped up in standing before a class as an authority figure and delivering a lecture? Will the students think less of them if they turn some of the responsibility for learning over to them? The answers to these questions form the assumptions that determine behaviors, and unless the teacher begins with them, any changes made will likely be temporary ones.

One practical way to begin thinking about these issues critically is to write out "critical incidents" (Brookfield, 1987) based on experiences with students. These notes can help bring about a concrete look at the focus identified earlier and can also act as a preliminary step to brainstorming with colleagues or pursuing a process of self-reflection that may be continued personally. Frequently this strategy is limited to negative experiences, but if positive experiences are also included, it may be easier to see a contrast and perhaps envision a starting place for change.

One can begin by thinking back over the last several months of work. Having already identified a focus area, experiences should be limited to those related to it. Listing three experiences that left one with the feeling that something was not working or that teaching was not accomplishing what was intended can be the first set of critical incidents. Following this, three experiences in which everything seemed to work well can be identified. After six experiences have been articulated, a brief description of each one can be written to include when and where they took place, who was involved, and, most important, what the most significant aspect of the experience was.

If this is being done with a group of colleagues, the next step would be to read aloud from the descriptions. Although this may seem intimidating at first, one will quickly discover that experiences are probably not unique; most have commonalities. What may be discovered, however, is that the criteria being applied to determine success may differ among colleagues. If this is so, before proceeding any further the group will probably want to look at this in more detail.

For instance, if one person is measuring successful performance by the test scores of students but colleagues are using a different measure (for example, end-of-the-term student evaluations of their teaching), this is a significant enough difference to warrant an in-depth discussion. This "criteria analysis," as Brookfield (1987) labels it, is important for the whole unit. The criteria by which performance is measured personally as well as with students not only affect an individual's behavior but they reflect the values and philosophy of the whole unit. For this reason, there needs to be a range of consistency and consensus among those in the unit.

Discussions that come out of these types of analyses exemplify how significant the change process is and how it can ultimately lead to a strengthening of collegial communities. It also underscores the amount of time and energy that can go into the overall process. Coming to consensus on issues such as this one takes time and may include some uncomfortable sessions as it is thrashed out within the group.

Once there is agreement on what constitutes successful and not-so-successful experiences, the group can begin to construct lists of behaviors that fall into each category. For example, if the focus is on ways of knowing, the list of successful experiences could include the following: collaborative groups were formed and seemed to be actively engaged; student feedback on the collaboration was positive; collaborative projects were completed more creatively than those completed individually. Using the same focus of collaborative learning, a list of not-so-successful experiences could include the following: collaborative groups seemed "lost"; one person seemed to do all the work in the group; class attendance dropped significantly when collaborative projects were assigned.

So far the process has not gone much beyond looking at external behaviors. Time has been devoted to reflections on past behaviors related to successes and failures. By doing this after an interval of time has elapsed, experiences have been analyzed with less emotion than when they originally occurred. This helps to provide a clearer perspective and may also lead to some change simply by the increased level of self-awareness that has developed and also by the sharing with colleagues. This change may be short-lived, however, unless the process is continued and the underlying assumptions that drive the behaviors are examined carefully.

Identifying assumptions is a more complicated endeavor than reviewing experiences. Many of them are so deeply ingrained that several layers must be uncovered to find them. Brookfield (1995) suggests that when hunting for these assumptions, there are three layers to examine. The easiest one to identify is that of causal assumptions—those directly linked to the strategies used. For instance, collaborative groups may be used with students because of the assumption that small-group work will lead all participants to become active information processors.

Digging a little bit further, it is very likely that another assumption drives this one. This next layer, referred to as prescriptive, may contain the assumption that collaboration equals activity. In other words, there is a belief that collaborative activities are necessary for active learning to occur with students. Going beyond this and operating at the very deepest level are the assumptions that ultimately drive everything else. These are the paradigmatic assumptions. They connect all activities in the learning environment to a general, overall framework because it is believed students learn best within this framework.

Once these assumptions have been uncovered, it is time to go back to the earlier experiences and reexamine them within this new contextual framework. Let's take the example of not-so-successful experiences with collaborative projects and look at it through the levels of assumptions we have just discussed. Remember how one of these less-than-successful experiences described attendance being lower at sessions where collaboration was an expected activity? Assuming this actually happened, it was truly a mystery to the instructor who was involved because she felt that these activities should naturally be lively and stimulating for her students. She believed that for learning to occur, it must actively engage the learner which, of course, included more than listening to a lecture (paradigmatic assumption). Forming groups of students and giving them a task to complete together would naturally lead to active engagement (prescriptive assumption), and this would in turn increase each student's ability to become an active information processor (causal assumption).

It wasn't until a student came loudly barging into the instructor's office after class one day that she even considered the collaborative activities to be less than successful. The student, however, was angry and accused her of not doing her job as a teacher; rather, she was using his peers to teach him what he had paid tuition to learn from her. He contended that his fellow students didn't know any more than he did, and the class was simply a waste of his time. He wasn't planning to come back.

Alone in her office following this encounter, the instructor's first reaction was anger. After all, she was experienced and considered herself to be aware of current learning theory. She knew what she was doing, or at least she thought she did. She assumed that her students respected her for trusting them to work independently with little direction. Because she worked very hard at being a facilitator in the classroom rather than a lecturer, she was hurt to be told she was not doing her job. As her anger subsided, however, she began to hear what the student was really saying. The collaborative activities were not working for him. Why not? This is when she began to examine her own assumptions. To do this, she talked to colleagues to see what their experiences with collaborative learning had been. She also reviewed current literature related to collaboration in the classroom.

What she found surprised her and led her back to her assumptions. At the paradigmatic and prescriptive levels, she began to realize that perhaps her definition of active learning was too narrow. Although she still believed that active learning was a goal, the literature suggested that students could be actively engaged as they sat quietly and listened to a lecture. Taking notes, for instance, can be a very active form of engagement, depending on the students and their styles. In fact, for some of her students, probably including the protestor, the noise level surrounding some collaborative activities might impede their ability to process information. It could also create anxieties and confusion if not clearly structured and monitored.

This led her to think about exactly how she had structured the collaboration that she expected from her students. At this causal level of assumptions, she found that she had given very little thought to this aspect of it. She had simply assumed that collaboration was a good thing and that her students would see it the same way. Now she realized there was more to it than simply assigning tasks to groups and leaving them alone to figure them out.

It is evident that this process of uncovering assumptions is an arduous one. It takes time and includes personal reflection and reading as well as discussions with colleagues. It most likely involves both denial and rationalization at first because it really does get at the heart of the belief systems that shape one's practice and sense of professionalism. Ultimately it leaves a set of assumptions that can be examined, refined, and perhaps reaffirmed. Once this point has been reached, however, some real and permanent changes can be considered.

Step 3: Evaluate Practice

The process of evaluation has, of course, already started as one's self-awareness has been increased through thoughtful reflection. Colleagues have been included and learning has taken place, individually through informal conversations and collectively through brainstorming and examining overall values. Now the lens needs to open even further by inviting someone who is trusted to provide critical feedback on one's interaction with students in the learning environment. Ideally, a culture of trust has been built through the process of critical reflection, and colleagues will be enthusiastic, not threatened, about this next crucial stage of development.

What is the best way to structure a component of critical feedback? One way to begin is to continue the process of self-evaluation by analyzing behavior in a particular area through a written survey that outlines observable activities. (The surveys that appear at the end this chapter provide examples.) It is best to concentrate this self-evaluation on one area to encourage a more in-depth analysis rather than looking at an entire range of behaviors in a broader, more diluted manner.

To help objectify this process of self-evaluation, providing examples for each ranked behavior is useful. If such examples cannot be generated, that may suggest that an activity is not happening and deserves further examination. Once this individual analysis has been completed, it will be easier to assess current strengths and areas that need development. At this point, inviting a colleague into the conversation will move the process to the next stage of evaluation.

Finding a colleague who is perceived to be strong in the areas that need development is one way of deciding whom to invite, but if this is not feasible, another approach may be to simply identify someone who is a good listener and who is willing to spend the time it takes to provide valuable feedback. Once the appropriate colleague has been identified, arranging an informal meeting to discuss mutual expectations for the process is the next step. Details such as the best time for a class visit, the amount of time for the visit, the focus of the visit, the format for feedback, and the outcomes expected by both colleagues need to be clarified ahead of time. For example, a set of expectations could include setting a time during the following week when a visit to a designated class could be arranged. The focus could be to pay careful attention to the nature of the collaborative groups in the class. Following the class visit, the feedback would be provided through a written analysis, followed up by a meeting to discuss the comments. The expectation for that meeting would be to discuss specific ideas for incorporating change.

This can work in other ways, but what is most important is developing a process that both agree to at the outset. Providing a written survey to the colleague who will be visiting helps establish common guidelines and can be most effective if it is the same survey that was used for the self-assessment. Reviewing the survey together before the visit ensures that both individuals have a similar understanding of the terms and criteria.

The surveys found in this chapter (see Exhibits 1 through 6 at the end of the chapter) have been organized and adapted from the sets of principles developed in Part Two within the following areas: self and identity, motivation, interaction with the environment, ways of knowing, learning styles and preferences, and self-regulation and goal setting. Some of the principles have been combined, whereas others have been divided into separate parts in order to provide discrete, observable behaviors. These surveys can be used as-is or as models that can be adapted to meet individual needs.

Step 4: Analyze Evaluation Results

Soon after the class visit, while memories are still fresh, it is helpful to sit down and compare notes with the colleague who visited. A discussion followed by written comments helps to ensure mutual understanding and produces a permanent record for future reference. It is always interesting to review the earlier self-assessment at this point to look for any significant discrepancies.

During the discussion, the "examples" section from both the visitor's survey and the self-assessment document deserves the most attention. Does the visitor have similar examples to those of the teacher? Does the visitor include examples of behavior that were unknown altogether to the teacher? As the examples are analyzed in detail, specific suggestions for change will emerge. If some examples seem confusing or in conflict, another source for input at this point is the students themselves. Depending on the level of sensitivity, this feedback could be solicited anonymously in writing or gathered orally by someone other than the teacher.

An additional source of information is another classroom. With a clear focus in mind and specific examples from one's own teaching for comparison, observing someone else may provide the missing link to move the analysis forward into an action plan.

Step 5: Incorporate New Teaching Behaviors into Practice

Let's assume that from the readings and reflections completed and from the examples provided through the surveys it has been determined that collaborative activities need more structure. What criteria can be used to measure success in providing this structure? A list can be developed that will help design a new format for the collaborative experiences with students. In this case, the list of criteria might include the following: students will demonstrate understanding of the assignment before they begin working; students will know how to work together to complete this assignment; the project will be broken into smaller tasks.

Knowing how to measure success, one can now sit down with old activities and begin to revise them. For instance, instead of simply providing verbal instructions to students grouped for collaboration, one could write out specific directions with the task outlined clearly in a written format. In addition, a time line could be provided to the students for completing each part of the assignment; suggestions for assigning specific roles of responsibility to group members could also be provided. A system for adjusting individual credit based on level of participation could also be built in at this point.

These are very specific plans of action related to one area of practice, and it will take time to fully integrate them. Keeping a journal related to these changes helps during this time of transition. This can include a short descriptive narrative following each session that includes the new activities. The narrative can follow a format similar to the earlier critical incident notes detailing who was involved, where, and when activities took place, as well as the significant aspects. This will help make progress more visible.

Once one feels a level of confidence related to the change, it is time to invite a colleague to visit again and to provide additional feedback. The more description provided prior to the visit that is related to the intended change, the more meaningful the feedback will be. The criteria that have been developed as a framework for the change should also be shared, so examples can be noted of how each one is being met.

Is this the end? Once colleagues have reinforced that a particular change has successfully been implemented, is the process of critical reflection finished? The answer is a resounding *no.* This is only the beginning. For one thing, the change that has been incorporated is likely to affect other aspects of teaching that also need to be considered and possibly refined. Second, the process of critically thinking about practice and looking for the assumptions that drive behaviors will continue to be influential. There should never be room for complacency again. Also, the process probably has engaged everyone enough so that the entire unit will continue to regularly review its practices and conduct professional development sessions routinely.

Exhibit 1. Self and Identity Survey.

Please indicate the frequency with which the following principles are present in the current learning environment. Following each principle, provide at least one example to describe what you mean.

1	2	3	4	5
always	frequently	sometimes	rarely	never

1. Issues of self-esteem are addressed
   to reduce anxiety in learning.
   Example:

   | 1 | 2 | 3 | 4 | 5 |
   | O | O | O | O | O |

_____

2. Environment is accepting and provides
   consistent and positive feedback.
   Example:

   | 1 | 2 | 3 | 4 | 5 |
   | O | O | O | O | O |

_____

3. Self-efficacy beliefs are discussed and
   linked to realistic self-assessments.
   Example:

   | 1 | 2 | 3 | 4 | 5 |
   | O | O | O | O | O |

_____

4. Opportunities exist for active involvement
   in order to promote positive self-concept
   development.
   Example:

   | 1 | 2 | 3 | 4 | 5 |
   | O | O | O | O | O |

_____

5. Encouragement is given to help develop
   positive self-images.
   Example:

   | 1 | 2 | 3 | 4 | 5 |
   | O | O | O | O | O |

_____

6. Support is provided to develop identity
   achievement, self-confidence, and maturity.
   Example:

   | 1 | 2 | 3 | 4 | 5 |
   | O | O | O | O | O |

_____

7. Different developmental patterns and factors
   related to diversity are taken into account.
   Example:

   | 1 | 2 | 3 | 4 | 5 |
   | O | O | O | O | O |

_____

Exhibit 2. Motivation Survey.

Please indicate the frequency with which the following principles are present in the current learning environment. Following each principle, provide at least one example to describe what you mean.

1	2	3	4	5
always	frequently	sometimes	rarely	never

1. Students are encouraged to develop mastery goals in order to increase engagement in learning.

    1 2 3 4 5
    ○ ○ ○ ○ ○

    Example:

    _____

2. Consistent feedback is given regarding goal attainment.

    1 2 3 4 5
    ○ ○ ○ ○ ○

    Example:

    _____

3. Individual choice and control is encouraged in learning activities.

    1 2 3 4 5
    ○ ○ ○ ○ ○

    Example:

    _____

4. Self-worth beliefs are considered in learning assignments.

    1 2 3 4 5
    ○ ○ ○ ○ ○

    Example:

    _____

5. Opportunities are provided for peers to model effective learning.

    1 2 3 4 5
    ○ ○ ○ ○ ○

    Example:

    _____

Exhibit 3. Interaction with the Environment Survey.

Please indicate the frequency with which the following principles are present in the current learning environment. Following each principle, provide at least one example to describe what you mean.

1	2	3	4	5
always	frequently	sometimes	rarely	never

1. Concrete examples and practical applications are suggested to help learners connect their prior knowledge to new information.
   Example:

   1 2 3 4 5
   ○ ○ ○ ○ ○

2. Opportunities are provided for social integration and community building.
   Example:

   1 2 3 4 5
   ○ ○ ○ ○ ○

3. Critical dialogue, integrative learning, and risk taking are part of the learning environment.
   Example:

   1 2 3 4 5
   ○ ○ ○ ○ ○

4. Peer teaching is promoted.
   Example:

   1 2 3 4 5
   ○ ○ ○ ○ ○

5. Adult learners are provided assignments requiring self-direction.
   Example:

   1 2 3 4 5
   ○ ○ ○ ○ ○

6. Students with disabilities are encouraged to self-identify and receive necessary accommodations.
   Example:

   1 2 3 4 5
   ○ ○ ○ ○ ○

7. Instruction considers diverse cultural backgrounds.
   Example:

   1 2 3 4 5
   ○ ○ ○ ○ ○

Exhibit 4. Ways of Knowing Survey.

Please indicate the frequency with which the following principles are present in the current learning environment. Following each principle, provide at least one example to describe what you mean.

1	2	3	4	5
always	frequently	sometimes	rarely	never

1. Activities are provided to facilitate students' development across cognitive stages.

    1   2   3   4   5
    O   O   O   O   O

    Example:

    _____

2. Challenges for cognitive development are provided within a supportive system.

    1   2   3   4   5
    O   O   O   O   O

    Example:

    _____

3. Working in groups is encouraged to enhance learning outcomes.

    1   2   3   4   5
    O   O   O   O   O

    Example:

    _____

4. A variety of intelligences is acknowledged and valued.

    1   2   3   4   5
    O   O   O   O   O

    Example:

    _____

5. A teacher-student relationship of collaboration is evident.

    1   2   3   4   5
    O   O   O   O   O

    Example:

    _____

Exhibit 5. Learning Styles and Preferences Survey.

Please indicate the frequency with which the following principles are present in the current learning environment. Following each principle, provide at least one example to describe what you mean.

1	2	3	4	5
always	frequently	sometimes	rarely	never

1. Cultural transitions are provided for students by giving them opportunities to link their personal experiences to the learning environment.
Example:

| 1 | 2 | 3 | 4 | 5 |
| O | O | O | O | O |

_____

2. Different cultural styles of communication in the learning environment are recognized and respected.
Example:

| 1 | 2 | 3 | 4 | 5 |
| O | O | O | O | O |

_____

3. Sensitivity to cultural differences is evident.
Example:

| 1 | 2 | 3 | 4 | 5 |
| O | O | O | O | O |

_____

4. Recognition is evident that all learners from particular cultures are individuals and do not necessarily share similar patterns of expectations or behavior.
Example:

| 1 | 2 | 3 | 4 | 5 |
| O | O | O | O | O |

_____

5. Different approaches to learning and processing information are valued.
Example:

| 1 | 2 | 3 | 4 | 5 |
| O | O | O | O | O |

_____

6. A range of instructional styles is provided to accommodate the range of student learning styles.
Example:

| 1 | 2 | 3 | 4 | 5 |
| O | O | O | O | O |

_____

7. Direct instruction related to learning strategies is provided.
Example:

| 1 | 2 | 3 | 4 | 5 |
| O | O | O | O | O |

_____

Exhibit 6. Self-Regulation and Goal-Setting Survey.

Please indicate the frequency with which the following principles are present in the current learning environment. Following each principle, provide at least one example to describe what you mean.

1	2	3	4	5
always	frequently	sometimes	rarely	never

1. Self-regulated learning is encouraged in order for students to control their learning.
   Example:

   1 2 3 4 5
   ○ ○ ○ ○ ○

2. Learners are encouraged to make a direct connection between their use of strategies and subsequent outcomes.
   Example:

   1 2 3 4 5
   ○ ○ ○ ○ ○

3. Learners are encouraged to set learning goals that enhance motivation.
   Example:

   1 2 3 4 5
   ○ ○ ○ ○ ○

4. Learners are encouraged to access their prior knowledge as it connects to content.
   Example:

   1 2 3 4 5
   ○ ○ ○ ○ ○

5. Learners' sense of self-efficacy is addressed and strategies are used to help strengthen it.
   Example:

   1 2 3 4 5
   ○ ○ ○ ○ ○

6. Instruction is provided with authentic materials.
   Example:

   1 2 3 4 5
   ○ ○ ○ ○ ○

7. Learners are given opportunities to build an internal commitment to the usefulness of self-regulation.
   Example:

   1 2 3 4 5
   ○ ○ ○ ○ ○

Chapter Twelve

Educator as Innovator, Researcher, and Change Agent

Throughout this book we have emphasized the need to integrate theory and research into practice. We began with a view of students today; we then looked at theories related to six topics in student learning and development: self and identity, motivation, environmental interactions, ways of knowing, learning styles, and self-regulation and goal setting. In Part Two, we summarized research related to these topics and used the TRPP model to develop principles and apply research findings to case studies. Finally, in Chapter Eleven we provided a framework for transforming practice. Now we look forward and examine what is known and not known about student learning and development, suggest some specific questions for further exploration, and discuss an expanded role of educator as researcher, innovator, and change agent for the years ahead.

It is not enough to be content to practice as before. Teaching and learning are dynamic activities that are always responding to changing conditions and situations. Furthermore, teachers cannot bring about change alone. Looking forward, we see learning in postsecondary education as a complex undertaking involving teachers, administrators, staff, and the students themselves. Cross (1998) talks about learning communities and puts forth a "changing philosophy of knowledge" (p. 4). She refers to the changing view of knowledge as a fundamental revolution in thinking that pits opposing beliefs against each other: egalitarianism versus hierarchies, collaboration versus competitiveness, and active learning versus passive acceptance.

Most important, recent research indicates that effective instruction is learner-centered, with the learner sharing responsibility for educational activities. No longer is the banking approach—the teacher deposits knowledge and the learner receives or withdraws it—to education accepted. The move to learner-centered education has profound implications for how classrooms are conducted, how learning occurs now, and how it will occur in the future. Although the lecture remains a prominent approach, too often it is supportive of the banking approach unless it is combined with other, more interactive, ways of processing material.

The idea of taking learning seriously was a major theme at the March 1998 meeting of the American Association for Higher Education (AAHE). The association announced that what is said about learning and student-centeredness is not evidenced in reality. A call is being made for a shift from the instruction paradigm to the learning paradigm. Theory and research on student learning and development provide a foundation for moving practice closer to the learning paradigm, but many questions remain. We will raise some of the questions as they arise around each of our major topics.

Self and Identity

Although recent research has advanced knowledge about self and identity, much is still unknown. The work of Chickering (1969) and Chickering and Reisser (1993), along with that of Erikson (1968) and Josselson (1987) conceptualizes identity as a psychosocial process involving the encounter of challenges and reactions to them. Others have viewed identity development primarily as a cognitive process whereby identity is defined through the process of thinking as one makes meaning of one's experiences (Loevinger, 1976).

It is likely that both of these perspectives operate uniquely with individuals at different times and in various situations. How does a student become more fully formed as a person and identify meaningful goals for life? It is known that women and persons of color form their identities in unique ways, but what processes dominate in their identity formation, and how do different processes interact?

Postsecondary education plays a role in helping students develop their self-concepts and identities as fully formed, mature persons.

Future research is needed to provide information on the various ways student cultures and peer relationships contribute to this development.

Motivation

Much is known about what motivates students. Goals, self-perceptions, and contextual factors play roles in motivation. Furthermore, interests, values, and expectancies affect it. The work of Covington and Omelich (1991) has provided us with typologies for the success-oriented student, the failure-avoider, the failure-accepter, and the overstriver. Although it is helpful to know the dynamics of motivation for each of these types of learners, it is not fully known how to move a failure-avoider or failure-accepter toward success-oriented behavior. The process of transformation from failure to success is complex. Further research in the mechanisms of change is needed to better understand how to promote growth and development. If, as expected, belief systems must be changed in order to move from failure to success, what can teachers do to achieve this?

Finally, given the role of culture, context, and gender in motivation, how do persons from different cultures adjust to learning when they are in unfamiliar situations? What effect does a foreign culture have on one's motivation to learn, and how does this vary across cultures and contexts? With increasing globalization, this question takes on particular significance. Students more freely access education in countries and cultures different from their own, and this is likely to increase as international exchange and cooperation expand at all levels in our society. Educational and work settings are equally affected by this phenomenon, so the issue of motivation as it concerns learning and work is important in many different contexts.

Interaction with the Environment

Environmental factors, including teaching behaviors, classroom climate, sense of community, peer teaching, and engagement in learning, are prominent in the discussion of enhancing learning and development. The importance of mentoring emerges in many studies of environmental interaction. Further exploration into the process of mentoring, the training of mentors, and how mentoring affects self-concept, identity, and motivation are of critical importance.

The role of the environment with specific student populations continues to be of great interest. As more students with disabilities, adults, and students of color pursue advanced education, it is important to be mindful of features of the environment that affect them. Padilla's (1991, 1994) work shows how successful students of color interact with the environment to be successful. It is important to study other groups of successful students, including women, adults, and students with disabilities, to better understand their coping mechanisms in order to help students who continue to struggle.

The engagement approach to learning (Haworth and Conrad, 1997) includes the idea of connected program requirements. This relates to the notion of learning communities where individuals interact together to pursue learning. Much interest is centered on the development of learning communities in higher education, but we need to know more about how they are effectively constructed, what problems are likely to occur, and which are the best methods for addressing these issues. The development of learning communities is a relatively new phenomenon. Such communities have the potential for promoting increased collaboration and active learning, but the process of developing and implementing them has not been fully assessed and understood.

Finally, research on environmental interaction emphasizes the importance of specific teacher behaviors that promote learning. Teaching behaviors in collaborative learning situations is an area for continued study and investigation. How do teachers help students overcome resistance to active participation and the expectation that learning is receiving information and not constructing it? How, exactly, is this accomplished, and are these approaches the same across all disciplines? Critical dialogue, integrative learning, and risk taking are central to enhanced learning, but how is this achieved in and out of the classroom?

Ways of Knowing

A great deal is known about how students learn. In Chapter Eight we discussed the notion of cognitive development and specifically the work of stage theorists and researchers who promote better understanding of the way learning takes place. We continued with a conversation about intelligence and differing notions of its meaning, including ideas about multiple intelligences and emotional intelligence. We stressed that intelligence is more than a unitary factor and operates in many different ways. Finally, we emphasized that knowledge is constructed through the process of active learning.

However, questions persist. For example, how are active learning and collaboration affected by new technology in instruction? With a diverse student population, how is the work of cognitive stage theorists like Perry relevant to these students? Knowing that emotional intelligence is important in learning, how is it integrated with cognitive development, and what instructional settings best promote this integration? Last, the idea of multiple intelligences and the importance of context in learning is particularly intriguing. The work of Gardner (1983, 1990, 1994) was conducted primarily on children, but the learning phenomena of older adolescents and adults must still be explored. The questions continue to emerge, and we have presented only a few for further exploration.

Learning Styles and Preferences

We discussed learning styles and preferences in Chapter Nine from three perspectives: cultural, physiological, and personality-based. From the cultural framework we know that differences exist in the way people from diverse backgrounds approach learning. Physiologically, learners have been described as left-brain or right-brain learners, and distinct differences are evident in the way the two types of learners process information. The work of Witkin (1976) addresses styles and preferences from the perspective of personality, indicating that a predisposition to process from either a field-dependent or field-independent position is prevalent in individuals. Finally, differing instructional styles and preferences are evident in that they either fit or challenge the learning styles of students experiencing them.

Knowledge of learning styles and preferences needs to be expanded to include more research with adults and diverse populations. In addition, more needs to be known about how different learning and teaching styles interact in order to better meet the needs of a diverse student body. Most of the research in learning styles and preferences describes students but does not tell enough about how to address differences. Classroom research is needed to address the question of how best to meet learning style preferences and how to provide environments that promote flexibility and adaptation when preferences are not supported. Finally, the construct "learning styles" is conceived of differently by researchers. The various notions and constructs need to be examined more fully with an eye to determining how the components of different constructs are linked and interact within one person.

Self-Regulation and Goal Setting

Self-regulated learners are those who see the relationship between strategies used and outcomes realized. They set goals for themselves and know how to go about achieving them. The use of self-regulatory strategies is complex and develops over time. It is not expected that learners easily acquire self-regulatory behavior. Sometimes self-regulation is achieved in one learning situation but not readily transferred to another.

Self-regulated learning can be taught, but learners must be motivated to learn it. In addition, prerequisite knowledge and understanding of the task must be present in order for self-regulation strategies to be useful.

Much still needs to be learned about how self-regulation occurs and how it transfers across different content areas. Furthermore, it is important to determine how students can be helped to see the connection between personal self-control over learning and the positive outcomes that result. Finally, ways must be explored to help students see the value of setting mastery goals over performance goals because we know that mastery goals are more likely to promote successful achievement.

Educator as Innovator, Researcher, and Change Agent

The primary purpose of this book is to review theory and research as it applies to teaching in order to enhance learning and development for all students in postsecondary education. Research has shown that teachers are an integral part of the education process, but they do not function alone. Even so, they are primary players and exert significant influence in how learning takes place. It is our position that new directions for teaching and learning include the evolution of teacher as innovator, researcher, and change agent. Each of these roles is presented here, with suggestions for how teachers need to function in these capacities.

Educator as innovator involves the notion that past ways of teaching are not enough. The traditional lecture is not effective in and of itself and must be complemented by interactive student engagement, critical dialogue, and more active learning approaches, including collaborative learning, to meet the needs of all students. The innovator role requires an openness to examine past approaches and an element of risk taking. In Chapter Eleven, we provided a framework called RE-CREATE including five components to guide the process of innovation. We define the role of innovator as one who applies research principles to practice in a dynamic way, questions what works and what doesn't, and finds new approaches to addressing challenges in teaching and learning.

Educator as researcher includes the idea of classroom as laboratory. Students are carefully considered for fuller understanding, and learning tasks are evaluated to determine their effectiveness in different settings and with diverse populations. Learning outcomes are identified and evaluated as they contribute to enhanced learning and development. We stress that the assumption of one way for all be discarded and replaced with different approaches for different needs.

Educator as change agent is a natural outgrowth of the innovator and researcher roles. To be a change agent one must be open to innovation and be concerned with the effectiveness of new ways. Change agents challenge the status quo. They are not satisfied with repeating past successes or accepting failures. Most important, they motivate themselves and others, including students, administrators, and colleagues, to explore new directions and take risks. We support this view as a foundation for making changes in practice and using theory and research to guide the way.

References

Adams, M., & Zhou-McGovern, Y. (1994). *The sociomoral development of undergraduates in a 'social diversity' course: Developmental theory, research and instructional applications.* Paper presented at the annual meeting of the American Educational Research Association, New Orleans.

Adelman, P. B., & Vogel, S. A. (1990). College graduates with learning disabilities: Employment attainment and career patterns. *Learning Disability Quarterly, 13,* 154–166.

Alexander, P. A. (1995). Superimposing a situation-specific and domain-specific perspective on an account of self-regulated learning. *Educational Psychologist. 30,* 189–193.

Alexander, R. A., & Barrett, G. V. (1982). Equitable salary increase judgments based upon merit and non-merit considerations: A cross-cultural comparison. *International Review of Applied Psychology, 31,* 443–454.

Ames, C. (1990). Motivation: What teachers need to know. *Teachers College Record, 91,* 409–421.

Apps, J. W. (1988). Adult education and the learning society. *Educational Considerations, 14*(2–3), 14–18.

Arnold, K. (1996). *Lives of promise: What becomes of high school valedictorians.* San Francisco: Jossey-Bass.

Astin, A. (1982). *Minorities in American higher education: Recent trends, current prospects, and recommendations.* San Francisco: Jossey-Bass.

Astin, A. W. (1993). *What matters in college: Four critical years revisited.* San Francisco: Jossey-Bass.

Atkinson, J. W. (1964). *An introduction to motivation.* Princeton, NJ: Van Nostrand.

Atkinson, J. W., & Feather, N. T. (1966). *N.T.A. theory of achievement motivation.* New York: Wiley.

Bachman, J. G., & O'Malley, P. M. (1986). Self-concepts, self-esteem, and educational experiences: The frog pond revisited (again). *Journal of Personality and Social Psychology, 50,* 35–46.

Baker, H. (1987). Underachievement and failure in college: The interaction between intrapsychic and interpersonal factors from the perspectives of self psychology. *Adolescent Psychiatry, 14,* 441–460.

Bandura, A. (1977). Self-efficacy: Toward a unifying theory of behavior change. *Psychological Review, 84,* 191–215.

Bandura, A. (1982). Self-efficacy mechanism in human agency. *American Psychologist, 37,* 122–147.

Bandura, A. (1986). *Social foundations of thought and action: A social cognitive theory.* Englewood Cliffs, NJ: Prentice Hall.

Bandura, A. (1989). Conclusion: Reflections on nonability determinants of competence. In R. J. Sternberg & Kolligian, J. (Eds.), *Competence considered.* New Haven, CT: Yale University Press.

Barnett, J. E. (1997). *Self-regulation of reading college textbooks.* Paper presented at the annual meeting of the American Educational Research Association (AERA). Chicago, IL.

Baxter Magolda, M. B. (1988). Measuring gender differences in intellectual development: A comparison of assessment methods. *Journal of College Student Development, 29,* 528–537.

Baxter Magolda, M. B. (1992). *Knowing and reasoning in college: Gender-related patterns in students' intellectual development.* San Francisco: Jossey-Bass.

Baxter Magolda, M. B. (1997). *Constructive-developmental pedagogy: Linking knowledge construction and students' epistemological development.* Paper presented at the annual meeting of the American Educational Research Association, Chicago.

Baxter Magolda, M. B. (1998). *Constructing adult identities.* Paper presented at the annual meeting of the American Educational Research Association (AERA). San Diego, CA.

Belenky, M. F., Clinchy, B. M., Goldberger, N. R., & Tarule, J. M. (1986). *Women's ways of knowing: The development of self, voice, and mind.* New York: Basic Books.

Berger, J. B. (1997). *The relationship between organizational behavior at colleges and student outcomes: Generating a quantitatively grounded theory.* Unpublished doctoral dissertation. Nashville, TN: Thunderbolt University.

Berger, J. B., & Milem, J. F. (1998). *Undergraduate self-concept: Differences between historically black and predominantly white colleges.* Paper presented at the annual meeting of the American Educational Research Association. San Diego, CA.

Biggs, J. B. (1987). *Student approaches to learning and studying.* Hawthorn, Victoria: Australian Council for Educational Research.

Black, A., and Ammon, P. (1992). A developmental-constuctivist approach to teacher education. Journal of Teacher Education. V43 n5, 323–335.

Blanc, R. A., DeBuhr, L. E., & Martin, D. C. (1983). Breaking the attrition cycle: The effects of supplemental instruction on undergraduate performance and attrition. *Journal of Higher Education, 54*(1), 80–90.

Blimling, G. S. (1993). The influence of college residence halls on students. In J. Smart (Ed.), *Higher education: Handbook of theory and research* (pp. 356–396). New York: Agathon Press.

Blohm, P. J., & Colwell, C. G. (1984). *Effects of readers' cognitive style, text structure and signaling on different recall patterns in social studies content.* (ERIC Document Reproduction Service No. ED 237 957)

Bonham, B., & Boylan, H. (1993). A new look at learning styles. *Research in Developmental Education, 10*(4), 1–4.

Bosworth, K. (1994). Developing collaborative skills in college students. In K. Bosworth & S. J. Hamilton (Eds.), *Collaborative techniques.* (New Directions for Teaching and Learning, No. 59). San Francisco: Jossey-Bass.

Boyer, E. L. (1987). *College: The undergraduate experience in America.* New York: Harper & Row.

Branch-Simpson, G. (1984). A study of the patterns in the development of black students at the Ohio State University. *Dissertations Abstracts International, 45*, 2422A.

Braxton, J., Brier, E., Herzog, L., & Pascarella, E. T. (1988). *Occupational attainment in the professions: The effects of college origins and college experiences on becoming a lawyer.* Paper presented at a meeting of the Association for the Study of Higher Education, St. Louis.

Brennan, J., & McGeever, P. (1988). *Graduates at work: Degree courses and the labour market.* London: Jessica Kingsley.

Brockett, R. G., & Hiemstra, R. (1991). *Self-direction in adult learning: Perspectives on theory, research, and practice.* London and New York: Routledge & Kegan Paul.

Brookfield, S. D. (1986). *Understanding and facilitating adult learning: A comprehensive analysis of principles and effective practices.* San Francisco: Jossey-Bass.

Brookfield, S. D. (1987). *Developing critical thinkers: Challenging adults to explore alternative ways of thinking and acting.* San Francisco: Jossey-Bass.

Brookfield, S. D. (1990). *The skillful teacher: On technique, trust, and responsiveness in the classroom.* San Francisco: Jossey-Bass.

Brookfield, S. D. (1995). *Becoming a critically reflective teacher.* San Francisco: Jossey-Bass.

Brophy, J., & Good, T. L. (1986). Teacher behavior and student achievement. In M. C. Wittrock (Ed.), *Handbook of research on teaching* (3rd ed.). New York: MacMillan.

Brown, A. L., Armbruster, B. B., & Baker, L. (1986). The role of metacognition in reading and studying. In J. Orasanu (Ed.), *Reading comprehension: From research to practice.* Hillsdale, NJ: Erlbaum.

Brown, B., Steinberg, L., Mounts, N., & Phillips, M. (1990). *The comparative influence of peers and parents on high school achievement: Ethnic differences.* Paper presented at the biennial meeting of the Society for Research on Adolescence, Atlanta.

Brown, J. S., Collins, A., & Duguid, P. (1989). Situated cognition and the culture of learning. *Educational Researcher,* Jan.-Feb., *18*(1), 32–42.

Brown, W. C. (1987). *Measuring tutoring effectiveness using interaction analysis research techniques.* Unpublished doctoral dissertation, University of California, Berkeley.

Brown, W. C. (1997). *Measuring tutoring effectiveness using interactive analysis research techniques.* Unpublished doctoral dissertation, University of California, Berkeley.

Browne, D. (1986). *Learning styles and Native Americans.* (ERIC Document Reproduction Service No. ED 297 906)

Bruffee, K. A. (1993). *Collaborative learning: Higher education, interdependence, and the authority of knowledge.* Baltimore: Johns Hopkins University Press, 3.

Bursuck, W. D., Rose, E., Cowen, S., & Yahaya, M. A. (1989). Nationwide survey of postsecondary education services for students with learning disabilities. *Exceptional Children, 56*(3), 236–245.

Burwell, L. B. (1991). The interaction of learning styles with learning control treatments in an interactive videodisc lesson. *Educational Technology, 31*(3), 37–43.

Butler, D. L. (1997). *The roles of goal setting and self-monitoring in students' self-regulated engagement in tasks.* Paper presented at the annual meeting of the American Educational Research Association. New Orleans, LA.

Candy, P. C. (1991). *Self-direction for lifelong learning: A comprehensive guide to theory and practice.* San Francisco: Jossey-Bass.

Canfield, A. (1988). *Canfield learning styles inventory.* Los Angeles: Western Psychological Services.

Carmen, R. A. (1975). *A long-term study of developmental mathematics.* Santa Barbara, CA: Santa Barbara City College.

Carroll, J. (1988). Freshman retention and attrition factors at a predominately black urban community college. *Journal of College Student Development, 29,* 52–59.

Carter, D. J., & Wilson, R. (1996–97). *Minorities in higher education: 15th annual status report.* Washington, DC: American Council of Education.

Carthy, J. H. (1993). *Relationships between learning styles and academic achievement and brain hemispheric dominance and academic performance in business and accounting courses.* (ERIC Reproduction Document Service No. ED 374 412)

Casazza, M. E., & Silverman, S. L. (1996). *Learning assistance and developmental education.* San Francisco: Jossey-Bass.

Center for Academic Development (1991). *Graduation rates for students who entered UN-KC, Fall 1983.* Kansas City, MO: University of Missouri-Kansas City.

Chavis, D. M., Hogge, J. H., McMillan, D. W., and Wardeisman, A. (1986). "Sense of Community through Brunswick's Lens: A First Look." *Journal of Community Psychology, 14,* 24–40.

Chen, C., Stevenson, H. W., Hayward, C., & Burgess, S. (1995). Cultural and academic achievement: Ethnic and cross-national differences. In M. L. Maehr & P. R. Pintrich (Eds.), *Advances in motivation and achievement* (pp. 119–151). Greenwich, CT: JAI Press.

Chew, C. A., & Ogi, A. Y. (1987). Asian American college student perspectives. In D. J. Wright (Ed.), *Responding to the needs of today's minority students.* (New Directions for Student Services, No. 38). San Francisco: Jossey-Bass.

Chickering, A. W. (1969). *Education and identity.* San Francisco: Jossey-Bass.

Chickering, A. W., & Reisser, L. (1993). *Education and identity.* San Francisco: Jossey-Bass.

Chisman, F. P., Wrigley, H. S., & Ewes, D. T. (1993). *ESL and the American dream.* Washington, DC: The Southport Institute for Policy Analysis.

Christensen, L. M. (1991). *Cognitive style and hemispheric dominance: Piecing the puzzle together-toward practical application in teaching the social studies.* (ERIC Document Reproduction Service No. ED 337 392)

Chronicle of Higher Education Almanac, 1998–99. Vol. XLV. No. 1. August 28, 1998. Chronicle of Higher Education, Washington, D.C.

Clinchy, B. (1994). Issues of gender in teaching and learning. In K. A. Feldman & M. B. Paulsen (Eds.), *Teaching and learning in the college classroom.* (ASHE Reader Series). New York: Ginn.

Cooper, J. L. (1995). Cooperative learning and critical thinking. *Teaching of Psychology, 22*(1), 7–9.

Covington, M. V. (1985). Ability and effort valuation among failure-avoiding and failure-accepting students. *Journal of Educational Psychology, 77,* 446–459.

Covington, M. V. (1992). *Making the grade: A self-worth perspective on motivation and school reform.* Cambridge, NY: Cambridge University Press.

Covington, M. V. (1993). A motivational analysis of academic life in college. In J. C. Smart (Ed.), *Higher education handbook of theory and research* (Vol. 9, pp. 50–93). New York. Agathon Press.

Covington, M. V., & Omelich, C. L. (1988). Achievement dynamics: The interaction of motives, cognition, and emotions over time. *Anxiety Journal, 1,* 165–183.

Covington, M. V., & Omelich, C. L. (1991). Need achievement revisited: Verification of Atkinson's original 2 × 2 model. In C. D. Spielberger, I. G. Sarason, Z. Kulcsar, & G. L. Van Heck (Eds.), *Stress and emotion: Anxiety, anger, and curiosity* (Vol. 14, pp. 85–104). Washington, DC: Hemisphere.

Coyne, J. C., & Lazarus, R. S. (1980). Cognitive style, stress perception, and coping. In I. L. Kutash & L. B. Schlesinger (Eds.), *Handbook on stress and anxiety.* San Francisco: Jossey-Bass.

Cranton, P. A., & Hillgartner, W. (1981). The relationship between student ratings and instructor behavior: Implications for improving teaching. *Canadian Journal of Higher Education, 11,* 73–81.

Crawford, J. S. (1989). *Perry levels and Belenky's findings: Their possibilities in the teaching of art and history.* Paper presented at the Getty Conference on Discipline Based Art Education, Austin, TX.

Creswell, J. L., Gifford, C., & Huffman, D. (1988). Implications of right/left brain research for mathematics educators. *School Science and Mathematics, 88*(2), 118–131.

Croker, R. E., Bobell, J., & Wilson, R. A. (1993). *Learning style, brain modality, and teaching preference of incarcerated females at the Pocatello Women's Correctional Center.* A research project presented at the annual conference of the American Vocational Association, Denver.

Cross, K. P. (1971). *Beyond the open door: New students to higher education.* San Francisco: Jossey-Bass.

Cross, K. P. (1987). Teaching for learning. *AAHE Bulletin, 39,* 3–7.

Cross, K. P. (1998). Why learning communities? Why now? *About Campus,* Jul.–Aug. (Vol. 3, pp. 4–11).

Cross, K. P., & Steadman, M. H. (1996). *Classroom research: Implementing the scholarship of teaching.* San Francisco: Jossey-Bass.

Cross, W. E., Jr. (1971). Toward a psychology of black liberation: The Negro-to-black conversion experience. *Black World, 20* (9), 13–27.

Cross, W. E., Jr. (1991). *Shades of black: Diversity in African American identity.* Philadelphia: Temple University Press.

Cross, W. E., Jr. (1995). The psychology of nigrescence: Revising the Cross model. In J. G. Ponterott, J. M. Casas, L. A. Suzuki, & C. M. Alexander (Eds.), *Handbook of multicultural counseling* (pp. 93–122). Thousand Oaks, CA: Sage.

Cuoco, A. A., and others (1996). Habits of mind: An organizing principle for mathematics curricula. *Journal of Mathematical Behavior.* Vol. 15, N4, 375–402.

Damasio, A. (1994). *Descartes' error.* New York: Grosset/Putnam.

Darkenwald, G. G. (1987). Assessing the social environment of adult classes. *Studies in the Education of Adults, 19*(2), 127–136.

Darkenwald, G. G. (1989). Enhancing the adult classroom environment. In E. Hayes (Ed.), *Effective teaching styles.* (New Directions for Continuing Education, No. 43). San Francisco: Jossey-Bass.

Davey, B. (1989). *Answering questions after reading: The effects of reader and task interactions on reading comprehension.* (ERIC Document Reproduction Service No. ED 305 650)

Davis, A. H., & Daugherty, M. S. (1992). *A framework for residence hall community development.* Unpublished manuscript. University of California, Davis.

Davison, J. E., & Sternberg, R. J. (1984). The role of insight in intellectual giftedness. *Gifted Child Quarterly, 28,* 58–64.

Dean, T. (1989). Multicultural classrooms, monocultural teachers. *College Composition and Communication, 40,* 23–37.

De Vos, G. A. (1973). *Socialization for achievement: Essays on the cultural psychology of the Japanese.* Berkeley: University of California Press.

Dings, J. D. (1989). Faculty members' assumptions about college students' reasoning using the reflective judgment model. Unpublished master's thesis, Department of College Student Personnel, Bowling Green State University.

Donley, J. (1992). *Effects of instructional context on academic performance and self-regulated learning in underprepared college students.* Paper presented at the annual meeting of the American Educational Research Association (AERA). San Francisco, CA.

Doring, A., Bingham, B., & Bramwell-Viol, A. (1997). *Transition to university: A self- regulatory approach.* Paper presented at the annual conference of the Australian Association for Research in Education, Brisbane.

Dornbusch, S. M., Ritter, P. L., Liederman, P., Roberts, D., & Fraleigh, M. (1987). The relation of parenting style to adolescent school performance. *Child Development, 58,* 1244–1257.

Dukes, F., & Gaither, G. L. (1984). A campus cluster program: Effects on persistence and academic performance. *College and University, 59,* 150–166.

Dunkin, M. J., & Biddle, B. J. (1974). *The study of teaching.* New York: Holt, Rinehart and Winston.

Dunn, R. (1993). Learning styles of the multiculturally diverse. *Emergency Librarian, 20*(4), 25–31.

Dunn, R., & Dunn, K. (1988). Presenting forewords backwards. *Teaching K–8,* Vol. 19. 71–73.

Dunn, R., Sklar, R. I., & Beaudry, J. S. (1990). Effects of matching and mismatching minority developmental college students' hemispheric preference on mathematics scores. *The Journal of Educational Research, 83*(5), 283–288.

Dweck, C. S. (1986). Motivational process affecting learning. *American Psychologist, 41*(10), 1040–1048.

Dweck, C. S. (1989). Motivation. In A. Lesgold & R. Glaser (Eds.), *Foundations for a psychology of education.* Hillsdale, NJ: Erlbaum.

Dwyer, F. M., & Moore, D. M. (1992). *Effect of color coding on cognitive style.* (Eric Document Reproduction Service No. 347 986)

Eccles, J. (1983). Expectancies, values and academic behaviors. In J. T. Spence (Ed.), *Achievement and achievement motives* (pp. 75–146). San Francisco: Freeman.

Eison, J., & Pollio, H. (1989). *LOGO II: Bibliographic and statistical update.* Mimeographed. Cape Girardeau, MO: Southeast Missouri State University, Center for Teaching and Learning.

Elliot, E. S., & Dweck, C. S. (1988). Goals: An approach to motivation and achievement. *Journal of Personality and Social Psychology, 54,* 5–12.

Emerson, A., Phillips, J., Hunt, C., & Bowman, A. A. (1994). Case studies. In K. Bosworth & S. J. Hamilton (Eds.), *Collaborative learning: Underlying processes and effective techniques* (p. 194). San Francisco: Jossey-Bass.

Ennis, C. D. (1989). Educational climate in elective adult education: Shared decision making and communication patterns. *Adult Education Quarterly, 39,* 76–88.

Erikson, E. H. (1968). *Identity: Youth and crisis.* New York: Norton.

Ethington, C., Smart, J., & Pascarella, E. T. (1986). Persistence to graduate education. *Research in Higher Education, 24,* 287–303.

Farr, C., & Moon, C. E. (1988). *New perspective on intelligence: Examining field dependence/independence in light of Sternberg's triarchic theory of intelligence.* (ERIC Document Reproduction Service No. 294 893)

Fehrenbach, C. R. (1994). Cognitive style of gifted and average readers. *Roeper Review, 16*(4), 290–292.

Fiore, M. (1998). Scores on one college-admissions test rise for the second straight year. *Chronicle of Higher Education,* 31.

Flannery, J. L. (1994). Teacher as co-conspirator: Knowledge and authority in collaborative learning. In K. Bosworth & S. J. Hamilton (Eds.), *Collaborative techniques.* (New Directions for Teaching and Learning, No. 59). San Francisco: Jossey-Bass.

Fleming, K. (1984). *Blacks in college: A comparative study of students' success in black and in white institutions.* San Francisco: Jossey-Bass.

Fordham, S. (1988). Racelessness as a factor in black students' school success: Pragmatic strategy on pyrrhic victory? *Harvard Educational Review, 58*(1), 54–84.

Fordham, S., & Ogbu, J. U. (1986). Black students' school success: Coping with the burden of acting white. *The Urban Review, 18,* 176–206.

Frank, B. M., & Keene, E. (1993). The effect of learners' field independence, cognitive strategy instruction, and inherent word-list organization on free recall memory and strategy use. *Journal of Experimental Education, 62*(1), 14–25.

Freire, P. (1970). *Pedagogy of the oppressed.* New York: Continuum.

Fritz, R. L. (1992). *A study of gender differences in cognitive style and conative volition.* (ERIC Document Reproduction Service No. 354 379)

Fullilove, R. E., & Treisman, P. U. (1990). Mathematics achievement among African American undergraduates of the University of California Berkeley: An evaluation of the mathematics workshop program. *Journal of Negro Education, 59*(3), 463–478.

Gabelnick, F., MacGregor, M., Matthews, R. F., & Smith, B. L. (1990). Learning communities: Creating connections among students, faculty, and disciplines. (New Directions for Teaching and Learning, No. 41). San Francisco: Jossey-Bass.

Gaddis, M. D., & Elliott, T. (1997). An alternative pedagogical approach to teaching at-risk and underachieving upper-level accounting students. Paper presented at the University of Kentucky Teaching and Learning Conference, Lexington, KY.

Gallimore, R. (1981). Affiliation, social context, industriousness, and achievement. In R. L. Munroe, R. H. Munroe, & B. Whiting (Eds.), *Handbook of cross-cultural human development,* pp. 120–131. New York: Garland.

Gallimore, R., & Howard, A. (1968). The Hawaiian life-style: Some qualitative considerations. In R. Gallimore & A. Howard (Eds.), *Studies in a Hawaiian community: Namakamaka o nanakuli* (pp. 10–16). Pacific Anthropological Records No. 1. Honolulu: B. P. Bishop Museum.

Gamson, Z. F., & Associates. (1984). *Liberating education.* San Francisco: Jossey-Bass.

Gardner, H. (1983). *Frames of mind: The theory of multiple intelligences.* New York: Basic Books.

Gardner, H. (1990). National educational goals and the academic community. *The Education Digest,* Vol. 55, 41–43.

Gardner, H. (1994). *Creating minds.* New York: Basic Books.

Gardner, H., Krechevsky, M., Sternberg, R. J., & Okagaki, L. (1994). Intelligence in context: Enhancing students' practical intelligence for school. In K. McGilly (Ed.), *Classroom lessons: Integrating cognitive theory and classroom practice* (pp. 105–128). Cambridge, MA: MIT Press.

Garner, R. (1987). Strategies for reading and studying expository text. *Educational Psychologist, 22*, 313–332.

Garner, R. (1990). When children and adults do not use learning strategies: Toward a theory of settings. *Review of Educational Research, 60*, 517–529.

Geary, W. T. (1998). *From dependence toward independence via interdependence.* Paper presented at the annual meeting of the American Educational Research Association, San Diego.

Gilligan, C. (1982). *In a different voice: Psychological theory and women's development.* Cambridge, MA: Harvard University Press.

Glatfelter, M. (1982). *Identity development, intellectual development and their relationship in reentry women.* Unpublished doctoral dissertation, University of Minnesota. (MnU-D 82–290)

Goldberger, N. R. (1996). Cultural imperatives and diversity in ways of knowing. In N. Goldberger, J. Tarule, B. Clinchy, & M. Belenky (Eds.), *Knowledge, difference, and power* (pp. 335–371). New York: Basic Books.

Golden, J. G. (1987). Acculturation, biculturalism and marginality: A study of Korean-American high school students. (University of Colorado at Boulder). *Dissertation Abstracts International, 48*, 1135A.

Graham, S. (1994). Motivation in African Americans. *Review of Educational Research, 64*, 55–117.

Gray, M. J., Rolph, E., & Melamid, E. (1996). *Immigration and higher education: Institutional responses to changing demographics,* Santa Monica, CA: RAND.

Greeley, A. T., & Tinsley, H.E.A. (1988). Autonomy and intimacy development in college students: Sex differences and predictors. *Journal of College Student Development, 29*, 512–590.

Grow, G. (1991). Teaching learners to be self-directed: A stage approach. *Adult Education Quarterly, 41*(3), 93–124.

Guild, P. B., & Garger, S. (1985). *Marching to different drummers.* Alexandria, VA: ASCD (Association for Supervisional Curriculum Development).

Hafner, A. L. (1989). The traditional undergraduate woman in the mid–1980s: A changing profile. In C. S. Pearson, D. L. Shavlik, & J. G. Touchton (Eds.), *Educating the majority: Women challenge tradition in higher education* (pp. 32–46). New York: ACE-MacMillan.

Hagen, A. S., & Weinstein, C. E. (1995). Achievement goals, self-regulated learning, and the role of classroom context. In P. R. Pintrich (Ed.), *Understanding self-regulated learning* (pp. 43–55). San Francisco: Jossey-Bass.

Hagtvet, K. A. (1984). Fear of failure, worry and emotionality: Their suggestive causal relationships to mathematical performance and state anxiety. In H. M. van der Ploeg, R. Schwarzer, & C. D. Spielberger

(Eds.), *Advances in test anxiety research* (Vol. 3, pp. 211–224). Hillsdale, NJ: Erlbaum.

Hahn, J. S. (1983–84). An exploratory study of the relationship between learner cognitive styles and three different teaching methods used to teach computer literacy with the Pittsburgh information retrieval system. *International Journal of Instructional Media, 11*(2), 147–158.

Hall, R. M., & Sandler, B. R. (1984). *Out of the classroom: A chilly campus climate for women?* Report of the Project on the Status and Education of Women. Washington, DC: Association of American Colleges.

Hamilton, S. J. (1994). Freedom transformed: Toward a developmental model for the construction of collaborative learning environments. In K. Bosworth & S. J. Hamilton (Eds.), *Collaborative learning: Underlying processes and effective techniques* (pp. 93–102). San Francisco: Jossey-Bass.

Hammond, M., & Collins, R. (1991). *Self-directed learning.* London: Kogan Page.

Harackiewicz, J. M., Sansone, C., & Manderlink, G. (1985). Competence, achievement orientation, and intrinsic motivation: A process analysis. *Journal of Personality and Social Psychology, 48,* 493–508.

Hau, K., & Salili, F. (1990). Examination result attribution, expectancy, and achievement goals among Chinese students in Hong Kong. *Educational Studies, 16*(1), 17–31.

Hausfather, S. J. (1996). Vygotsky and schooling: Creating a social context for learning. *Action in Teacher Education,* Summer, *18*(2), 1–10.

Haworth, J. G., & Conrad, C. F. (1997). *Emblems of quality in higher education: Developing and sustaining high-quality programs.* Boston: Allyn & Bacon.

Hays, Janice N. (1988). Socio-cognitive development and argumentative writing: Issues and implications from our research project. Journal of Basic Writing. Vol. 7, N2, 42–67.

Helms, J. E. (1990). Toward a model of white racial identity development. In J. E. Helms (Ed.), *Black and white racial identity: Theory, research, and practice* (pp. 49–66). New York: Greenwood Press.

Henderson, S. (1994). *Theories of cognitive development and the teaching of argumentation in first-year composition.* Paper presented at the annual meeting of the Conference on College Composition and Communication, Nashville, TN.

Hewson, W., & Hewson, M. C. A'B (1988). An appropriate conception of teaching science: A view from studies of science learning. *Science Education.* Vol. 72, N5, 597–614.

Hines, C. V., Cruickshank, D. R., & Kennedy, J. J. (1985). Teacher clarity and its relationship to student achievement and satisfaction. *American Educational Research Journal, 22,* 87–99.

Hodges, S. (1994). Brain hemisphericity and school dropouts. (ERIC Document Reproduction Service No. ED412 271)

Holland, D., & Eisenhart, M. (1990). *Educated in romance: Women, achievement, and college culture.* Chicago: University of Chicago Press.

Howard, J., & Hammond, R. (1985). Rumors of inferiority: The hidden obstacles to black success. *The New Republic,* September, 17–21.

Hoyte, R. M., & Collett, J. (1993). "I can do it": Minority undergraduate science experiences and the professional career choice. In J. Gainen & R. Boice (Eds.), *Building a diverse faculty.* (New Directions for Teaching and Learning, No. 53). San Francisco: Jossey-Bass.

Hussar, W. J., & Gerald, D. E. (1996). *Projections of education statistics to 2006* (25th ed.). Washington, DC: U.S. Department of Education, Office of Educational Research and Improvement. (NCES, National Center for Educational Statistics, 96–661)

Hvitfeldt, C. (1986). Traditional culture, perceptual style, and learning: The classroom behavior of Hmong adults. *Adult Education Quarterly, 36*(2), 65–77.

The Institute for Higher Education Policy. (1996). *Life after forty: A new portrait of today's—and tomorrow's—postsecondary students.* The Educational Resources Institute. Washington, D.C.

Irwin, D. E. (1981). Effects of peer tutoring on academic achievement and affective adjustment. In G. Enright (Ed.), *Proceedings of the Thirteenth Annual Conference of the Western College Reading Association, XIII,* 42–45. Dallas, TX.

Jaffe, Barbara (1997). *Student success in college composition through the Puente Project Model.* ERIC Document Reproduction Series No. 336 251.

Johnson, D. W., Johnson, R. T., & Smith, K. A. (1991). *Cooperative learning: Increasing college faculty instructional productivity.* Washington, DC: The George Washington University, School of Education and Human Development. (ASHE-ERIC Higher Education Report, No. 4)

Jordan-Cox, C. A. (1987). Psychosocial development of students in traditionally black institutions. *Journal of College Student Development, 28,* 504–512.

Josselson, R. (1987). *Finding herself: Pathways to identity development in women.* San Francisco: Jossey-Bass.

Josselson, R. (1996). *Revising herself: The story of women's identity from college to midlife.* New York: Oxford University Press.

Kaiser, B. T. (1971). *Student life styles and their impact on college union planning.* Paper presented at National Exposition of Contract Interior Furnishings, The Merchandise Mart, Chicago, Illinois on June 24, 1971.

Kanfer, R., & Ackerman, P. L. (1989). Motivation and cognitive abilities: An integrative/aptitude-treatment approach to skill acquisition. *Journal of Applied Psychology, 74,* 657–690.

Kardash, C. M., Lukowski, L., & Bentmann, L. (1988). Effects of cognitive style and intermediate testing on learning from a lecture. *Journal of Educational Research, 81*(6), 360–364.

Kegan, R. (1994). *In over our heads: The mental demands of modern life.* Cambridge, MA: Harvard University Press.

Kenny, M. E., & Donaldson, G. A. (1991). Contributions of parental attachment and family structure to the social and psychological functioning of first-year college students. *Journal of Counseling Psychology, 38,* 479–486.

King, P. M., & Kitchener, K. S. (1994). *Developing reflective judgment: Understanding and promoting intellectual growth and critical thinking in adolescents and Adults.* San Francisco: Jossey-Bass.

Kitchener, K. S., & King, P. M. (1990). The reflexive judgment model: Transforming assumptions about knowing. In J. Mesirow & Associates (Eds.), *Fostering critical reflection in adulthood: A guide to transformative and emancipatory learning* (pp. 159–176). San Francisco: Jossey-Bass.

Kitchener, K. S., King, P., Wood, P., & Davison, M. (1989). Sequentiality and consistency in the development of reflective judgment: A six year longitudinal study. *Journal of Applied Developmental Psychology, 10,* 73–95.

Kitchener, K. S., Lynch, C. L., Fischer, K. W., & Wood, P. K. (1993). Developmental range of reflective judgment: The effect of contextual support and practice on developmental stage. *Developmental Psychology, 29,* 893–906.

Kitchens, A. N., Barber, W. D., & Barber, D. B. (1991). Left brain/right brain theory: Implications for developmental math instruction. *Review of Research in Developmental Education, 8*(3).

Knefelkamp, L. L. (1984). *A workbook for the practice-to-theory mode.* Unpublished manuscript, University of Maryland, College Park.

Knowles, M. S. (1980). *The modern practice of adult education: From pedagogy to andragogy* (2nd ed.). New York: Cambridge Books.

Koehler, L. (1987). *Helping students to succeed: A report on tutoring and attrition at the University of Cincinnati.* ERIC Document Reproduction Service. ED 290370.

Kolb, D. A. (1984). *Experiential learning: Experience as the source of learning and development.* Englewood Cliffs, NJ: Prentice Hall.

Kroll, B. (1992). *Teaching hearts and minds: College students reflect on the Vietnam war in literature.* Carbondale: Southern Illinois Press.

Kuh, G. D. (1991). Snapshots of campus community. *Educational Record.* Winter, 40–44.

Kuh, G. D., Schuh, J. D., Whitt, E. J., Andreas, R. E., Lyons, J. W., Strange, C. C., Krehbiel, L. E., & MacKay, K. A. (1991). *Involving colleges:*

Successful approaches to student learning and development outside the classroom. San Francisco: Jossey-Bass.

LaCounte, D. W. (1987). American Indian students in college. In D. J. Wright (Ed.), *Responding to the needs of today's minority students*. (New Directions for Student Services, No. 38). San Francisco: Jossey-Bass.

LaFromboise, T., Coleman, H.L.K., & Gerton, J. (1993). Psychological impact of biculturalism. *Psychological Bulletin, 114,* 395–412.

Lan, W. Y., Bradley, L., & Parr, G. (1994). The effects of a self-monitoring process on college students' learning in an introductory statistics course. *Journal of Experimental Education, 62,* 26–40.

Land, M. L. (1979). Low inference variable of teacher clarity: Effects on student concept learning. *Journal of Educational Psychology, 71,* 795–99.

Langer, J. A., & Applebee, A. N. (1987). *How writing shapes thinking: A study of teaching and learning*. Urbana, IL: National Council for Teachers of English Research Report No. 22.

Laux, L., & Glanzmann, P. (1987). A self-presentational view of test anxiety. In R. Schwarzer, H. M. van der Ploeg, & C. D. Spielberger (Eds.), *Advances in test anxiety research* (Vol. 5, pp. 3–37). Hillsdale, NJ: Erlbaum.

Lave, J., Murtaugh, M., & de la Roche, O. (1984). The dialectic of arithmetic in grocery shopping. In B. Rogoff & J. Lave (Eds.), *Everyday cognition: Its development in social context*. Cambridge, MA: Harvard University Press.

LeDoux, J. (1996). *The emotional brain*. New York: Simon & Schuster.

Lewin, K. (1936). *Principles of topological psychology*. (F. Heider & G. M. Heider, Trans.) New York: McGraw-Hill.

Lindner, R. W., & Harris, B. R. (1992). *Teaching self-regulated learning strategies*. Washington, DC: U.S. Department of Education, Educational Resources Information Center. (ERIC Document Reproduction Service No. 362 182)

Lipsky, S. (1989). *Effect of field independence/dependence on two* textbook note-taking techniques. (ERIC Document Reproduction Service No. 311 983)

Locke, E. A., & Latham, G. P.(1990). *A theory of goal setting and task performance*. Englewood Cliffs, NJ: Prentice Hall.

Loevinger, J. (1976). *Ego development: Conceptions and theories*. San Francisco: Jossey-Bass.

Lounsbury, J. W., & DeNuie, D. (1995). Psychological sense of community on campus. *College Student Journal, 29,* 270–277.

Lyons-Lawrence, C. L. (1994). Effect of learning style on performance in using computer-based instruction in office systems. *Delta Pi Epsilon Journal, XXXVI*(3), 166–175.

MacGregor, S. K., Shapiro, J. Z., & Niemic, R. (1988). Effects of a computer-augmented learning environment on math achievement for students with differing cognitive styles. *Journal of Educational Computing Research, 4*(4), 453–465.

Macrorie, K. (1984). *Twenty teachers.* New York: Oxford.

Maehr, M. L., & Anderman, E. M. (1993). Reinventing schools for early adolescents. *Elementary School Journal, 93,* 593–610.

Maehr, M. L., & Pintrich, P. R. (Eds.). (1995). *Advances in motivation and achievement* (Vol. 9, pp. 159–181). Greenwich, CT: JAI Press.

Marcia, J. E. (1966). Development and validation of ego-identity status. *Journal of Personal and Social Psychology, 3,* 551–558.

Marcia, J. E. (1980). Identity in adolescence. In J. Adelson, (Ed.), *Handbook of adolescent psychology* (pp. 159–187). New York: Wiley.

Marshall, H. H., & Weinstein, R. S. (1984). Classroom factors affecting students' self-evaluations: An interactional model. *Review of Educational Research, 54,* 301–325.

Marshall, S. & Johns, M. (1992). Left brain/right brain and school achievement. (ERIC Document Reproduction Service No. ED302 417)

Maslow, A. H. (1970). *Motivation and personality.* New York: HarperCollins.

Mayer, R. E. (1987). *Educational psychology: A cognitive approach.* Boston: Little, Brown.

Mayer, J. D., & Geher, G. (1996). Emotional intelligence and the identification of emotion. *Intelligence, 22,* 89–113.

Mayer, J. D., & Salovey, P. (1997). What is emotional intelligence? In P. Salovey & D. Sluyter (Eds.), *Emotional development and emotional intelligence: Implications for educators* (pp. 3–31). New York: Basic Books.

McCarthy, M. E., Pretty, G.M.H., & Catano, V. (1990). Psychological sense of community and student burnout. *Journal of College Student Development, 31*(2), 211–216.

McCarthy, B. (1980). *The 4MAT system: Teaching to learning styles with right/ left mode techniques.* Barrington, IL: EXCEL.

McCarty, T. L., Wallace, S., Lynch, R. H., & Benally, A. (1991). Classroom inquiry and Navajo learning styles: A call for reassessment. *Anthropology and Education Quarterly, 22*(1), 43–54.

McClelland, D. C. (1961). *The achieving society.* Princeton, NJ: Van Nostrand.

McClusky, H. Y. (1970). An approach to a differential psychology of the adult potential. In S. M. Grabowski (Ed.), *Adult learning and instruction.* Syracuse, NY: ERIC Clearinghouse on Adult Education.

McKeachie, W., Pintrich, P., Lin, Y., & Smith, D. (1986). *Teaching and learning in the college classroom: A review of the research literature.* Ann Arbor: University of Michigan, National Center for Research to Improve Postsecondary Teaching & Learning.

McKeachie, W. J. (1969). *Teaching tips: A guidebook for the beginning college teacher.* Lexington, MA: D.C. Heath.

McLeod, A. (1996). Discovering and facilitating deep learning states. *The National Teaching & Learning Forum, 5*(6), 1–7.

McMillan, D. W., & Chavis, D. M. (1986). Sense of community: A definition and theory. *Journal of Community Psychology, 14*(1), 6–23.

Mealey, D. L. (1990). Understanding the motivation problem of at-risk college students. *Journal of Reading, 33,* 598–601.

Meng, K., & Patty, D. (1991). Field dependence and contextual organizers. *Journal of Educational Research, 84*(3), 183–189.

Menges, R. J., & Svinicki, M. D. (Eds.). (1991) *College teaching: From theory to practice.* (New Directions for Teaching and Learning, No. 45). San Francisco: Jossey-Bass.

Merriam, S. B. (1993). *An update on adult learning theory.* San Francisco: Jossey-Bass.

Mezirow, J. (1991). *Transformative dimensions of adult learning.* San Francisco: Jossey-Bass.

Mezirow, J. D. (1981). A critical theory of adult learning and education. *Adult Education Quarterly, 32*(1), 3–24.

Miller, I. W., & Norman, W. H. (1979). Learned helplessness in humans: A review and attribution-theory model. *Psychological Bulletin, 86,* 93–118.

Miller, J. E., Trimbur, J., & Wilkes, J. M. (1994). Group dynamics: Understanding group success and failure in collaborative learning. In K. Bosworth & S. J. Hamilton (Eds.), *Collaborative techniques.* (New Directions for Teaching and Learning, No. 59). San Francisco: Jossey-Bass.

Mintzes, J. J. (1979). Overt teaching behaviors and student ratings of instructors. *Journal of Experimental Education, 48,* 145–153.

Moll, L. C. (1990). *Literacy research in community and classrooms: A socio-cultural approach.* Paper presented at the conference on Multi-Disciplinary Perspectives on Research Methodology in Language Arts, National Conference on Research in English, Chicago.

Moll, L. C., & Greenberg, J. B. (1990). Creating zones of possibilities: Combining social contexts for instruction. In L. C. Moll (Ed.), *Vygotsky and education.* Cambridge: Cambridge University Press.

Moos, R. H. (1979). *Evaluating educational environments.* San Francisco: Jossey-Bass.

Moos, R. H. (1986). *The human context: Environmental determinants of behavior.* Malabar, GL: Krieger.

Moos, R. H., & Gerst, M. (1974). *The university residence environment scale manual.* Palo Alto, CA: Consulting Psychologists Press.

Mruk, C. (1995). *Self-esteem research, theory, and practice.* New York: Springer.

Mullin, A. E. (1998). Another look at student writing and stages of intellectual development. *Journal of College Reading and Learning, 28*(2), 79–92.

Multon, K. D., Brown, S. D., & Lent, R. W. (1991). Relation of self-efficacy beliefs to academic 1 outcomes: A meta-analytic investigation. *Journal of Counseling Psychology, 38,* 30–38.

Murray, H. G. (1983). Low-inference classroom teaching behaviors and student ratings of college teaching effectiveness. *Journal of Educational Psychology, 75,* 138–149.

Murray, H. G. (1997). Effective teaching behaviors in the college classroom. In R. P. Perry & J. C. Smart (Eds.), *Effective teaching in higher education: Research and practice* (pp.171–204). New York: Agathon Press.

Myers, I., & Briggs, K. (1985). *Myers-Briggs type indicator.* Palo Alto, CA: Consulting Psychologists Press.

Myers, I. B. (1980). *Gifts differing.* Palo Alto, CA: Consulting Psychologists Press.

National Council of Teachers of Mathematics. (1989). *Curriculum and evaluation standards for school mathematics,* Reston, VA: NCTM.

Nisbett, R., & Ross, L. (1980). *Human inference: strategies and shortcomings of social judgment.* Englewood Cliffs, NJ: Prentice-Hall.

Nugent, S. (1993). *Stories told in a different voice: Women students as developing writers.* Washington, DC: U.S. Department of Education, Educational Resource Information Center. (ERIC Document Reproduction Service No. 361 042)

O'Brien, K., Brown, S. D., & Lent, R. W. (1989). *Self-efficacy beliefs to academic achievement and career development in at-risk college students.* Paper presented at the 97th annual convention of the American Psychological Association, New Orleans.

Okagaki, L., & Sternberg, R. (1993). Parental beliefs and children's school performance. *Child Development, 64*(1), 36–56.

Ogbu, J. (1990). Cultural model, identity, and literacy. In J. W. Stigler, R. A. Schweder, & G. Herdt (Eds.), *Cultural psychology: Essays on comparative human development* (pp. 520–541). Cambridge: Cambridge University Press.

Ostertag, B. A., Pearson, M. J., & Baker, R. E. (1986). Programs for learning disabled in California community colleges. *Reading, Writing, and Learning Disabilities, 2,* 331–347.

Padilla, R. V. (1991). Assessing heuristic knowledge to enhance college students' success. In G. D. Keller, J. R. Deneen, & R. J. Magallan (Eds.), *Assessment and access: Hispanics in higher education* (pp. 81–92). Albany, NY: State University of New York Press.

Padilla, R. V. (1994). The unfolding matrix: A technique for qualitative data acquisition and analysis. In R. G. Burgess (Ed.), *Studies in qualitative methodology: Vol. 4. Issues in qualitative research*. Greenwich, CT: JAI Press.

Padilla, R. V., Trevino, J., Gonzalez, K., & Trevino, J. (1997). Developing local models of minority student success in college. *Journal of College Student Development, 38*(2), 125–135.

Pai, Y., & Adler, S. A. (1997). *Cultural foundations of education* (2nd ed.). Upper Saddle River, NJ: Prentice Hall.

Palmer, P. (1983). *To know as we are known: A spirituality of education*. San Francisco: HarperCollins.

Palmer, P. (1998). *The courage to teach*. San Francisco: Jossey-Bass.

Paris, S. G., & Newman, R. C. (1990). Developmental aspects of self-regulated learning. *Educational Psychologist, 25*(1), 87–102.

Pascarella, E. T. (Winter 1980). Student-faculty informal contact and college outcomes. *Review of Educational Research, 50,* 545–590.

Pascarella, E. T., Ethington, C., & Smart, J. (1988). The influence of college on humanitarian/civic involvement values. *Journal of Higher Education, 59,* 412–437.

Pascarella, E. T., & Terenzini, P. T. (1991). *How college affects students: Findings and insights from twenty years of research*. San Francisco: Jossey-Bass.

Pascarella, E. T., & Terenzini, P. T. (1992). Designing college for graduate learning. *Planning for Higher Education, 20,* 1–6.

Pascarella, E. T., Whitt, E. J., Edison, M. I., Nora, A., Hagedorn, L. S., Yeager, P. M., & Terenzini, P. T. (1997). Women's perceptions of a chilly climate: And their cognitive outcomes during the first year of college. *Journal of College Student Development, 38*(2), 109–124.

Perry, R. P. (1985). Instructor expressiveness: Implications for improving teaching. In J. G. Donald & A. M. Sullivan (Eds.), *Using research to improve teaching* (pp. 35–49). San Francisco: Jossey-Bass.

Perry, R. P., & Penner, K. (1990). Enhancing academic achievement in college students through attributional retraining and instruction. *Journal of Educational Psychology, 82,* 262–271.

Perry, W. G., Jr. (1970). *Forms of intellectual and ethical development in the college years*. Troy, MO: Holt, Rinehart and Winston.

Peterson, P. L., Fennama, E., & Carpenter, T. (1989). Using knowledge about how students think about mathematics. *Educational Leadership,* Vol. 46, N4, 42–46.

Phinney, J. (1990). Ethnic identity in adolescents and adults: Review of research. *Psychology Bulletin, 108,* 499–514.

Pintrich, P. R. (1995). Understanding self-regulated learning. In P. R. Pintrich (Ed.), *Understanding self-regulated learning* (pp. 3–12). San Francisco: Jossey-Bass.

Pintrich, P. R., & Schunk, D. H. (1996). *Motivation in education.* Englewood Cliffs, NJ: Prentice Hall.

Portis, S. C., Simpson, F. M. and Wieseman, R. A. (1993). *Convergence or divergence? Perspective as experience and cognitive styles of prospective teachers.* (ERIC Document Reproduction Service No. 354 236)

Pounds, A. W. (1987). Black students' needs on predominantly white campuses. In D. J. Wright (Eds.), *Responding to the needs of today's minority students.* (New Directions for Student Services, No. 38). San Francisco: Jossey-Bass.

Pratt, D. D. (1981). Andragogy as a relational construct. *Adult Educational Quarterly, 38,* 160–181.

Pressley, M. (1995). More about the development of self-regulation: Complex, long-term, and thoroughly social. *Educational Psychologist, 30*(4), 207–212.

Pressley, M., El-Dinary, P., Brown, R., Schuder, T. L., Pioli, M., Green, K., SAIL Faculty and Administration of Montgomery County Public Schools, Rockville, MD, and Gaskins, I. (1994). *Transactional instruction of reading comprehension strategies. Perspectives in reading research No. 5.* National Reading Research Center. Athens, GA. (ERIC Document Reproduction Service No. 375 391)

Price, G., & Jang, Y. S. (1998). *ZPD tango.* Paper presented at the annual meeting of the American Educational Research Association, San Diego.

Prosser, M., & Millar, R. (1989). The how and why of learning physics. *European Journal of Psychology of Education, 4,* 513–28.

Quevedo-Garcia, E. L. (1987). Facilitating the development of Hispanic college students. In D. J. Wright (Ed.), *Responding to the needs of today's minority students.* (New Directions for Student Services, No. 38). San Francisco: Jossey-Bass.

Rainer, J., & Guyton, E. (1998). *Teacher change: The strategies and effects of a constructivist teacher education program.* Paper presented at the annual meeting of the American Educational Research Association, San Diego.

Ramsden, P. (1992). *Learning to teach in higher education.* New York: Routledge.

Reagan, D. (1992). *The academic dismissal student and the self-worth theory of achievement motivation.* Unpublished doctoral dissertation, University of California, Berkeley.

Ross, A. O. (1992). *The sense of self.* New York: Springer.

Rotter, J. (1966). Generalized expectancies for internal versus external control of reinforcement. *Psychological Monographs, 80* (1, Whole No. 609).

Rush, G. M., & Moore, D. M. (1991). Effects of restructuring training and cognitive style. *Educational Psychology, Vol. 11,* N3–4, 309–321.

Salame, R. (1984). Test anxiety: Its determinants, manifestations and consequences. In H. M. van der Ploeg, R. Schwarzer, & C. D. Spielberger (Eds.), *Advances in test anxiety research* (Vol. 3, pp. 240–256). Hillsdale, NJ: Erlbaum.

Salili, F. (1995). Explaining Chinese students' motivation and achievement: a socio-cultural analysis. In M. L. Maehr & P. R. Pintrich (Eds.), *Advances in motivation and achievement* (Vol. 9, pp. 73–118). Greenwich, CT: JAI Press.

Salili, F., & Mak, P.H.T. (1988). Subjective meaning of success in high and low achievers. *International Journal of Intercultural Relations, 12,* 125–138.

Sanford, N. (1967). *Where colleges fail: A study of the student as a person.* San Francisco: Jossey-Bass.

Scheurman, G. (1996). *Constructivist strategies for teaching educational psychology.* Paper presented at the annual meeting of the American Educational Research Association, New York.

Schiller, P. M. (1987). *Biculturalism and psychosocial adjustment among Native American university students.* The University of Utah. *Dissertation Abstracts International, 48,* 1542A.

Schmalt, H. D. (1982). Two concepts of fear of failure motivation. In R. Schwarzer, H. M. van der Ploeg, & C. D. Spielberger (Eds.), *Advances in test anxiety research* (Vol. 1, pp. 45–52). Lisse: Swets and Zeitlinger.

Schmidt, J. (1985). Older and wiser? A longitudinal study of the impact of college on intellectual development. *Journal of College Student Personnel, 26,* 388–394.

Schraw, G., & Bruning, R. (1996). Readers' implicit models of reading. *Reading Research Quarterly, 31*(3), 290–305.

Schroeder, C. C. (1994). Developing learning communities. In C. C. Schroeder & P. Mable (Eds.), *Realizing the educational potential of residence hall.* San Francisco: Jossey-Bass.

Schunk, D. H. (1991a). Self-efficacy and academic motivation. *Educational Psychologist, 26,* 207–231.

Schunk, D. H. (1991b). Goal setting and self-evaluation: a social cognitive perspective on self-regulation. In M. L. Maehr & P. R. Pintrich (Eds.), *Advances in motivation and achievement* (Vol. 7, pp. 85–113). Greenwich, CT: JAI Press.

Schunk, D. H., & Hanson, A. R. (1985). Peer models: Influence on children's self-efficacy and achievement. *Journal of Educational Psychology, 77,* 313–322.

Schunk, D. H., & Meece, J. L. (Eds.). (1992). *Student perceptions in the classroom.* Hillsdale, NJ: Erlbaum.

Schunk, D. H., & Swartz, C. W. (1993). Goals and progress feedback: Effects on self-efficacy and writing achievement. *Contemporary Educational Psychology, 18,* 337–354.

Scott, H. V. (1993). *A serious look at the 4MAT model.* (ERIC Document Reproduction Service No. 383 654)

Scribner, S. (1984). Studying working intelligence. In B. Rogoff & J. Lave (Eds.), *Everyday cognition* (pp. 9–40). Cambridge MA: Harvard University Press.

Sharan, S. (1980). Cooperative learning in small groups: Recent methods and effects on achievement, attitudes, and ethnic relations. *Review of Educational Research, 50,* 241–271.

Shavelson, R. J., Hubner, J. J., & Stanton, G. C. (1976). Self-concept: Validation of construct interpretation. *Review of Education Research, 46,* 407–441.

Shell, D. F., Horn, C. A., & Severs, M. K. (1988). Effects of a computer-based educational center on disabled students' academic performance. *Journal of College Student Development, 29,* 432–440.

Shoff, S. (1979). The significance of age, sex, and type of education on the development of reasoning in adults. University of Utah. *Dissertation Abstracts International, 40,* 3910A.

Simpson, F. M., Portis, S. C., & Mills, L. (1995). *Evolution of cognitive styles for pre-professional educators.* (ERIC Document Reproduction Service No. 392 788)

Sivan, E. (1986). Motivation in social constructivist theory. *Educational Psychologist, 21*(3), 209–233.

Slavin, R. E. (1989). Cooperative learning and student achievement. In R. E. Slavin (Eds.), *School and classroom organization* (pp. 129–156). Hillsdale, NJ: Erlbaum.

Smagorinsky, P. (1991). *Expressions: Multiple intelligences in the English class.* Urbana, IL: National Council of Teachers of English.

Smart, J. C. (1985). Holland environments as reinforcement systems. *Research in Higher Education, 23,* 279–292.

Smith, D. (1990). Women's colleges and coed colleges: Is there a difference for women? *Journal of Higher Education, 61,* 181–197.

Smith, L. S., & MacGregor, J. T. (1992). What is collaborative learning? In A. Goodsell, M. Maher, V. Tinto, B. Smith, & J. MacGregor, *Collaborative learning: A sourcebook for higher education* (pp. 9–22). The National Center on Postsecondary Teaching, Learning and Assessment, Pennsylvania State University.

Smith, T., & Easterday, K. E. (1994). *Field dependence-independence and holistic instruction in mathematics.* (ERIC Document Resource Service No. 377 072)

Spence, J. T. (1985). Achievement American style: The rewards and costs of individualism. *American Psychologist, 40,* 1,285–1,295.

Spitzberg, I. J., & Thorndike, V. V. (1992). *Creating community on college campuses.* Albany, NY: SUNY Press.

Springer, L., Miller, H., & Wright, R. (1997). *Structural active learning.* Paper presented at the annual meeting of the American Educational Research Association, Chicago.

Steinberg, L., & Brown, B. B. (1989). *Beyond classroom: Family and peer influences on high school achievement.* Paper presented at the annual meeting of the American Educational Research Association, San Francisco.

Steinberg, L., Mounts, N., Lamborn, S., & Dornbusch, S. (1991). Authoritative parenting and adolescent adjustment across various ecological niches. *Journal of Research on Adolescence, 1,* 19–36.

Stephenson, B., & Hunt, C. (1977). Intellectual and ethical development: A dualistic curriculum intervention for college students. *Counseling Psychology, 6,* 39–42.

Sternberg, R. J. (1988). *The triarchic mind: A new theory of human intelligence.* New York: Penguin Books.

Sternberg, R. J. (1996). What should we ask about intelligence? *The American Scholar, 65,* 205–207.

Sternberg, R. J., & Lubart, T. I. (1991). Creating creative minds. *Phi Delta Kappan, 72*(8), 609–614.

Sternberg, R. J., Wagner, R. K., Williams, W. M., & Horvath, J. (1995). Testing common sense. *American Psychologist, 50,* 912–927.

Sternberg, R. J., & Williams, W. M. (1995). Parenting toward cognitive competence. In M. H. Bornstein (Ed.) *Handbook of Parenting* (Vol. 4, pp. 259-275). Mahwah, NJ: Erlbaum.

Stevenson, H. W., Chen, C., & Uttal, D. H. (1990). Beliefs and achievement: A study of black, white, and Hispanic children. *Child Development, 61,* 508–523.

Stevenson, H. W., & Stigler, J. W. (1992). *The learning gap: Why our schools are failing and what we can learn from Japanese and Chinese education.* New York: Summit Books.

Stikes, C. S. (1984). *Black students in higher education.* Carbondale: Southern Illinois University Press.

Stoecker, J., Pascarella, E. T., & Wolfe, L. (1988). Persistence in higher education: A nine-year test of a theoretical model. *Journal of College Student Development, 29,* 196–209.

Straub, C. A., & Rodgers, R. E. (1986). An exploration of Chickering's theory and women's development. *Journal of College Student Personnel, 27,* 216–224.

Strichart, S. S., & Mangrum, C. T., II. (1986). College for the learning disabled student: A new opportunity. *Reading, Writing, and Learning Disabilities, 2,* 251–266.

Talbot, G. L. (1996). *A grounded research perspective for motivating college students' self- regulated learning behaviors: Preparing and gaining the coop-*

eration, commitment of teacher. Washington, DC. (ERIC Document Service No. 414 788)

Taub, D. J. (1997). Autonomy and parental attachment in traditional-age undergraduate women. *Journal of College Student Development, 38,* 645–654.

Taub, D. J., & McEwen, M. K. (1991). Patterns of development of autonomy and interpersonal relationships in black and white undergraduate women. *Journal of College Student Development, 32,* 502–508.

Tennant, M., & Pogson, P. (1995). *Learning and change in the adult years: A developmental perspective.* San Francisco: Jossey-Bass.

Tharp, R. G., and Gallimore, R. (1988). *Rousing minds to life: Teaching, learning, and schooling in social context.* Cambridge: Cambridge University Press.

Tharp, R. G. (1989). Psychocultural variables and constants: Effects on teaching and learning in schools. *American Psychologist, 44*(2), 349–359.

Thomas, A., & Chess, S. (1989). Genesis and evolution of behavioral disorders: From infancy to early adult life. *American Journal of Psychiatry, 141*(1), 1–9.

Tinto, V. (1975). Dropout from higher education: A theoretical synthesis of recent research. *Review of Educational Research, 45,* 89–125.

Tinto, V., & Riemer, S. (1998). *Learning communities and the reconstruction of remedial/education in higher education.* Paper presented at the Conference on Replacing Remediation in Higher Education sponsored by the National Center for Postsecondary Improvement and the Ford Foundation, Stanford University.

Tobias, S. (1990). *They're not dumb, they're different.* Tucson, AZ: Research Corporation.

Tom, F.K.T., & Cushman, H. R. (1975). The Cornell diagnostic observation and reporting system for student description of college teaching. *Search 5*(8), 1–27.

Trawick, L. (1992). *Effects of a cognitive-behavioral intervention on the motivation, volition, and achievement of academically underprepared college students.* Washington, DC: U.S. Department of Education, Educational Resource Information.

Treisman, U. (1986). A study of mathematics performance of black students at the University of California Berkeley (doctoral dissertation, University of California, Berkeley). *Dissertation Abstracts International, 47,* 1641A.

Triandis, H. C. (1995). Motivation and achievement in collectivist and individualist cultures. In M. L. Maehr & P. R. Pintrich (Eds.), *Advances in motivation and achievement,* Vol. 9, pp. 1–30) Greenwich, CT: JAI Press.

U.S. Bureau of the Census. (1993). *Hispanic Americans today: Current population reports* (pp. 23–183). Washington, DC: U.S. Government Printing Office.

U.S. Department of Education. (1995). *College freshmen with disabilities.* Health Resource Center: A Program of the American Council of Education, *14*(2,3).

van Etten, S., Pressley, M., & Freebern, G. (1998). An interview study of college freshmen [sic] beliefs about their academic motivation. *European Journal of Psychology of Education, Vol XIII,* 105–130.

Van Glasersfeld. (1995). A constructivist approach to teaching. In L. P. Steffe & J. Gale (Eds.), *Constructivism in education* (pp. 3–15, 361–383). Hillsdale, NJ: Erlbaum

Vernez, G., & Abrahamse, A. (1996). *How immigrants fare in U.S. education.* Santa Monica, CA: RAND.

Vincent, V. C. (1983). *Impact of a college learning assistance center on the achievement and retention of disadvantaged students.* ERIC Document Reproduction Service. ED 283 438.

Vogel, S. (1982). On developing LD college programs. *Journal of Learning Disabilities, 15*(9), 518–528.

Vygotsky, L. S. (1965). *Thought and language.* New York: Wiley.

Warkentin, R. W., & Bol, L. (1997). *Assessing college students' self directed studying using self- reports of test preparation.* Paper presented at the annual meeting of the American Educational Research Association, Chicago.

Waterman, A. S. (1982). Identity development from adolescence to adulthood: An extension of theory and a review of research, *Developmental Psychology, 18,* 342–358.

Watson, G., & Glaser, E. (1980). *The Watson-Glaser critical thinking appraisal.* Cleveland, OH: The Psychology Corporation.

Weiner, B. (1972). *Theories of motivation: From mechanism to cognition.* Chicago: Rand McNally College Publishing.

Weiner, B. (1984). Principles for a theory of student motivation and their application within an attributional framework. In R. Ames and C. Ames (Eds.), *Research on motivation in education. Vol. 1. Student motivation.* Orlando, FL: Academic Press.

Weiner, B. (1986). *An attributional theory of motivation and emotion.* New York: Springer-Verlag.

Weiner, B. (1990). History of motivational research in education. *Journal of Educational Psychology, 82,* 616–622.

Weiner, H. S. (1992). Collaborative learning in a classroom: A guide to evaluation. In A. Goodsell & others (Eds.), *Collaborative learning: A sourcebook for higher education* (pp. 90–96). The National Center on

Postsecondary Teaching, Learning and Assessment, Pennsylvania State University.

Weinstein, C. E. (1997). *A model of strategic learning.* Keynote address at the annual conference of National Association of Developmental Education. Denver, CO.

Weinstein, C. E., & Mayer, R. E. (1986). The teaching of learning strategies. In M. C. Wittrock (Ed.), *Handbook of research on teaching* (3rd ed., pp. 315–327). New York: MacMillan.

Wells, R. N. (March 1989). *The Native American experience in higher education: Turning around the cycle of failure.* Paper presented at the Minorities in Higher Education Conference, New York.

Wertsch, J. V. (1991). *Voices of the mind: A socio-historical approach to mediated action.* Cambridge, MA: Harvard University Press.

White, S., & Tharp, R. G. (1988). *Questioning and wait-time: A cross-cultural perspective.* Paper presented at the annual meeting of the American Educational Research Association, New Orleans.

Whitman, N. A. (1988). *Peer teaching: To teach is to learn twice.* Washington, DC: ASHE- ERIC Higher Education Report No. 4.

Whitt, E. J. (1994). I can be anything: Student leadership in three women's colleges. *Journal of College Student Development, 35*(3), 198–207.

Wieseman, R. A., Portis, S. C., & Simpson, F. M. (1992). *A follow-up study on learning styles: Using research to facilitate educational excellence.* (ERIC Document Reproduction Service No. 343 867)

Wilkerson, R. M. (1992). Integrated teaching and learning: A developmental perspective. *Kappa Delta Pi Record, 28,* 93–96.

Williams, C. (1997). *Genetic wild card: A marker for learners at risk.* (ERIC Document Reproduction Service No. 409 695)

Williams, W. M., & Sternberg, R. J. (1988). Group intelligence: Why some groups are better than others. *Intelligence, 12,* 351–377.

Winne, P. H. (1995). Inherent details in self-regulated learning. *Educational Psychologist, 30*(4), 173–187.

Witkin, H. A. (1949). The nature and importance of individual differences in perception. *Journal of Personality, 18,* 145–170.

Witkin, H. A. (1950). Individual differences in ease of perception of embedded figures. *Journal of Personality, 19,* 1–15.

Witkin, H. A. (1976). Cognitive style in academic performance and in teacher-student relations. In S. Messick & Associates (Eds.), *Individuality in learning* (pp. 38–72). San Francisco: Jossey-Bass.

Wlodkowski, R. J., & Ginsberg, M. B. (1995). *Diversity & motivation: Culturally responsive teaching.* San Francisco: Jossey-Bass.

Wren, C., Williams, N., & Kovitz, V. (1987). Organizational problems at the college level. *Academic Therapy, 23*(2), 157–165.

Wright, D. J. (1987). Minority students: Developmental beginnings. In D. J. Wright (Ed.), *Responding to the needs of today's minority students.* (New Directions for Student Services, No. 38). San Francisco: Jossey-Bass.

Wyatt, D., Pressley, M., El-Dinary, P. B., Stein, S., Evans, P., & Brown, R. (1993). Comprehension strategies, worth and credibility monitoring and evaluations: Cold and hot cognition when experts read professional articles that are important to them. *Learning and Individual Differences, 5,* 49–72.

Yakimovicz, A. D., & Murphy, K. L. (1995). Constructivism and collaboration on the Internet: Case study of a graduate class experience. *Computer Education, 24*(3), 203–209.

Yardley, K., & Honess, T. (1987). *Self and identity: Psychosocial perspectives.* New York: Wiley.

Yekovich, F. R. (1994). *Current issues in research on intelligence.* Washington, DC: Office of Educational Research and Improvement. (ERIC Document Reproduction Service No. 385 605)

Young, M. C., & Gardner, R. C. (1990). Modes of acculturation and second language proficiency. *Canadian Journal of Behavioral Science, 22,* 59–71.

Zenhauseon, R. (1978). Imagery, cerebral dominance, and style of thinking: a unified field model. *Bulletin of the Psychonomic Society, 12,* 381–384.

Zimmerman, B. J. (1990). Self-regulated learning and academic achievement: An overview. *Educational Psychologist, 25*(1), 2–17.

Zimmerman, B. J., & Paulsen, A. S. (1995). Self-monitoring during collegiate studying: An invaluable tool for academic self-regulation. In P. R. Pintrich (Ed.), *Understanding self- regulated learning* (pp. 13–28). San Francisco: Jossey-Bass.

Name Index

Subject Index